MONSTROUS WOMEN

MONSTROUS WOMEN
Reimagining the Female Monster in Greek Mythology

Elisabeth Brooke

AEON

First published in 2025 by
Aeon Books

Copyright © 2025 by Elisabeth Brooke

The right of Elisabeth Brooke to be identified as the author of this work has been asserted in accordance with §§ 77 and 78 of the Copyright Design and Patents Act 1988.

All rights reserved. No part of this publication may be reproduced, stored in a retrieval system, or transmitted, in any form or by any means, electronic, mechanical, photocopying, recording, or otherwise, without the prior written permission of the publisher.

British Library Cataloguing in Publication Data

A C.I.P. for this book is available from the British Library

ISBN-13: 978-1-80152-186-4

Typeset by Medlar Publishing Solutions Pvt Ltd, India

www.aeonbooks.co.uk

CONTENTS

ACKNOWLEDGEMENTS	vii
INTRODUCTION	ix
DRAMATIS PERSONAE (IN DATE ORDER)	xix
MYTHICAL FIGURES	xxiii
TIMELINE	xxix
CHAPTER ONE Roots of the Gorgon	1
CHAPTER TWO The Embodied Gorgon	19
CHAPTER THREE The Dancing Gorgon	39

CHAPTER FOUR
The Terror of Hades   63

CHAPTER FIVE
The Furies   77

CHAPTER SIX
Hekate   95

CHAPTER SEVEN
The Sirens   117

CHAPTER EIGHT
Eris and the Daemons   135

ENDPIECE   149

APPENDIX ONE
Truth, Lies, and Opinions   151

APPENDIX TWO
The political situation in Athens in the 5th century and its effect on the *aegis*   163

APPENDIX THREE
Daemons   167

BIBLIOGRAPHY   175

INDEX   191

ACKNOWLEDGEMENTS

Many thanks to the team at Aeon Books, Alice Rathbone and Oliver Rathbone, for their patience in waiting for this manuscript to arrive. Especial thanks to the staff of University College Hospital who cared for me so kindly and efficiently. I have to mention that the staff I encountered were nearly all migrants from Philippines, Japan, Thailand, South Africa, Nigeria, France, Australia and France amongst others. This book formed part of my dissertation for an MA in Classical Studies at the Open University, I would like to thank my tutors, Cathy Morris and Eireann Marshall, for their help and support.

INTRODUCTION

> Ancient Greek myths remain part of us, despite all the differences between their culture and ours. I would never have become interested in the lives of ancient women had I not been interested in the way in which women's roles have been defined by modern society.[1]

Why does Greek mythology matter? Because it has coloured European and indeed Western thought for millennia. Ancient Greece's most important legacy is their mythology. The Greek gods live on in our imagination no matter how much Christians and others tried to dismiss them as frivolous and harmful. Mostly we encounter Greek myths through the eyes of the Romans in a watered down and filtered form.

Bricolage, a term developed by Claude Levi-Strauss, the structuralist anthropologist, describes the way myth is endlessly reinvented by adding and subtracting elements, making new stories from old ones.[3] Old myths haunt us by the common assumptions about the shape of human experience. The superiority of men is expressed in almost every Greek myth. Indeed, the misogyny of Greek thought "relates the mastery of the female to higher social goals".[4] This is despite the fact that Greek religion had many powerful goddesses who appeared to antedate their male counterparts.

The myth of a matriarchy was used as justification for the status quo.[5] Women, so the myth goes, once ruled but brought chaos because of their dishonesty and licentiousness and therefore they needed to be contained and subjugated. They were counterintuitively both weak and powerful, ineffective and dangerous.

Patriarchal marriage was at the heart of this control. Women who rejected the marriage bond, either warrior Amazons, the Danaids who murder their suitors and see marriage as rape and enslavement, or Klytemnestra who murders her husband Agamemnon because he sacrificed her daughter, are perceived as a threat to men and "civilisation". Men then, needed to create myths which showed the danger women represented and the need to control them. Women of course, through their fertility, were the only way a society might prosper. But women's unbridled sexuality was dangerous and subversive. Women represented a double bind in other words. They were both totally necessary and a source of chaos and rebellion.

Myth then is a way to show "how things have always been" and how badly things go wrong when "unnatural" forces seize power. As we shall see with Metis and the Gorgon Medusa, Greek male gods absorbed and appropriated women's powers by force and then rewrote history to claim them as their own. In mythology, men often steal sacred objects like masks, trumpets, and keys from women, and make them their own exclusive possessions. In this way, Apollo seized the Delphic oracle by killing the female dragon *Pytho* who protected it. Although Apollo can never prophesy, he can control. The oracle, the Pythia, is always a woman.

> In a society dominated by men who sequester their wives and daughters, denigrate the female role in reproduction, erect monuments to the male genitalia, have sex with the sons of their peers, sponsor public whorehouses, create a mythology of rape, and engage in rampant sabre rattling it is not inappropriate to refer to the reign of the phallus.[6]

The story of phallic rule at the root of Western civilisation has been supressed as a result of the near monopoly, until recently, that men have held in the field of classics. This forgetting was achieved by neglect of rich pictorial evidence through prudery and censorship, and by a desire to protect an idealised image of Athens.

As we examine Monstrous Women, we need to be mindful of our own prejudices. The presumed legacy of Ancient Greece penetrated Christian Europe and was interpretated with their bias into religion, philosophy, statesmanship, law, and science.[7] Greece has been used to represent any value and outlook the writer chose to ascribe to it[8] and exploited to fit a modern agenda.

> ... their [the Greeks'] legacy, what we have chosen to inherit or see ourselves as having inherited from them, is still an active process and requires constant scrutiny and re-evaluation.[9]

For example, the type of female experience favoured and reported by classicists is that of the apparently secluded and powerless Athenian woman. She was later chosen by scholars as the "Greek woman" and not her freer and more empowered sister, the Spartan woman. Bias is exposed, as the Greek ideal man was based on Spartan men. The reason for this was that it suited the agendas or prejudices of nineteenth-century classicists and twentieth-century psychologists and anthropologists to represent women in this way.[10]

Classicists often show a double bias, that is male analysis of women's lives, by men who had little access to their lives, which is later interpreted by other similarly prejudiced scholars.[11] For example, Walter Burkert[12] writing on women-only ritual observed, 'the absence of men gives a secret and uncanny quality to the festival of women'. Burkert is expressing the twentieth-century male fear of what women do when men are not around to monitor them. This viewpoint, however, may have been alien to the Greeks who left women the perform their own rituals unsupervised. The voice of Greek women is silent or silenced.

In matters of gender roles, culture overrode nature, Barbarian males were considered to be feminine.[13] Athenian men identified themselves through the polarities of male, female, human, divine, Pythagorean and Aristotelian, Dionysian and Apollonian, and *nomos* versus *phusis*.[14] The complementary positions of men and women, honour, and shame, public and domestic were altered by later scholars into binary oppositions, and they lost their significance as essentially manipulable and rhetorically subtle symbols.

The new science of biology (Aristotle[15] et al) determined that women were inferior and this biological fact was used to legitimise the subordination of women. It follows that whatever cannot be accommodated in the dominant ethos and risks subordinating that order, is claimed as false, a distortion, or a lie, leaving the dominant ethos unchallenged as the correct or natural reality. The norm of course is based on the dominant group's resemblance to themselves and damning others depending on their level of difference. As symbols of aberrations, or abnormality, monsters are defined by socially recognised conventions[16] and are characterised by contrast with the norm. Science, philosophy, religion, and the arts then create discourses which support this view.

The rigid sex-based divisions recorded by later scholars may have far surpassed those of the people they sought to describe.[17]

> A woman in the shape of a monster
> a monster in the shape of a woman
> the skies are full of hate[18]

Historians have viewed Women Monsters as emblematic of Otherness.[19] Art played an indispensable role in defining Otherness in Greek culture.[20] Images leave a deep and abiding impression on both the conscious and subconscious mind, particularly in what was a mainly illiterate culture. Images in material culture are part of a mesh of related ideas, cultural, political, and religious, and thus become part of the established order of things.[21] Art embodies changing attitudes, and in the late Classical period the Gorgo/Medusa changed from hideous to pitiable.[22]

For women and illiterate men, art and storytelling were the main vehicles for the transmission of myth and social and religious mores. Images can reveal what texts omit or cannot articulate. Literacy and intellectual pursuits were generally reserved for Greek citizen males.[23] Through imagery, women learned their place and the penalty for transgressing social norms.[24] Analysing ancient symbols, like women monsters, logically is less helpful than to consider what the *paideutic* (educative) value of the myth was, both in its time and in our own era. In other words, exploring what Athenian society was teaching or trying to teach its members with any given myth gives insight into the values of the *polis* (city).

And it is always important to remember that the Olympian gods, according to Herodotus writing in the fifth century, were created by Homer and Hesiod. They

> created a theogony for the Greeks. They gave names to the gods, decided what their special skills were and what honours they should be given and described their appearance.[25]

The nature of monsters must be seen in relation to the meanings given to monstrosity within the particular culture. I argue for a fresh look at monsters and what they meant to the Greeks, particularly the Athenians. How they originated and how modern scholars have interpreted them.

> ... monstrosity ... [is] the class of things contrary to nature.[26]

Every culture has coded systems of display and concealment, and scripts which prescribe class, gender, social status, age, and ethnicity roles. What is considered a norm could be different in another time. We cannot know how much that is taken for granted and normalised is in fact correct, but we can profitably speculate and question the certainties of previous generations and re-evaluate the material which survives. Monsters, because they are Other, embody the difference between what is normal in a culture and what is not; in other words, monsters serve to define the human normal by bringing the norm into sharper clarity.[27]

Working within the material culture, historians can only decipher what remains. Who decided what to save and what to destroy can only be guessed at. With regard to women, the culture which followed the Greeks and Romans, Christianity, was ultra misogynist and doubtless a great deal of material on women's lives may have been lost or supressed as a result. The voice of Greek women is mostly missing and the words of women have been lost. Women did write and there were female poets in the Classical period (see appendix 2), but they were not saved or deemed important enough to copy.

The reason myths persist is that they represent archetypes which are understood beyond language.[28] They are a vehicle for conversations around general cultural concerns (like women's autonomy) through the narration of particulars.²⁹ The majority of the monsters in ancient Greece were female. Mythic narrative was one way the ancients made sense of the irrational and women, as they situate disorderly monsters and anchor any symbolic force they may have. This narrative logic is heuristic; the plots of myths are not random and the mode of operation is teleological: they are purposeful and functional. Again, we have to question whether our interpretations are chronologically inappropriate.³⁰

Gorgo/Medusa has been seen as a symbol of the conflictual relationship between men and women or masculinity and femininity.³¹ Medusa's demise through the trickery of Perseus has been seen as a male initiation,³² or the removal of a monster representing the Dionysian dark principle by an Apollonian hero, the light principle. Others argue that Gorgo/Medusa records the destruction of the Neolithic Great Goddess Culture at the hands of the invading hordes of patriarchal Greeks.³³ Gorgo/Medusa may exemplify the social archetypes men and women learnt from her deadly gaze, her association with serpents, death, hauntings, her voice, her movements, and her aberrant, non-conformist female nature; which suggest Greek ideas concerning female monstrosity and, in turn, male fear of women.

Symbols are decisive in shaping cultures and provide a crucial nexus between individual and society. Each culture has its own symbolic language.³⁴ The symbolism of Gorgo/Medusa derives from many pasts, and her image may have meant something completely different to the Ancient Greeks from what it does to modern scholars. Lazarou³⁵ identifies six types of Gorgons: the *Gorgoneion,* mixed monsters, Gorgo with animals, winged Gorgo *Knielauf,* Chthonic Gorgon, and the Gorgon from the myth of Hesiod. The classification is useful, and this investigation will consider each of these Gorgons. Lazarou³⁶ provides a thorough critical overview of the research to date.

Chapter One concerns the original demon, gendered female: the *Gorgoneion* or Gorgon's head. It appears several times in Homer and presages doom to warriors. The mouth screams like a banshee, and it is the sound of her fearful roar which chills the blood of those who hear it. The chapter considers silence and noise, and women's relationship to being heard.

Chapter Two describes how the *Gorgoneion* becomes embodied. She is given a woman's body, serpent's hair and becomes the object of the hero's quest. Her head, only recently attached to a body, is detached again by the warrior prince, and is fixed to the breastplate on the *aegis* of the parthenogenic goddess Athena. We consider the deadly gaze of women.

Chapter Three continues the hunt for Gorgo Medusa, and we consider her running, or dancing, her life in the Hesperides with her sisters, and how sacred dance, women's ritual defence, and warrior dance are found in the Maori *Haka* and the temples of India. We consider dance as a sacred vehicle to express women's power.

Chapter Four considers the Greek ideas of the dead which changed over time, and the restless dead who wander between the worlds causing havoc. We consider women living lives of the living dead, paralysed and numbed.

In Chapter Five we meet the Furies, the *Erinyes*, who are also mentioned in Homer. They star in Aeschylus' play *The Eumenides*, written and performed in Classical Athens in 458 BCE. The Erinyes bring death to the living, and avenge oath breakers and those who murder kin. In the play they are neutralised, because they represent the old Chthonic goddesses. They epitomise female rage at injustice and the revenge they take on men, hounding them into insanity. We consider women and revenge.

In Chapter Six I discuss the several manifestations of Hekate. From the Great Shining One, to Queen of the Witches, to the Cosmic Soul. Another Titan goddess, Hekate predates the Olympians and represents Cosmic Order and compassion, and guidance for lost souls and the unquiet dead. We consider ancient chthonic powers, and death and rebirth.

In Chapter Seven we meet the Sirens who are neither ugly nor terrifying. They are beautiful, seductive, and deadly. Their voices draw men to their meadow where they lie captivated and slowly starve to death. Sirens control the weather and lead men astray with the beauty of their song. We consider the beauty of a woman's voice, and its danger.

Chapter Eight we consider other *daemones*. Eris who rages, provokes fights, and embodies the furious woman, who craves bloodshed and discord. The women warrior, the harridan with a big stick. Also Scylla who captures sailors and eats them. We consider fighting and using animals to attack men.

There follow three appendices. Appendix one, Truth and Lies and Opinions, considers how women's voices as credible knowers is a recent phenomenon looks at how knowledge has been transmitted through the centuries and how biases affect what has arrived in our time. Appendix two considers the political background to the changes in fifth-century Athens which affect how myths, particularly those concerning women, evolved, and why that may have been. Appendix three lists the *daemons*.

Interest in Greece has never been greater, and scholars are re-writing or further investigating the past with fresh eyes.[37] *Monstruous Women* aims to provide another viewpoint on Greek mythology and how female monsters change according to the *zeitgeist* or prevailing social mores and how lies and misrepresentation have characterised women through the ages and continue to do so.

Fitzrovia, April 2025.

Notes

1. Lefkowitz 2002:ix.
2. Ovid's *Metamorphoses* is the "standard text" for Greek and Roman mythology. In my opinion, the Roman versions of Greek myths carry their militaristic and cruel culture. Not that the Greeks were not fighters, but the cruelty I feel, is peculiarly Roman.
3. Doherty 2001:129.
4. Zeitlin 1978:150.
5. Bamberger 1974:267.
6. Keuls, Eva, *The Reign of the Phallus. Sexual Politics in Ancient Athens.* (Berkeley CA: University of California Press, 1993).
7. Berggreen 1995:5.
8. Turner 1981:3f.
9. Cartledge 2002:7.
10. Berggreen 1995:6.
11. Berggreen 1995:7, Lyons 2007:36, Butler 1990:136.
12. Burkert 1985:242.
13. Cartledge 2002:11.
14. Cartledge 2002:14–15.
15. See Aristotle *De Generatione* where he contends the father has the major role in the form of the child, the mother is the incubator, a trope which is endlessly used to demean and marginalise women.
16. Morgan 1984:15.
17. Garber 1992:29.

18. Adrienne Rich, Planetarium in *Collected Early Poems 1950–1970* Norton NY 1993:361.
19. Giallongo 2018:3.
20. Giallongo 2018:5.
21. Gombrich 1963:66.
22. Morgan 1984:19.
23. Giallongo 2018:82.
24. Morgan 1984:6.
25. Herodotus *Histories* 3.38.
26. Aristotle *De Generatione* 770 b 10.
27. Morgan 1984:5.
28. Jung 1948:207–254.
29. Morgan 1984:7.
30. Morgan 1984:812–183.
31. Alban 2023:50, Giallongo 2018:3.
32. Marinatos 2000.
33. Gimbutas 1982, Harrison 1903, Frothingham 1911.
34. Giallongo 2018:2.
35. Lazarou 2022:60 figs. A–F.
36. Lazarou 2022:47–62.
37. e.g. Josephine Quinn's monumental history, *How the World Made the West*. (London: Bloomsbury, 2025) who traces much of "Greek" culture and mythology from Phoenician and other states in the Levant.

DRAMATIS PERSONAE (IN DATE ORDER)

The Pythia (c. 1400 BCE): the High Priestess at the shrine at Delphi. It was seized by Apollo, (c. 8th C BCE) who killed the sacred serpent (the Python) who guarded the shrine. The Pythia was the name of the priestess who read the oracle and gave her divination in poetic dactylic hexameters. Later writers (post Greece) claimed the male priests translated these, but there is no basis for this assumption (except misogyny).

Homer (c. 700 BCE): author, disputed by some, of the *Iliad* and the *Odyssey* but probably not the *Homeric Hymns*. Said to have been born in Chios, he was a blind rhapsode or bard who travelled about singing his poems which were written as dactylic hexameters and accompanied by the lyre or *kithra*.

Hesiod (c. 700 BCE): born in Ascra, Boetia (Central Greece). He was a farmer who worked a smallholding near Mount Helicon, where he claimed the Muses visited him. Author of *Theogony* and *Works and Days*, written in the form of poetry. Unclear if he is the author of the *Shield of Heracles* and the *Catalogue of Famous Women*.

Sappho (born circa 612 BCE): lyric poet of Mytilene in Lesbos, centre of a group of women and girls around the cult of Aphrodite.

Author of seven or ten books of poetry, on the themes of love, Aphrodite, marriage, and mythology. Her work is mostly lost, although poems are continually being discovered on buried papyri in the Egyptian desert at Oxyrhynchus.

Pythagoras (c. 530 BCE): Greek philosopher and mathematician born in Samos. Started a community in Croton, southern Italy for men and women as equal members. An influence on Plato, especially on the movement of the spheres (see Sirens). He left no writing. Euclid set out the theory which has his name but was Babylonian in origin (dated to 1800 BCE).

Pindar (518–438 BCE): Greek lyric poet, born in Boetia, educated in Athens. Composer of *Odes*, choral songs which celebrated winners in athletic games.

Bacchylides (c. 6th C BCE): Greek lyric poet from Keos, who wrote poems, victory odes, and choral hymns.

Aesop (6th C BCE): creator of fables. Herodotus said he was a slave from Samos.

Herodotus (c. 484–420 BCE): from Halicarnassus (modern day Bodrum in Turkey). Called the "father of history", he travelled widely in Europe and Egypt. He was the first to write in prose, as far as we know. Author of the *Histories* which are considered the first history and ethnography books.

Aeschylus (525–456 BCE): Athenian tragic dramatist, author of over eighty plays, seven of which survive: *Persians, Suppliants, Seven Against Thebes, Prometheus Bound* and the trilogy, *The Oresteia*, which is three plays, *Agamemnon, The Libation Bearers* and *The Eumenides*. All these were performed publicly at the annual patronal festival in Athens, the *Panathenaea*.

Pericles (d. 429 BCE): Pericles was a Greek politician and general during the 'Golden Age of Athens'. He was important during the Greco-Persian Wars and the Peloponnesian War and was responsible for most of the building on the Acropolis. His famous Funeral Speech was recorded by Thucydides, a contemporary historian, who called him 'the first citizen of Athens'. He was the husband/partner of Aspasia.

Sophocles (496–406 BCE): Athenian tragic dramatist, friend of Herodotus. Author of one hundred and twenty three plays of which seven survive: *Ajax, Antigone, King Oedipus, Women of Trachis, Electra, Philoctetes,* and *Oedipus at Colonis*. All were performed at the *Panathenaea*.

Euripides (480–406 BCE): Athenian tragic dramatist. Author of ninety-two plays of which nineteen survive including *Medea, Phaedra, The Bacchae, The Trojan Women, Alcestis, Hippolytus,* and *Electra*. Known for his sympathetic portrayal of women.

Aristophanes (450–385 BCE): Greek comic dramatist. He wrote over forty comedies of which eleven survive. They were wicked satires and parodies of famous Athenians, performed at the *Dionysia* (plays in honour of the god Dionysius) at the *Panathenaea*, usually in front of his victims (male citizens were expected to attend these plays). They include *Frogs, The Birds, Lysistrata* (about a sex-strike by the women of Athens), *Wasps, Archanians* and *Clouds*. He was a friend of Socrates, who he mocked in *Clouds* and from where the expression "cloud-cuckoo land" comes from.

Thucydides (c. 460–400 BCE): Greek historian, general, author of *The History of the Peloponnesian War*, in which the famous *Funeral Speech* is found.

Socrates (469–399 BCE): Athenian philosopher. He left no writing, and we know him through the books of Plato and Xenophon. Socrates taught on love according to the teachings of Diotima, a priestess (nothing more is known about her). He was executed by taking a lethal dose of hemlock by the Athenians for corrupting the youth and bringing false gods into the city.

Diotima (c. 440 BCE): a female philosopher who instructed Socrates in *eros*. Her teachings were the basis of what later became known as Platonic Love (after Plato in *The Symposium*). Later scholars believed she was fictional, while more modern scholarship suggests she was based on Aspasia (Pericles). She was called wise (*sophos*) and a prophetess (*mantis*). Her teaching on the daimon (that which is between mortal and immortal) and giving birth to the beautiful appear in Plato.

Plato (429–347 BCE): Athenian philosopher, pupil and friend of Socrates, and teacher of Aristotle. He wrote on Socrates's teachings and his death in the *Apology* and on the ideal state in the *Republic*. His metaphysical views were influenced by Pythagoras, especially the *Myth of Er* in the *Republic* (see Sirens). His works were translated by Marsilio Ficino in Florence in the fifteenth century and influenced western thought thereafter for good or ill.

Xenocrates of Chalcedon (396–314 BCE) was a Greek philosopher, mathematician, and leader of the Platonic Academy from 339/8 to 314/3 BCE. His teachings followed those of Plato, which he attempted to define more closely, often including mathematical elements.

Aristotle (384–322 BCE): Greek scientist and philosopher. He studied with Plato and taught Alexander the Great.

Callimachus (c. 305–240 BCE): Hellenistic poet, he worked at the library of Alexandria and produced a 120-volume catalogue.

Theocritus (c. 300–260 BCE): Greek pastoral poet working mostly in Cos and Alexandria.

Apollonius of Rhodes (3rd C BCE): Alexandrian poet named after the island he retired to. Head of the famous library of Alexandria, he wrote the *Argonautica*, a four-book epic dealing with Jason's quest for the Golden Fleece and his relationship with Medea. He was a big influence on the Roman poet Ovid.

Virgil (70 BCE–19 BCE): Roman poet author of the *Aeneid*, which follows Aeneas to Rome after the fall of Troy.

Ovid (43 BCE-17/18 CE): Roman poet from whom much of our knowledge of Greek myths comes. His book *Metamorphoses* brings a Roman slant to the myths and is substantially more bloodthirsty and cruel than the Greek originals.

Seneca (4 BCE–65 CE): Roman philosopher and writer. Wrote tragedies based on the Greek, *Medea*, *Phaedra* and *Oedipus*.

Plutarch (c. 46–126 CE): Greek essayist and biographer living in Rome. His essays include *Moralia* and *Parallel Lives*.

Dio Chrysostom (c. 40–115 CE): orator, writer, philosopher, and historian.

Porphyry (c. 233–309 CE): Greek philosopher.

MYTHICAL FIGURES

(I go into the mythology of goddesses in more depth in my book *Goddess Astrology*.)

Achilles: the Greek warrior who fought in the Trojan War and had 'the longest sulk in history' when Agamemnon took away his slave Briseis. He died at Troy.

Agamemnon: King of the Mycenae who led the Greek forces in the Trojan War. He sacrificed his daughter Iphigenia to Artemis when the Greek fleet was becalmed. In revenge, his wife, Klytemnestra (or her lover) murdered him, when Agamemnon returned from Troy.

Aphrodite: goddess of love and beauty, either the daughter of Zeus and Dione or foam-born from the severed penis of Uranus. She has close affinity with Semitic Astarte.

Apollo: twin of Artemis, son of Leto. He took over the Delphic Oracle by killing the serpent guardian.

Artemis: pre-Olympian goddess. Olympians give her as the daughter or Zeus and Leto, twin sister of Apollo. Often conflated with Hekate or

Selene, the Moon goddess. Hunter, dancer, protector of the young and birthing women.

Athena: Greek goddess of war, of cities especially Athens, and of crafts and wisdom. Daughter of Zeus and Metis, who Zeus swallowed to appropriate her knowledge. She was born from his head. She wears the *aegis* which has the Gorgon's head on it.

Dionysus: perhaps pre-Greek and Greek god of wine and the ecstatic cult of his Mysteries. His origin myths are various; in one he was the son of Zeus and Semele. Taken from the dead body of Semele and brought to Mount Nysa in India where he was raised by the nymphs and taught the use of vine by Silenus and the Satyrs, and of ivy which is intoxicating and a symbol of the afterlife. Carrying his ivy-entwined staff, he led his maenads from India to Greece. Other myths say he was born in Thebes, that he was the son of Persephone. He was celebrated in the Great Dionysia in Athens where plays were performed. Other sources indicate he was worshipped in Mycenaean culture.

Electra: daughter of Klytemnestra and Agamemnon, said to be the driving force behind Orestes' matricide driven by her hatred of her mother. Subject of Euripides' *Electra* and source of Freudian "Electra Complex", hatred of the mother.

Gaia: pre-Greek Gaia is the ancestral mother, sometimes parthenogenically, sometimes of all life. She is the mother of Uranus (Ouranus, personification of the sky). They produced the Titans (parents of the Olympians), the Cyclopes and the Giants, as well as Pontus (sea). She mated with him to bear the primordial sea gods. The mating and marrying is probably a way to explain how the older goddesses lost or had their powers and spheres of influence taken by the Olympians.

Jason: son of king Aeson in Thessaly, his uncle usurped the throne, and he was raised by Chiron. When he returned to claim the throne, his uncle sent him to fetch the Golden Fleece. He assembled his crew, the Argonauts, and their adventures were recorded by Apollonius of Rhodes's *Argonautica*. He was helped by Medea, princess of Colchis, who killed her brother to obtain it.

Kalypso (Calypso): a nymph daughter of Atlas living on the island of Ogygia where she keeps Odysseus captive for seven years. Her name means hidden. She was a chthonic goddess who offers Odysseus eternal life, but he refuses her offer as he wishes to return home to his wife, Penelope.

Kassandra (Cassandra): daughter of Queen Hecuba and King Priam of Troy, priestess of Apollo, who was fated never to be believed. After the fall of Troy, she was the sex slave of Agamemnon. She warned him his wife would kill him, but he ignored her, and they were both murdered by Klytemnestra and her lover Aegisthus.

Kirke (Circe): goddess and sorceress, daughter of the Sun who lived on an island of Aeaea with wild animals. She changed Odysseus' men into pigs with her wild herbs. He resisted her magic using the herb *moly* given to him by Hermes. Odysseus lived with her for a year, and she tells him how to get to the Underworld and warns him about the Sirens. Medea and Jason visit, so Medea can get some herbs which she later uses to kill her rival.

Klytemnestra (Clytemnestra): sister of Helen (of Troy), wife of Agamemnon king of Mycenae. While he was away fighting, she took his cousin Aegisthus as a lover, and when Agamemnon returned they killed him (jointly or severally). She was the mother of Orestes, Electra and Iphigenia, who Agamemnon sacrificed to Artemis to move the becalmed fleet sailing to attack Troy.

Kronos (Cronos): the youngest of the first generation of Titans, descendants of Gaia and Uranus. He castrated his father with a sickle and seized power. He was then overthrown by his own son, Zeus.

Medea: daughter of the King of Colchis and granddaughter of Helios the sun god. She was a high priestess of Hekate and a witch. She helped Jason to steal the Golden Fleece. She killed her brother in the process, and they travelled to Kirke who cleansed her of the blood guilt. They then travelled to Corinth where Jason abandoned her for the King's daughter. Medea killed her and her father with a poisoned robe and diadem and murdered her own two sons. She escaped in a chariot of the Sun to Athens and then Asia.

Metis: goddess of wisdom, wife of Zeus and mother of Athena. She was swallowed by Zeus who gave birth to Athena through his head.

Muses: The nine muses of the creative arts who taught Hesiod his poetry (or he channelled theirs). Daughters of Zeus and Mnemosyne (memory) according to Hesiod, while Alcman (c. 7th C BCE) said they were daughters of Gaia and Ouranos and hence deities of Delphi, long before Apollo, who was later said to control them. Named in Hellenistic times, they were given spheres of influence: Calliope (heroic epic), Clio (history), Euterpe (flute and music), Terpsichore (lyric poetry and dance), Erato (hymns), Melpomene (tragedy), Thalia (comedy), Polyhymnia (mime), and Urania (astrology).

Nyx (Night) is a primaeval goddess, the daughter of Chaos, and sister of Erebus. According to some sources, Nyx and Erebus become the parents of Aether and Hemera (Day). Parthenogenetically she gives birth to Moros, Ker, Thanatos, Hypnos, Oneiroi, Momus, Oizys, the Hesperides, the Morai, the Keres, Nemesis, Apate, Philotes, Geras, and Eris (see appendix 3). Other sources make her the mother of the Erinyes and Hekate.

Odysseus: protagonist of *The Odyssey* which concerns his journey home after the fall of Troy. King of Ithaca, husband of Penelope (she of the endless weaving). On his journey he meets goddesses Kirke (Circe) and Kalypso (Calypso), encounters the Cyclops, Scylla and the Sirens, and travels to Hades.

Orestes: son of Agamemnon and Klytemnestra. To avenge his father's murder, he murders his mother and is pursued by the *Erinyes* (see Erinyes).

Poseidon: god of the sea, brother of Zeus and Hades, rival to Athena.

Perseus: son of Zeus and Danae. He rescued Andromeda and killed the Gorgon Medusa.

The Python (Pytho) was a dragon or serpent (*Drakina*) said to be living at the centre of the earth (Delphi) represented by a stone, the *omphalos* or navel/womb, which Python guarded. Python was the good daemon of the shrine and appears in Minoan religion. There were Minoan priestesses at Delphi in the early days.

Rhea: the Titan daughter of Gaia and Uranus, himself a son of Gaia. She is the older sister of Kronos (Cronos) who married her. She is the mother of the six eldest Olympian gods, Hestia, Demeter, Hera,

Poseidon, Hades and Zeus. Kronos learnt that he would be overthrown by one of his children like his father before him, so he swallowed all his children with Rhea as they were born. When Rhea had her sixth and final child, Zeus, she spirited him away and hid him in Krete substituting a stone for the baby. The stone was later installed at Delphi as the *omphalos* or navel stone of the world. Zeus overthrew his father by castrating him.

Scylla (or Skylla) and **Charybdis:** Scylla was a man-eating monster who lived on one side of a narrow channel of water, opposite her counterpart, the sea-swallowing monster Charybdis. The two sides of the strait are within an arrow's range of each other, so close that sailors attempting to avoid the whirlpools of Charybdis would pass dangerously close to Scylla. Scylla's parentage is unclear. Three times a day, Charybdis swallowed a huge amount of water, before belching it back out again, creating large whirlpools capable of dragging a ship underwater. Her parents were said to be Poseidon and Gaia (brother and sister).

Titans: pre-Olympian gods. They were the twelve children of the primordial parents Gaia (Earth) and Uranus (Sky). The six female Titans were Theia, Rhea, Themis, Mnemosyne, Phoebe, and Tethys. The male Titans were Oceanus, Coeus, Crius, Hyperion, Iapetus and Kronos. They fought a ten-year battle against the Olympians (the Titanomachy) and lost and were imprisoned in Tartarus. Some remained free.

Zeus: a primaeval rain and thunder god, son of Kronos and Rhea. He fought against the Titans and ousted the pre-Olympian gods. Rapist and seducer of many.

TIMELINE[1]

Middle Bronze Age 2100–1600 BCE

2100 Incursion of Indo-European speakers into Greece.

2100 Indo-European gods introduced.

1900 first palaces on Krete. Mainland contacts with Krete and Near East.

1800 Linear A writing developed on Krete.

1600–1150 late Bronze Age: flourishing of important centres, Mycenae and Pylos. Linear B writing. Major settlement at Troy: Troy VI, modern day Hisarlik, Turkey.

1500–1450 Mycenaeans take over Krete.

1450 destruction of the pre-Greek Minoan palaces.

1375 Knossos destroyed.

1250–1225 Trojan War, possible oral composition of the Homeric poems *Iliad* and *Odyssey*.

1200 invaders loot and destroy Mycenaean palace centres.

1200–1100 collapse of the Mycenaean palatial civilization.

"Early Dark Age" c. 1100–900 BCE

900 buildings at Nichoria and Lefkandi.

800–770 early Geometric Period. Greeks begin using Phoenician (from the Levant) phonetic alphabetical writing.

776 traditional first date of the Olympic games.

Archaic Period 750–480 BCE

750–700 creation of large geometric pots in the Kerameikos cemetery, Athens.

725–675 Homeric poems oral composition and oral preservation by Homeridae (followers of Homer) in Chios.

720 orientalising period.

700–650 Hesiod's *Theogony* and *Works and Days*. Period of lyric poetry.

650 temples built. Corinthian black figure pottery.

600 Presocratic philosophy and science.

582–573 Pythian and Nemean games.

560–514 Peisistratus, the tyrant of Athens, expands religious festivals.

530 Athenian red figure pottery.

530–510 interest in Homeric poems in Athens under Peisistratus (c. 530–510 BCE), possible recitation at the Panathenaic festival.

Classical period 480–323 BCE

500–400 Athenian tragedies dramatize Greek legendary stories including Homeric.

458 first performance of Aeschylus' *Oresteia*.

451 Pericles' laws on citizenship. Herodotus' *Histories*.

447–432 Parthenon built.

400–320 much literary criticism with reference to Homer, Plato and Aristotle, suggesting they were well-known.

399 Socrates executed.

387 Plato founds the Academy at Athens.

343 Aristotle, tutor to Alexander the Great.

Hellenistic Period 323–30 BCE

300–100 Alexandrian scholarship in Egypt. Homeric Texts edited and studied and divided into 24 books. The earliest papyrus fragments date from the 3rd century BCE.

100 BCE-1300 CE Graeco-Roman and Byzantine scholars at Pergamon, Rome. Athens then Constantinople publish commentaries on Homer. The oldest complete surviving manuscript date back to the 10th–11th century.

Modern Scholarship of Homer

1488 First printed Homer in Florence.

1917 Standard scholarly text, the "Oxford Texts".

Note

1. For an excellent, detailed and researched history and background of the development of Greece see: Quinn, Josephine, *How the World Made the West.* (London: Bloomsbury, 2025). Many of the dates are speculative or open to debate but the general timelines are correct.

CHAPTER ONE

Roots of the Gorgon

> Myths are strange things that never happened but always are.
>
> Sallust

Gorgo/Medusa has been called the first female monster.[1] She is found in the earliest Greek written sources, Homer and Hesiod. The *Gorgoneion* or disembodied head of the Gorgon was the symbol of death. The use of the disembodied head as an apotropaic symbol (having the power to avert evil influences) protected warriors on their armour and on temples and coinage and elsewhere.

The *Gorgoneion* (Figure 1.1) is the head of the gorgon without the body. It is believed to have originated in the prehistoric Greek mainland and Aegean. The earliest example of a pre-*Gorgoneion* dates to the Middle Neolithic era (4100–2500 BCE), found in Sesklo, central Greece. It is a ceramic mask with bulging eyes, elongated mouth, wide nostrils, and a prominent teeth and tongue.[2]

2 MONSTROUS WOMEN

Figure 1.1. *Gorgoneion*, Red figure *Gorgoneion* Hydra, c. 490 BCE. Notice the twenty-eight snakes.

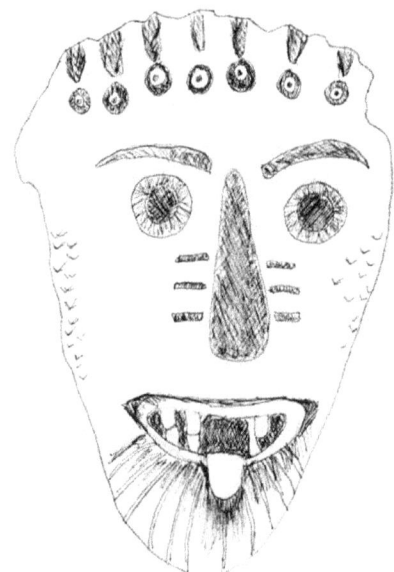

Figure 1.2. Pre-*Gorgoneion*, Gorgon mask. Mainland Greece 628–580 BCE.

Certainly, the figure resembles the *Gorgoneion*. But so do the Baubo figures on a seal impression from Uruk dated to the end of the fourth millennium BCE.[3] Arguably the *Gorgoneion* either derived from a combination of these sources or represents an ancient archetypal demonic figure found in several cultures.

Figure 1.3. Baubo figure, Baubo figure. Asia Minor 5th century BCE.

Homer's epics glorify warrior culture, or rather the bravery of individual warriors, but overall they can be seen as anti-war poems. There are individual heroics, but also stupidity. By the time of Homer[4] the pantheon of Olympian deities had been established.

Homer mentions the *Gorgoneion* four times.[5] He does not fully describe the *Gorgoneion*, and as a result each artist created their own version albeit with similar iconography. Eventually, a common symbol was developed, and it was reproduced all over the Greek-speaking world.

4   MONSTROUS WOMEN

Figure 1.4. Achilles and Ajax playing a boardgame. Athenian Black figure Amphora. 575–550 BCE. From Vulci. Vatican Museum.

This amphora shows the side view of the warriors' shields, both of which have the *Gorgoneion* on them. But the *Gorgoneion* appears to be male, and it has male-like features, with abundant, but not snaky, hair and a bushy beard which is similar to the beards of the two warriors, luxurious and detailed. Both shields show other *Gorgoneion* iconography: the left, a panther or leopard and a bearded snake, and the right two bearded snakes. The face on the right has two tusks and a protruding tongue, while the left shield shows a thick hairstyle and a luxurious beard. Ajax or Achilles (on the left) has a panther icon tattoo on his upper right arm, which would be his spear- and sword-holding arm. Although the *Gorgoneion* is gendered female in the text, this illustration shows hyper masculine faces.

This amphora and its iconography relate to the description of Agamemnon's shield strap which has the *Gorgoneion* and a blue snake above it, but not part of it. The *Gorgoneion*[6] is described as ferocious-faced, *blosuropis* (also bushy-faced) or "of hairy appearance", which probably describes the beard.[7] Also "bristly-haired" or "shaggy".[8] Interestingly[9] *blosuropis* can be translated as "wicked faced", which gives a more neutral sense of intent to cause harm and to protect warriors from danger.

Shields are the largest image a warrior will present to an enemy in hand-to-hand fighting, so the symbols on them are intended to alarm the enemy. The symbolism of the snake represents Hades, where the enemy is headed; the panther shows the warrior's strength, courage, and deadly fighting skills; and the head of a screaming supernatural figure with fangs which is intended to petrify the enemy.

Figure 1.5. Shaggy faced *Gorgoneion*, c. 525 BCE.

The *Gorgoneion* is described as fearful and wondrous (*deinde*).[10] Homer is not speaking of an embodied Gorgo/Medusa but a head without a body. A disembodied head is horrifying and bloodthirsty, and embodies terror, hatred, courage and agression. *Smerdne* means terrible to look at and terrible to hear. Its roots are probably cognate with the Sanskrit *mardati* (to crush or crumble), which can also be translated as "blasting", evoking both noise and smashing. Fearful noise is the signature of the *Gorgoneion* as much as its terrible appearance. The *Gorgoneion* screams or shouts at men, which explains her open mouth and lolling tongue.[11] The word "Gorgon" is derived from the Sanskrit stem *garg* which relates to gargle, gurgling, gorge, gargoyle, and growl in English. So, not only does the *Gorgoneion* have a deadly glare, but monstrous sounds also come from her wide-open mouth, a terrifying roar, a guttural animalistic howl. Fearful noise is then part of her terror. Gorgo's mouth is always open wide. The 'blasting thing' gives the cry added force. In Homer, the *aegis* (Athena's breastplate) and the *Gorgoneion* are 'terror, hatred and battle strength, heart-freezing onslaught, the grim gigantic Gorgon, a thing of fear and horror'.[12]

Figure 1.6. The Chigi vase, detail of shields Corinth c. 640 BCE.

Figure 1.7. Gorgoneion anti-fix roof tile, South Italy c. 540 BCE. Notice the 13 snakes, the number of full moons in a year.

The *Gorgoneion*, therefore, is an apotropaic symbol. As an apotropaic symbol, it both terrifies and repels.[13] It is found on armour, cooking implements, chariots, coinage, cosmetics, antefixes on temples and houses, and its use and meaning are clear: it protects and keeps danger away.[14] Thus, the *Gorgoneion* was distinct from the Gorgo/Medusa.[15] The *Gorgoneion* has a clearly defined area of influence, its purpose to create confusion and repel the enemy and evil forces by doing this.[16]

Gorgoneions were among the most ancient monsters.[17] Those of the 7th century BCE often featured large heads, gaping mouths and wide, generally almond-shaped eyes surmounted by prominent brows, all the hallmarks of a dangerous and bestial nature. They may have derived from a peasant society and the natural fear of aggressive wild animals.[18] Or perhaps the *Gorgoneion* originated in North Africa and depicted Bes the lion. Alternatively the terror on seeing the *Gorgoneion* was a fear found amongst all primates, the fear of decapitation.[19] The mask could also represent human fear or be a symbol of human aggression designed to keep wild beasts and enemies away.[20] Her head not only glares but it is shaggy-maned like a wild animal. Her hair is integral to her iconography.[21]

In the *Odyssey* (2.634) the *Gorgoneion* is described as the 'gigantic shape of fear'. An interesting theory considers it to be a threshold guardian wearing the mask of Hekate who protects the sacred sanctuaries dedicated to her worship.[22] Behind the mask of Hekate is the void, the great nothingness from which everything arose; thus the mask blocks what is 'too potent and deadly to be seen' and no mortal can look behind the mask or into her eyes and 'escape paralysis or disintegration'. It seems more likely that the demon the *Gorgoneion* illustrates is exactly that and has no need for a mask, as the terrors and meaninglessness of death are well known to the warrior.

The *Gorgoneion's* most important role is policing the boundary between the living and the dead.[23] She does not simply petrify (from "petra" meaning rock), she engulfs the soul of the dead and deposits it in Hades. Odysseus refers to the *Gorgoneion* as 'the terrible monster' because she is sent by Persephone from Hades to collect the dead, and he was terrified of the nothingness of death.[24] So terrible was the vision of the *Gorgoneion* that Odysseus fled the Underworld,

> '... lest August Persephone might send out from the house of Hades the head of the Gorgon, that awful monster.'[25] Odysseus, who was untroubled by the mass of ghosts who flew to him in Hades,

was terrified by the thought the Gorgon might appear. Homer understood the greatest of heroes still had the frightened little boy inside, who would flee in terror from monsters.[26]

In the epic view, death was divided into positive heroic deaths with *kleos* (glory or fame), like Achilles who chose a short but glorious life rather than a safe old age.[27] Heroes went to the Elysian Fields[28] which were exclusive to elite males. For most people, until the Mystery cults of the Classical era, death was oblivion.[29] In Hades the *eidolon* (spectre, phantom) of the dead wandered for eternity. The dead were shadows, dependent on *choai* or libations[30] poured by the living.[31] Thanatos was the god of peaceful death.[32]

The *Keres* were the goddesses of death from violence or disease, and were malevolent forces which swept into people's lives, bringing a harsh and painful demise. Ignominious death was considered female. The *Keres* were female then, suggesting they were concerned with the unheroic, miasmic[33] areas of life, like sickness and childbirth. The *Gorgoneion* does not represent Thanatos, which is the warrior's noble death, a civilised death with lavish funerals, expensive tombs, heroic myths, and songs to remember them by, but the ignominious death of the defeated, eaten by carrion, or the unnoticed death of the insignificant, and the repulsion and fear of the human transformed into a corpse, the 'horror of unspeakable Night'.[34] The *Gorgoneion* represents a putrefying corpse with bulging staring lifeless eyes and flaccid, swollen tongue.[35] And she symbolises the ignominy of the death of the defeated warrior.[36]

As an apotropaic symbol the *Gorgoneion* shows the enemy what is in store for them as they die, and this is why they are found projected outwards on shields and weapons. The *Gorgoneion's* gaping mouth evokes chaos, the empty space of nothingness and the primordial night (Nyx). This is the worst fate a hero could imagine, where *kleos* and *arete* (fame and renown) after death are paramount. Chaos is related to *chaino* (to gape) and *chasma* "chasm" which are evoked by the open mouth of the *Gorgoneion*.[37] When Ker[38] swallows Patroklus,[39] the verb used is *amphichaino* which suggests she swallows him back to the original abyss, the realm of Night (Nyx) who emerges from the primaeval chaos, born parthenogenically.[40] The *Gorgoneion* is called *khthonia* (the origin of "chthonic"), dwelling in Hades.[41]

Homer describes *Gorgoneion's* eyes as 'grim of aspect, glaring terribly'.[42] The *Gorgoneion's* frontal face emphasises her lethal gaze. The Homeric epics call it *brotoloigou* which translates as the 'bane' of men, implying a lethal danger.[43] This suggests a sudden disintegration caused by the power of the eyes that unnerves men and makes them collapse. The *Gorgoneion* has the wide eyes of the predator, the owl who sees in the dark, the snake who fascinates and hypnotises its prey before killing it.[44] Eyes also have a protective function against the malignant gaze of others. Bulging eyes and protruding tongues deter predators in the animal kingdom. Wrathful gods across the world are shown with fangs and protruding tongues.[45] The Greeks imbued the gaze with extraordinary powers.

Figure 1.8. Bulging eyes of the *Gorgoneion*. Attic Black Figure Eye cup. c. 530 BCE.

A woman's gaze was connected with female power. An epic hero's knees loosen with the desire that comes from a woman's eyes.[46] The Greeks had much to say about the eye: biologically (Aristotle), philosophically (Plato), and mathematically (Euclid).[47] They believed that the eye emitted rays that could interact with the object being viewed. The eyes were perceived as a kind of cold-fire furnace, radiating positive or negative influences into the world outside. The look of the *Gorgoneion* mobilises its terrifying rays to destroy the malignant gaze of the enemy.[48]

There is an intimacy in meeting the gaze of another and, as windows to the soul, the eyes reveal our innermost nature and our vulnerabilities. The unflinching full-frontal stare of the *Gorgoneion* draws the man in. Like the hypnotising eyes of a snake, he cannot withdraw his gaze, but is mesmerised by the power her eyes emit. He is spellbound by those terrible eyes and dominated by her gaze. Possessed, he ceases to be himself, loses his humanity and is consumed by the awful power of the *Gorgoneion*. Through the eyes of the *Gorgoneion* the man enters a 'radical alterity'[49] and is lost. Warriors could evoke the deadly Gorgon stare. Homer describes Trojan Hector's eyes as he goes in for the kill; he had 'Gorgon eyes or those of man-destroying Ares'.[50]

So the eye was a powerful instrument of the body. It showed personal character and could channel the supernatural, acting as both predator and prey. It was thought of as the most trustworthy part of the body.[51] Facial expressions and the eyes were, in effect, useful tools for studying human character.[52] It was believed a man should never look certain women (maybe dangerous ones), death or the gods in the eyes because their unmediated power is too great.[53] The *Gorgoneion* subverts the male gaze, which is dominant in patriarchal societies.

> Men do not simply look; their gaze carries with it the power of action and possession.[54]

The male gaze controls the actions of women and threatens them. Being watched, judged and stalked is an everyday experience for women and girls. The gaze can be appreciative, but also threatening and confrontational. Women are expected to lower their eyes, look away. Too bold a look threatens fragile male egos or is seen as an 'invitation'. Thus women are relegated to objects to be viewed and controlled by the male gaze. But when women stare back, they make men the object which threatens their power. A woman's stare is the antidote to the power and threat of the male gaze. Men do not simply look; their stare is about possession.

> The Look of the Other, which reveals to me my object side, judges me, categorises me; identifies me with my external acts and appearances ... it threatens ... to reduce me to the status of a thing in the world. In short, it reveals my physical and my psychic vulnerability, my fragility.[55]

The Look is so disturbing because it is another judging us and we have no control or any idea what their judgement is.[56] The hard male gaze is a defence against men's vulnerability being revealed through the female gaze. Like those staring contests we had as children, whoever can hold out the longest is the 'winner'.

The stare of women and the *Gorgoneion* reminds weak men of the awesome power women had in pre-Olympian times. She was the serpent goddess of Libyan Amazons, perhaps even from a Black Amazon tribe[57] and the destroying aspect of the Triple Goddess.[58] She was all that has been, that is, and that will be.[59]

Her fearsome gaze reminds that one must not look a goddess in the face, nor certain women, witches, and wizards, as their eyes held a terrible power and they may fascinate, hypnotise, and kill. Interestingly, amulets to banish the 'evil eye' (*ophthalmòs báskanos*) included objects in the shape of a phallus, which suggests only the power of the masculine could avert its awesome power. Phallic charms were found on finger rings and pendants as well as being carved on buildings.[60]

Similarly there are several Greek myths of gods and heroes blinding monsters. Zeus ends the Titanomachy (the Titan rebellion against the Olympians) by blinding the Titans with his flash of lightning. His enemy Typhoeus is a threat because of his hundreds of flame-spurting eyes. Zeus' ability to blind his enemies heralds their comprehensive defeat.[61]

People are often blinded for offences against the gods, as with Erymanthos after he saw Aphrodite bathing. Stesichorus is supposed to have been blinded for insulting Helen. Poseidon put a mist before Achilles' eyes to stop him killing Aeneas.[62] Orion is blinded as a punishment for rape, but he regains his sight upon seeing Helios, the sun. Often prophets and seers are blind or blinded by the gods. Tiresias is blinded because he sees Athena bathing, but she gives him the gift of prophecy in return. Homer was said to be blind, and this gave him the gift of poetry.

12   MONSTROUS WOMEN

Figure 1.9. Kylix Black-Figure pot. Athens c. 560 BCE.

This pot shows Cadmus, Apollo, or Achilles carrying a shield bearing the face of the *Gorgoneion*, in the act of slaying a bearded snake twined around the pillar of a temple or something hidden behind a curtain. There is a second snake behind the building, two water birds on the roof, and two raptors, one before and one behind the hero. Below is a hare and two flower-like medallions, or sunbursts. The *Gorgoneion* on his shield has a full beard, staring, large eyes, and a protruding tongue, but the snakes are all external to it, on the building.

The *Gorgoneion* is not using serpentine power but is destroying it via a warrior. The snake is the enemy of the warrior who is using the apotropaic force of the *Gorgoneion* in his battle. Both the snake and the bird are symbols often associated with Gorgo/Medusa. Snakes may be connected with the Neolithic bird/snake goddess and symbolise a continuum of birth, death, and rebirth.[63] The birds represent the sky and the snakes represent the earth, and the Underworld. Snakes are oviparous[64] and carry deep symbolism.[65] They hibernate in the earth which connects them to death and burial, the bearded snake is found in tombs in Greece. Snakes shed their skin which shows regeneration. The sudden appearance of snakes in spring, when they emerge from hibernation (darkness), is followed by a vigorous mating.[66] Snakes then can be associated with death, regeneration and fertility and sexuality. Greek theogony swarms with malevolent snake-women: the reptile which guarded the garden of the Hesperides, the monster Echidna, half-nymph half-snake, who bore the Chimera, one-third snake, and the Drakina a female snake-dragon Apollo killed to take over the oracle at Delphi.

> Wherever the Greeks came, in every valley, every isle, and every cove, there was a local manifestation of the goddess-mother.[67]

Myths concerning heroes' killing snakes and dragons, of which there are many, tell of the destruction of the ancient snake-cults of women and replacing them with hero-cults of men. The invading Hellenes destroyed the shrines and tore off the masks of the priestesses of the goddess. It can be argued the original *Gorgoneion* was an apotropaic mask worn by priestesses to protect their secret rituals from interlopers.

The Goddess Athena had a *Gorgoneion* on her *aegis*. The *aegis* comes from the stem *aisso*, meaning to move or rush violently, and could signify a rushing storm or hurricane or frightening like the shaking of an *aegis* to warn, threaten and announce. It also comes from *aix* which means little goat and may refer to it being a goat-skin cloak. The aegis was originally Athena's and was 'transferred to' or stolen by Zeus when he arrived in Greece.[68] Herodotus wrote that the source of the *aegis* was in Libya, which was always a distant territory of ancient magic for the Greeks.

> Athena's garments and aegis were copied by the Greeks from the Libyan women, who are dressed in exactly the same way, except that their leather garments are fringed with thongs, not serpents.[69]

Libya, of course was one home of the Amazons, the other being Scythia on the Black Sea. Goat-skin aprons were the usual clothes of Libyan maidens, and the *aegis* a magical goat-skin bag containing a snake and protected by a Gorgon mask.[70] It may have contained a sacred disc with the Pelasgian alphabet written on it[71] and was Athena's long before her father stole it. The original *Gorgoneion* then had a sacred purpose, to protect secrets of the goddess.

A poem by Stesichoros (6th C BCE) called the *Birth of Athena*[72] suggests that Athena was born with the *aegis*, while Hesiod argues, perhaps in his predictably misogynist manner, that Athena, jealous of the armour of Zeus, carried the *aegis* that Metis had in some way conceived *in utero*.[73] Zeus is referred to as *aigiochos* (aegis bearing), and this name occurs at least fifty times in the *Iliad* and *Odyssey*.[74] The *aegis* then reflects the special relationship of Zeus and Athena, although it was used by Apollo to repel enemies.[75] No other gods could wear it.

The power of the *Gorgoneion* is in her gaze and her voice. Hilariously, psychoanalytic theory has decided that the *Gorgoneion* is a symbol of the vulva and that this is the origin of the horror on seeing it. The symbol of the virgin Athena who repels all sexual advances is that of the genitals of the Mother and because 'Greeks were strongly homosexual' this horrific symbol of 'castration' frightens and repels them.[76] This is laughable because this male perspective misses the obvious. It is not the penis women envy, but the power and privileges than accompany it. The face of the *Gorgoneion* with her staring eyes, boldly looking into the eyes of men causes them to 'feel that my free subjectivity has been paralyzed, this is as if I had been turned to stone.'[77] The baleful eyes make the warrior the object; he sees himself and is rendered powerless and then dead.

Later, the *Gorgoneion* becomes Gorgo/Medusa. She develops a body, but it is not clear why that should be.[78] Why was this terrible symbol female? And why was Athena, the parthenogenic goddess, the one to kill her (or not) and wear her decapitated head on her chest? In the next chapter I will examine how the iconography of the embodied Gorgon/Medusa ran parallel with the enshrining of women's marginality in law.

Diving into the abyss

The *Gorgoneion* invites us to embrace the darkness and dive in. On the other side is our creativity, a diminishing of our ego and a connection with the collective unconscious. She argues for connection with the source, Mother and the hideous darkness of chaos, which leads to our creative power, a hidden treasure in Hades. Bringing it into the daylight frees us. The task is to unbury and then re-member yourself by confronting and acknowledging the darkness within us.[79]

Notes

1. Giallongo 2018:2.
2. Lazarou 2019:353–385.
3. Marinatos 2000:57.
4. Marler 2002:16.
5. Homer *Iliad* 5. 738ff, *Iliad* 11:36, *Odyssey* 11:633.
6. *Iliad* 11:36–37.
7. Howe 1954:211.
8. Marler 2012:16.
9. Lazarou 2019:354.
10. *Iliad* 5:741.
11. Feldman 1965:488.
12. *Iliad* 5:733–742.
13. Lazarou 2022:48.
14. Marinatos 2000:55.
15. Howe 1954:209–221 and Feldman 1965:487.
16. Siebers 1983:8–9.
17. Giallongo 2018:86.
18. Howe 1954:220.
19. Feldman 1965:498.
20. Howe 1954:58.
21. Other theories include: Giallongo (2018:13) considers the *Gorgoneion* originated as an Assyrian male deity (citing Hopkins 1934:341–358). Rose (1928:29–30) described her as the "nightmare phantom" while Wilk (2000) gives several naturalistic and rather fantastical and unconvincing explanations including the octopus, the star Algol, terrors of the sea, the ocean waves, volcanic eruptions, a symbol of the Moon eruptions, and the empty wastes of Libya. Etymologically, Gorgo derives from the Indo-European '*garag*' which means horror, dread, terrible (Zolotnikova 2016:359). Dexter (2010:35) claims she is related to the Near Eastern demon Humbaba believed to have been brought to Sparta by the Phoenicians (Carter 1987:91, 355, 359) Like the *Gorgoneion*, Humbaba is represented frontally, but it is masculine unlike the *Gorgoneion*.
22. Marler 2002:17.
23. *Od.* 11:633–5, Hagen 2007:29.
24. *Od.* 11:635.
25. *Od.* 11:636.

26. Feldman 1965:491.
27. Hagen 2007:30.
28. *Odyssey* 4:561–5.
29. Burkert 1985:199.
30. Liddell 1944:785.
31. Burkert 1985:195–7.
32. Vernant 1991:95.
33. Miasma is the Ancient Greek word for "stain, defilement, pollution". Women were seen as polluting during their periods and after childbirth, men after battle and killing, and both sexes after sexual intercourse. People needed to be ritually cleansed before entering sacred space.
34. Vernant 1990:97.
35. Lazarou 2022:56.
36. Wilks 2000:186–89.
37. Liddell Scott 1944:778, 779.
38. Kere were female death spirits drawn to bloody deaths of warriors. Daughters of Nyx and Erebus, they feasted on the dead.
39. *Iliad* 23:78.
40. Vernant 1990:98.
41. Alexandridou 2011:53.
42. *Iliad* 11:36.
43. Liddle and Scott 1944:137.
44. *Iliad* 8:349, Marler 2000:17–18.
45. Wilke 2000:172.
46. Homer *Iliad* 5:16, 11:579, 15:332, *Odyssey* 18:212.
47. Inge 2007:160.
48. Vernant 1991:149.
49. Vernant 1991:137.
50. *Iliad* 8:349.
51. Giallongo 2018:78.
52. Giallongo 2018:79.
53. Hall 1980:65.
54. Audre Lorde, *Sister Outsider*. (New York: Crossing Press, 1982) p. 53.
55. Barnes, Hazel, *The Meddling*. 23.
56. Bowers, Susan, *Medusa and the Female Gaze*. (1990) p. 219.
57. Emily Culpeper. Ancient Gorgons: A Face for Contemporary Women's Rage. *Women of Power 3*. (Winter/Spring 1986):22.
58. Bowers 1990:220.
59. *Larousse Encyclopaedia of Mythology*. London: Hamlyn, 37.

60. Johns, C. *The Phallus and the Evil Eye. Sex or Symbol? Erotic Images of Greece and Rome.* (London: British Museum Press, 1989).
61. Perseus continues the institution of blindness to subdue people in stealing the Graeae's eye and continuing his quest. Argos closes his eyes and Hermes decapitates him. When Odysseus blinds Polyphemus the Cyclops, he himself is punished. Metope is punished by her father Echetus with blindness and must work to regain her sight. Blinding is also used as revenge, as with Polymestor's punishment for murder in *Hecabe*.
62. *Atê*, the spirit of delusion and "blind" folly. She is known also as Ruin as she leads all who follow her astray by causing them to become "blinded" to their mistakes and often insane. Another of Greek mythology's numerous linkings of blindness and madness is in *Ajax*. Athena describes the madness she institutes in Ajax in very visual terms, saying she will make his eyes dark although he is still sighted. This rendering of blindness is in fact a means of saving Odysseus from Ajax. From: https://disabledfeminists.com/2010/12/22/blindness-in-greek-myth/.
63. Dexter 2010:25.
64. Dexter 2010:33.
65. Marler 2002:19.
66. Marler 2002:19.
67. Joseph Campbell, *Occidental Mythology*. (New York: Viking Press, 1964) 149.
68. Keuls 1993:39. *Iliad* 2:466–7.
69. Herodotus *Histories* 4:189.
70. Graves 1960:8.1, 44.
71. Graves 52.b, 181–2.
72. Stesichoros in Marx 1993:266.
73. Hesiod (fr. 343) in https://sententiaeantiquae.com/2016/11/17/the-consumption-of-metis-birth-of-athena-and-creation-of-the-aegis-hes-frag-343/.
74. *Iliad* 2:375, *Od.* 4.752.
75. *Iliad* 15:229, 307; 17.593. Hartswick 1993:274.
76. Freud Sigmund, (1927) Medusa's Head. Vol. 5 of *Collected Papers* Strachey (ed.) New York: Basic Books 1959:105–6. In Bowers 1990:219.
77. Paraphrased from Sartre, Jean-Paul, *Being and Nothingness*. (New York: Philosophicla Library, 1956).
78. I discuss the political background in Athens which may be a reason the *Gorgoneion* became the Gorgon in Appendix One.

79. Blau, Rachel De Plesis Medusa in *Wells* (New York: Montemora Press, 1980) 13–22. Also, consider the myth of Innana. She descends into the Underworld and is hung on a peg until her flesh rots, before being rescued, but not before she has to send another in her place. So she sends her husband who is fated to spend six months of the year there. That process may be familiar to many who have wandered Hades' halls at various times in their lives. See Sylvia Brinton Perera, *Descent to the Goddess* Inner City Books (1981) for a Jungian take on the myth. Also Diane Wolkstein *Inanna Queen of Heaven and Earth* (1983) for a retelling of the myth.

CHAPTER TWO

The Embodied Gorgon

In the previous chapter, we discussed how the *Gorgoneion* was a demonic or apotropaic symbol. If the Gorgons three (the single *Gorgoneion* later became the three Gorgons, who were sisters) were invented from the age-old symbol of the *Gorgoneion*, why would that be? The answer is politics. It can be argued that the *Gorgoneion* became a political symbol for Athens' growing power and independence and suggests that literary sources, the updated *Iliad*, and visual images were used to convey political and civic propaganda.

During the seventh and sixth centuries BCE Athenian society underwent major legal, political, social, and economic transformation that eventually led to democracy in the fifth century. Solon's legislation in 594 BCE began the process. In his effort to remedy the Athenian social and financial crises, Solon instituted a set of laws that directly affected women. The longevity and geographical spread of this legislation was influential in defining women's identity thereafter.[1] Solon's laws were intended to remove power from the aristocrats and put it in the hands of citizen men. One way to reduce their power was to restrict the display of their women who were social markers of wealth.

Solon banned the dowry and reduced women's appearances at festivals and in the public sphere, restricted public expressions of grief, limited the number of women at funerals, and banned female professional mourners.[2] Lavish funerals were used by the aristocracy as displays of wealth and power. Henceforth women were expected to be invisible and silent. It is no coincidence then that the embodied *Gorgoneion* in the form of Gorgo/Medusa and the aetiological myths that accompanied her made explicit the dangers of visible and noisy women. To consolidate the *polis*, lawmakers identified those who were 'in', that is male citizens, and who was 'out', women and barbarians. Thus, woman was legally Othered.

If as it is claimed[3] Gorgo/Medusa was a vestige of the Great Goddess, then the people needed to be persuaded that certain aspects of the feminine were not divine but demonic and that male gods were superior to female goddesses. Gorgo/Medusa implies that female demons epitomised the danger women represented, they were seen as both weak and strong. The implication was that masculine values, and the Olympian gods, were to be dominant in this brand-new world.

It is important to remember that according to Herodotus writing in the fifth century the Olympian gods were constructed by Homer and Herodotus who

> ... created a theogony for the Greeks. They gave names to the gods, decided what their special skills were and what honours they should be given and described their appearance.[4]

In other words, Homer and Hesiod created the myths about the gods to suit the agenda or *zeitgeist* of the times. Remember, their work was written down in the era of tyrants when 'enemies of the state' were routinely executed or exiled.

Why did the *Gorgoneion* grow a woman's body? A closer examination of the myth may give us some clues. Perseus and Medusa are never mentioned together in Homer. The poet lists Perseus' parentage from Zeus and Danae[5] giving him the stock epithet that he was 'predominant above all warriors'.[6] As discussed previously, there is no ambiguity in Homer's mention of the *Gorgoneion*, which appears to be a familiar menacing image and is presented with little description, as it was presumably a well-known symbol.

Perseus scarcely appears in myth or material culture before the second half of the seventh century when he suddenly arises in a variety of guises simultaneously throughout Greece. This suggests artists were experimenting with a new concept.[7] Artists reflect the culture they live in, and especially in the time of tyrants they would support the narrative or code of the day. Both written sources and material culture provide a snapshot of current social mores. The *Gorgoneion* was given a body and aetiological myths to explain this change. Enter Perseus the hero from Argos. Hesiod begins the story:

> ... concerning the Gorgons, they lived across the glorious Ocean towards the furthest Night, in the clear voiced Hesperides. Stheno, Euryale and mischievous and ill-used Medusa who was mortal and the other two immortal and ageless.[8]

Living on the watery fringes of the world, along with other marginal groups who are outside the pale of society, is the obvious and rational home of the Gorgons. They are outside the conventional world, the wild outdoors[9] which of course is no place for a respectable Greek woman who was ideally sequestered inside the house.[10] Here the single floating head, the *Gorgoneion*, becomes three sisters, two immortal, one mortal. The triad is reminiscent of the triple goddess of the matriarchal theories of Gimbutas, Harrison, et al.

Hesiod exhibits sympathy for Medusa in these verses: she is mischievous (*lugros*) rather than demonic (others translate this as baneful/mournful/sad). My translation suggests Medusa was irreverent or cheeky and not cowed or raped:

> She had lain beside the Dark Haired One [Poseidon] in a soft grassy meadow amid the spring flowers.[11] And when Perseus cut off her head, out came the great horse Perseus and Krysaor of the golden sword.[12]

Medusa lay with Poseidon. Hesiod suggests it was a consensual meeting in a beautiful meadow. For him, Medusa is a woman who enjoys her sexuality and is fertile. Celebrating her sexual power, she can attract the attention of a god, who desires her. They make love in nature which upsets the natural order where women were expected to be passive recipients of male sexual desire. Lust in a woman is an aberration and therefore monstrous. Women's sexual desires threaten the male order and risks a man raising children which are not his own, a deep and until recently unprovable peril, and as it turns out a substantiated fear.[13] Indeed Medusa's sexuality has an androgynous quality by virtue of her wildness, their sexual congress in nature and her sexual desire.

Hesiod does not suggest why Perseus decapitated Medusa. The head needed to be detached, having recently been attached, by a male warrior/hero killing a female demon/goddess to sever the ties with her (perhaps) powerful and illustrious past. The masculine present captured and destroyed ancient female power. Hesiod[14] calls Perseus *mestor phoboio*, lord over death. The *Gorgoneion* signalled an ignominious death, so it follows Gorgo/Medusa represents a shameful death as well.

The *Shield of Heracles* (believed to date from the 6th C BCE) is harsher in its description of the Gorgons:

> The monstrous and unapproachable Gorgons … on their belts a pair of snakes, their heads hanging down, with flickering tongues. Their sharpened teeth gleamed; their eyes flashed. And on the terrible heads of the Gorgons, Great Fear trembled.[15]

In the *Shield*, Gorgo/Medusa becomes monstrous, perhaps to provide a worthy opponent for the hero. Her ugliness is central to her monstrosity. Her physical features align her with the world of animal nature: wild, aggressive, fertile, with claws, big tongue, snakes, horns or fangs, wings and beast ears. Her snaky hair in particular represents licentiousness. Unbound hair flowing freely is reminiscent of the wild maenads of Dionysus. A respectable Greek woman bound her hair and kept her head covered in modesty.

It can be argued that the harsh lessons taught by the Greek myths emphasise the superiority of heroes such as Achilles, Heracles, and Perseus, as a way of judging not only the world, but also beauty.[16] The myths established that the ideal of beauty was male and good, and ugliness and female were evil. After all what was the principal characteristic of the oldest Gorgons in Greek myths and visual sources? A monstrous ugliness. When she became less ugly, in Hellenistic and Roman times, Gorgo/Medusa was seen as less of a threat, perhaps because patriarchy was by then so entrenched that no woman could represent a threat to the status quo, or rather her danger came from her sexuality and its ability to befuddle the brains of men, not her awesome power.

Hesiod did consider her sad or mischievous, but not beautiful. Although arguably she was alluring enough to attract Poseidon, the Olympian gods chose the most beautiful humans to mate with. The depiction of Gorgo/Medusa's ugliness may be connected with Solon's sumptuary laws, as he outlawed bejewelled and expensively dressed aristocratic and who were deemed 'ugly' in the new *polis*. This is in contrast to the *Gorgoneion* who was more terrifying in sight and sound.

Figure 2.1. Black figure pot. 625–600 BCE Athens. Winged Gorgon with protruding tongue, in motion.

Figure 2.1 shows the ugliness of the Gorgon, although if the backstory was not known the gender would be unclear, as she has no breasts. This image is reminiscent of the Homeric *Gorgoneion*: staring, bulging eyes, bearded, tongue protruding and fangs. She wears no snakes, like the *Gorgoneion*. It is an energetic and threatening figure, front-facing and glaring. A worthy opponent for the hero. The repulsive aspect of the Gorgo/Medusa visually represented and contextualised Otherness through female monstrosity. The new Athenian male citizens celebrated themselves with representations of Otherness on pots such as these.[17] The hideous Gorgo/Medusa highlighted the contrast between men and Others who were beneath contempt. She represented all that was ugly and degraded in the human and animal kingdoms, the polar opposite of what men considered themselves to be.

The half-human and half-animal depiction of Gorgo/Medusa was intended to provoke disgust.[18] This is a very different response to the fearful dread of the *Gorgoneion*. The *Gorgoneion* spread terror in the hearts of men, while Gorgo/Medusa was vanquished apparently easily by a Greek hero. Gorgo/Medusa became the devouring feminine of the Greek *polis*, not a terrifying monstrosity bringing death to men.

The hero needed to slay the monster, but why did it have to be a female monster? Surely, a hero killing a woman is easy and heroes need redoubtable opponents. Women were weak in mind and body; or were they? It may be that Gorgo/Medusa represented the Other as a woman warrior, who may or may not have existed but exemplified the Greek fear of a foreign threat to the *polis* and their patriarchal order. The decapitation of Medusa may reflect the Argive conquest of Libya by the first wave of Achaeans, who supressed a matriarchal rulership and violated the shrines of the Libyan snake goddess Lamia (Neath).[19] It may be that Medusa represented the destructive face of the same female Libyan trinity,[20] and Medusa was the Libyan queen killed by Perseus the 'cutter' or 'destroyer'.[21] The same Perseus who went on to become the mythical ruler of Mycenae, Tiryns, and Argos. Mycenae of course stands at the border between the old Minoan and new Argive cultures.

A later account from Palaiphatus explains this.[22] On the island of Cerne lived the Ethiopians. Their land is Libyan, found by the river Annon, straight across from Carthage. There were three islands in the kingdom. They were a people rich in gold. The king Phorcys made a golden statue of Athena (their name for her was Gorgon), but he died before he could dedicate the statue (did this make the goddess angry?). His three daughters Stheno, Euryale, and Medusa divided up their father's property between them. They had no wish to marry so each ruled over one island. They kept the Gorgon as their own treasure and did not dedicate it to the temple but took turns to keep it, again an insult to the goddess. The statue was six feet tall.

Perseus, an exile from Argos was making piratical raid along the coast when he heard there was a wealthy kingdom ruled by women. A man called the Eye,[23] a confidant of the late king, was sailing between the three islands. He was captured by Perseus. The Eye told Perseus that the only thing of value in the islands was the golden Gorgon. Perseus came to the sisters. He said he would kill the Eye unless they gave him the Gorgon. Medusa refused, but Stheno and Euryale agreed. Perseus killed Medusa.

Perseus cut the statue to pieces and put the golden head on his trireme and named his ship Gorgon. He sailed around the islands extorting money from other islanders and killed those who refused to pay (he was a pirate after all). Perseus landed on Seriphos (mentioned in Pindar) and demanded money. The villagers asked for a few days to collect the blackmail money, but instead they assembled man-sized stones and set them up in the marketplace and fled the island. When Perseus returned, all he found were these stones.

Thereafter, when any other of the island people refused to pay up, Perseus would say, 'be careful that you do not suffer as the people of Seriphos, who saw the Gorgon's head and were turned to stone'.

Admittedly, this is a late piece, believed to have been written in the fourth century BCE. Palaephatus belongs to the Pragmatic school, which analysed myths from a pragmatic viewpoint, following the sixth century authors Stesichorus and Xenophanes, who argued myth did not mean what it appeared to mean. The Pragmatic approach was developed by Herodotus and Herodorus, who wrote that speculation had to be based on experience and systematic research. Like Herodotus, Palaephatus travelled and spoke to 'old men [about] what they had heard about each of these stories'. He said 'I write here what I learned from them ... I think that everything which has been narrated happened. For if they were merely names, no story would have come to being about them. But first the deed occurred and then the story about it.'[24]

The myths are found in other sources, and they have many things in common. Of course it cannot be known if these stories were hoaxes with enough known facts to make them believable. But certainly Libya, Amazons, Seriphos, decapitation, snakes, stones, Gorgons, deadly gaze and three sisters all appear in earlier myths. In Pindar[25] Perseus turned all the inhabitants of Seriphos to stone: When Perseus shouted, he brought the third part of the sisters to sea-girt Seriphos and its people as its doom.[26]

This reading of the myth would explain how Medusa (and her sisters) were worthy opponents of Perseus. They were Amazons and female rulers, and they had wealth. The myth also explains why Medusa the rebel needed to die. She refused to obey a man and was not intimidated by him. Perseus is behaving exactly as the Greeks did in the *Iliad*, raiding poorly defended places, stripping them of their wealth and enslaving or killing the inhabitants.

Herodotus also placed the three sisters in Libya. Her name Medousa is perhaps derived from the feminine present participle *medousa* (guardian goddess, ruling) from the verb *medew* (to rule). This could reflect her royal status in Libya.[27] A later writer Diodoros described the Gorgons as Amazon queens whose kingdom was by Lake Tritonis in

Libya and who fought in snakeskin armour. The Gorgons were subdued by Perseus when Medusa was the ruler. Later they and the race of Amazons were destroyed by Heracles because he could not allow any nation to be ruled by women.[28]

Although this source was written several hundred years after our time period, it does show a continuity and the persistence of the Libyan myth of the Gorgons, and also their relationship to the Amazons, other female protagonists who are despatched by Greek 'heroes'.[29] It also relates to the threat from the East, namely the Persians who were barbarians. Similarly ancient myths such as Gorgo/Medusa were overhauled to instil confidence in new political or religious institutions, just as the surviving version of Homer's poems was.[30]

Of course, Greek women's voices are silent.[31] We can however look across the world to see other examples of women warriors.

Figure 2.2. New Zealand women's rugby team performing the *Haka* or war dance before a match to frighten their opponents.

There is a similarity here, women shouting insults and warning, with staring, bulging eyes, tongue out (not shown), arm gestures, bent knees, dancing not running. All intended to paralyse their opponents in fear. Part of their chant includes

> Women of strength/who will bear the future/Rise and press on!/ Move it!

Figure 2.3. Māori girl learning the *Haka*, Gottfried Lindauer, circa 1907 public domain. In this painting we see a young girl strike a pose very reminiscent of the Gorgo/Medusa. I argue that Gorgo/Medusa is doing the same, staring down the enemy face forwards, eyes blazing and screaming a blood curdling war cry.

Interestingly, a huge statue of the Mexica (Aztec deity) Earth Goddess Tlaltecuhtli has been unearthed, and she also resembles the Gorgon.[32]

28 MONSTROUS WOMEN

Figure 2.4. Monolith of Tlaltecuhtli discovered in Mexico city in 2006 (1502 CE).

Tlaltecuhtli means 'the one who gives and devours life'. She has the same lolling tongue and claws, and is often shown in a squatting position in the act of giving birth. She has several mouths over her body filled with sharp teeth, which are often spurting blood. On her elbows and knees are human skulls and, in many images, she has curly or snaky hair. This suggests there is a female archetype stretching from New Zealand to Mexico to the Middle East and Greece and of course India.[33]

In the Mexica myth, Tlaltecuhtli was dismembered by the male gods Tezcatlipoca and Quetzalcoatl who were disgusted by her ugliness. They changed themselves into snakes and tore her body apart. Like in Greece, patriarchs argue that ugly women deserve to die. But Tlaltecuhtli refused to die. The severed pieces of her body became part of the earth, her skin changed into grass and small flowers, her hair grew into the trees and herbs, her eyes turned into springs and wells, her nose grew to be the hills and valleys, her shoulders changed into the mountains, and her mouth became the caves and rivers.[34]

Thus, the earth goddess Tlaltecuhtli returns to the earth as fertile, abundant, beautiful nature. She outsmarts the men who only look superficially at her 'value'. Tlaltecuhtli required blood sacrifice to 'moisten the earth'. Her open mouth symbolizes the passage to the Underworld inside the earth, but in many images her lower jaw is missing, torn away by Tezcatlipoca to prevent her from sinking beneath the waters. She often wears a skirt of crossed bones and skulls with a great star sign border, symbol of her primordial nature; she is depicted with large teeth, bugling eyes, and a huge, protruding tongue.

Many Aztec sculptures, especially those of Tlaltecuhtli, were not meant to be seen by humans. They were made and then set up in a hidden place or carved on the underside of stone boxes and *Chacmool* sculptures. The sculptures were intended for the eyes of the gods only, perhaps because they were so powerful. Statues and carvings of Tlaltecuhtli were placed face down on the earth or in caves referencing her domain of the earth and nature.

As a warrior queen and an enemy of the *polis*, Medusa's warrior nature is absorbed or co-opted by Athena who cannot have a woman rival. In Euripides' play *Ion* (987–93) it is Athena herself who decapitates Medusa in the Battle of the Giants and places the *Gorgoneion* on her *aegis*. Interestingly, the *aegis* is described as a 'breastplate armed with coils of a viper' (993) and not an embodied monster. After killing Medusa, Athena does not absorb the monster (like her father did her mother Metis) but places it on her body, looking outwards.

Medusa is contrasted with the goddess Athena who is androgynous but has no sexual desire and is non-sexual, while Medusa had aberrant sexual desire, for a woman. Athena does however have the positive androgynous characteristic of being a warrior, as Medusa had once been. Athena is neither a wife nor a mother, but only the ever-virginal daughter, who was born through a male not a woman. Athena represents neither ideal humanity (maleness) nor monster, but she receives the monstrous head on her *aegis* and thus neutralises the powerful, sexual, disobedient warrior queen.

As we have seen, Gorgo/Medusa may have been a warrior queen. Other theories[35] suggest the Gorgon was a fertility goddess and link her with Artemis, the Great Mother, Demeter etc. The name *medousa* is a title which was also sometimes applied to Athena, Artemis, and Aphrodite.[36] Symbols around Medusa include images of fertility such as snakes, horses, plants, lions, deer, birds, wolves, sphinxes,

30 MONSTROUS WOMEN

Figure 2.5. Athena and aegis c. 430 BCE.

and beehives. Some of the earliest representations of the whole-body Gorgon/Medusa show her in this way.

To return to our question, why was the *Gorgoneion* given a body? The *Gorgoneion* expanded into a full figure around 580–550 BCE when the earliest examples of Gorgons on architecture appeared in Greece, the most famous being the eight-foot-high carving on the temple of Artemis at Corfu (Korkyra).

This massive sculptural relief[37] shows Medusa's enormous head, which is front-facing like the *Gorgoneion*. Her legs are in the *knielauf* or 'sky walking' position, and she looks as though she is flying through the air or perhaps dancing (see chapter 3). She wears a short tunic and has strong, muscled legs with winged boots. Around her waist are two bearded serpents facing one another, jaws open, while two more

Figure 2.6. Korkyra Gorgon, west pediment, temple of Artemis, Corfu c. 580 BCE.

snakes emerge from behind her ears. Two lions or panthers are on each side of the figure. The fact this was on the temple of Artemis begs several questions.

Firstly, is this another representation of Artemis, perhaps with a mask? She may be shown as Mistress of the Wild Things or *Potnia Theron*, whose lineage can be traced back to Palaeolithic times. *Potnia*, the protectress of all living creatures, is the embodiment of wild nature and is usually shown holding two wild animals, sometimes lions, panthers, or deer. Artemis is the virgin[38] goddess who presides over the hunt and also protects wild places. Temples of Artemis were often built in liminal, wild areas.[39] Artemis initiated girls and maidens, and perhaps they wore masks like those found in the Ortheia sanctuary in Sparta.[40] The lions, or panthers, may show Orientalising influence.[41]

It has been suggested there are parallels to Assyrian art which is found in Greece at that time. The lion was sacred to Ishtar, the Assyrian goddess of war and fertility. The woman between two big cats or birds is typical of Near Eastern depictions of *Potnia*, known in Greece since the second millennium BCE.[42]

Representations of women between animals are known from the geometric period. The earliest appearance of *potnia theron* in Greek art is in the Kretan repertoire dated from the end of the 8th C BCE which was adopted in Sparta, Boeotia, and the Cyclades in the first half of the seventh century. The earliest found on pottery are on Corinthian vases. In early examples she is naked and unwinged following the Kretan Mycenaean tradition, and later she is winged after oriental prototypes. She is associated with a number of creatures; lions and birds are the most common. *Potnia* is sometimes shown with mythical beasts like sphinxes and griffins which might point to a chthonic role.[43]

Figure 2.7. *Potnia Theron*, Artemis Orthea sanctuary, Sparta 7th C BCE.

A similar image is found on a seventh century plate from Rhodes. Painted red, it shows a figure with the Gorgon face or mask holding two birds, perhaps swans. She is dressed in a long skirt which has a slit up the side. She has double wings, unlike the Kretan Gorgon, and her mask/face shows the typical staring eyes, wide mouth, enlarged fangs or tusks, protruding tongue, shaggy beard, and snaky hair which resembles dreadlocks. This has led scholars to suggest that the Gorgon is the same as *Potnia Theron*.

Figure 2.8. Rhodian plate, c. 600 BCE.

However, there are differences between *Potnia* and Gorgons. Gorgons are front facing, *Potniae* face sidewards. Gorgons are shown moving, while the *Potniae* stand still in a priestess position. The Gorgons wear a short tunic, the *Potniae* have a long robe; finally the Gorgon has snaky hair, and *Potniae* wear their hair long. It may be the Gorgons of the Classical era are a combination of the bird and snake goddess.[44] The bird-woman is an ancient symbol; hundreds of terracotta figurines have been found in the Balkans, believed to be from the Vinca culture (5,000 BCE) showing a female body with a bird head or mask. Female figures in bone, stone and clay with bird heads were found in Neolithic graves and Early Bronze Age sites in Krete, Sicily, Sardinia, Spain and Portugal, Western Anatolia and the Cycladic islands.[45]

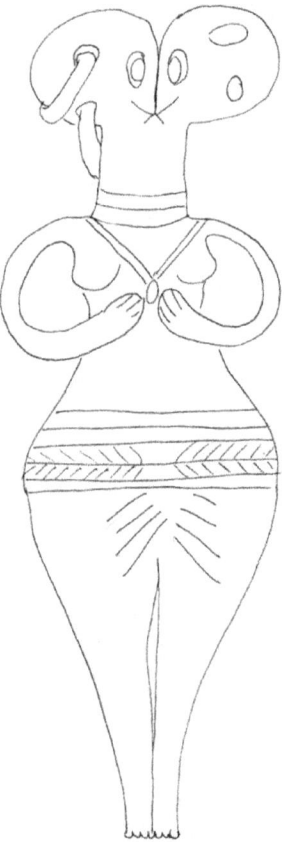

Figure 2.9. Bird Goddess, Cypress c. 2500 BCE.

Bird-women are found in burial sites and are therefore associated with death and perhaps the afterlife. Others consider the *Gorgoneion* to have originated as a Near East demon.[46] I am not sure I agree here, as there are too many similarities between the *Gorgoneion* and the embodied Gorgon. But we cannot know.

Although the Gorgon has an association with Artemis, the Olympian Artemis is distinct. Others have suggested that Gorgon represents the dark side of the goddess, and with Hekate makes up the triple goddess of the New Moon/Artemis, full Moon/Demeter, and Dark Moon/Hekate. This also fits, but again as we shall see in chapter six Hekate has her own, well-defined provenance and area of influence, and she is not monstrous in the same way at all. Personally, I see the embodied Gorgon as a woman warrior, who naturally subdues wild beasts.

Swallowing the Daemon: Down with the animals

Years ago, making my way around London as a young woman, with all that it entails as men seem to enjoy stalking and hunting women (who knows why?) I would imagine myself walking between two enormous, hungry, sleek, black panthers: the big cats, not the revolutionaries. And whenever I felt a threat, I would imagine them tearing the guy to shreds (yes it was always a man). Those hungry cats made me feel better, and no creeps or weirdos ever approached me. I walked the streets unmolested. It's interesting then that *Potnia* has the same big cats at her side. I knew nothing of her then, but wonder if the 'woman and cat thing' is in our collective memory. The cats are our protectors from predators, and we kept them as pets … Do you have a spirit animal? A protector? Maybe get one … any big cat or dog will do … or a bear.[47]

Notes

1. Tsakiropoulou-Summers 2018:2.
2. Tsakiropoulou-Summers 2018:1.
3. Gimbutas (1982), Harrison (1903), and Frothingham (1911).
4. Herodotus *Histories* 3:38.
5. *Iliad* 14:319.
6. *Iliad* 19:116.
7. Howe 1954:220.
8. Hesiod *Theogony* 274–283.
9. Morgan 1984:192.
10. Although this has been disputed in recent scholarship.
11. See the chapter on Sirens for a discussion of the symbolism of meadows.
12. *Theogony* 274–283.
13. DNA studies have found between 1–30% of children are not the children of their supposed fathers. https://www.theguardian.com/society/2005/aug/11/childrensservices.uknews.

14. *Catalogue of Women* 129:15.
15. *Shield of Heracles* 233–236.
16. Giallongo 2017:101.
17. Giallongo 2017:102.
18. This is similar to the disgust patriarchal religions have with menstruation, without which life would not exist. The endless pettifogging restrictions around periods, and the "uncleanliness" of menstruating women, when the reverse is true (menstruation cleanses the body), all replicate the disgust men feel about the female body as a way to elevate themselves and denigrate and disempower feminine, life-giving power.
19. Marler 2002:19.
20. Giallongo 2018:19.
21. Shearer 2018:19.
22. *Peri Apiston (On things not to Believe)* 31 *The Daughters of Porcys*. Keisling, Barry (trans.) (2002) from the 1902 Greek text. https://topostext.org/work/808.
23. See the previous chapter for a discussion of the Greek view of the eye.
24. Osmun 1956:133.
25. *Pythian Odes.* 12:11–12.
26. *Pythian Odes.* 12:11–12.
27. Herodotus *Histories* 2:91.
28. Diodorus Book III, 53–55 (in Dexter 2010:30).
29. Dexter 2010:30.
30. Lubell 1994:107.
31. Or is it? In a fascinating article on women to women relationships, Meryl Altman (2009) argues that imagery on a pot illustrates women making courtship gestures in a similar way that male to male relationships are shown on pots, suggesting a certain freedom between women.
32. This sculpture measures about 4 x 3.6 metres (13.1 x 11.8 feet) and weighs around 12 tons. It is the largest Aztec monolith ever discovered. Carved in a block of pink andesite it represents the goddess in the typical squatting position, and it is vividly painted in red ochre, and white, black, and blue colours.
33. The Hindu goddess Kali. Space means I cannot discuss all these goddesses, but the commonality of the "devouring female" is established.
34. Thevet, André (c. 1540). "IX". *Histoyre du mechique* (in French). pp. 31–34. Note that this is a very late source (16th c.) so the analysis and understanding reflect the time and mindset of the author.
35. Hagen 2007:15. Gimbutas 1982:152, Frothingham 1911:349.

36. Hagan 2007:16.
37. Joan Marler, 2002:19.
38. Virgin in this context implies unmarried rather than non-sexual.
39. See Appendix 2 for a discussion of Artemis.
40. Burkert 1998:150.
41. Hopkins 1934:345, 352.
42. Hagen (2007:16) *Potnia Theron* was a Bronze Age representation of the goddess, as protector and tamer of wild beasts. She is usually shown holding a lion or other big cat and a deer or hind. In the early Archaic era, Greek art and religious ideas were influenced by contact with the East (Burkert 1992:19). Marinatos (2000:10) places her origin in Syria, but her conclusions are debatable. Hagen (2007:17) suggests that this explains the depiction of Artemis as *Potnia* (the Francois vase p.17: fig. 2.1). Hagen (2007:17) suggests rather than signifying dominion or domination of the animals (Alexandridou and Marinatos), *Potnia* is a protector or *kourotrophos* who safeguarded young animals (are these young animals?) and shared this role with Artemis. Marinatos (2000:93–97) suggests that when Artemis became the patroness of hunting by the 6th C BCE, *Potnia* was absorbed by Artemis. Hagen suggests (2007:17) after Harrison 1955:193–4, fig. 3) that the depiction of Gorgo in the same pose emphasizes her connection to Artemis (in contrast to Alexandridou and Marinatos who see no such connection).
43. Alexandridou 2011:63.
44. Lazarou 2022:51.
45. Marler 2002:20.
46. Lazarou 2022:51.
47. There was, in 2024, meme going around social media, asking women if they would rather meet a bear alone in the forest or a man. 99.9% of women said a bear. Some men, around 50% in my reckoning, agreed, but the others were outraged and threated to kill/rape/harm the women who believed this to be true, which rather proved the women's point.

CHAPTER THREE

The Dancing Gorgon

How was Gorgo/Medusa represented? She had wild hair, snakes, a wide mouth, lolling tongue, a beard, moving in an unfeminine manner, staring eyes, fangs, and wings. Her manner and physical body could well be that of a female warrior, certainly not the 'soft-limbed' traditional Greek woman.

In this gemstone, her face and body are front-facing, her legs depicted side-on; her hands hold two serpents and there are two further serpents coming from the side of her head. She is shown as female, with breasts. And has four large wings indicating her divine nature and a wide-open, screaming mouth. She is wearing a fine diaphanous Greek chiton. She is both beautiful, and delicate and hideous.

Is this the face of a Libyan Queen? Well it could be, especially if she were a queen/priestess dancing, and she was wearing a mask to scare away interlopers. A gemstone such as this would have been carried as an amulet or protective symbol and so was imbued with power. This is a powerful female figure. She is not androgynous like some other Gorgons, but has the body of a young woman. She has winged boots, which demonstrate her power to fly between worlds and move swiftly.[1] With these boots Gorgo/Medusa travelled in all directions, to the farthest reaches of the world, from the shores to Okeanos to the

40   MONSTROUS WOMEN

Figure 3.1. Carved chalcedony gemstone Greece Attica c. 720–480 BCE.

land of the Hyperboreans, where Perseus found her. She appears to be very light on her feet and yet powerful in her stance. Although her gaze is hidden, perhaps behind a mask, it is nevertheless commanding. Her wide-open mouth appears to be screaming.

What is especially noticeable are the snakes she grasps in her hands. She is in command of them, and they submit to her grip. Snakes, as we discovered in Chapter One, have a chthonic association. But they may also represent sexuality, male[2] and female.[3] Morgan[4] argues that the Greeks saw them as or both phallic and chthonic. When analysing symbols, it is important to attempt to place ourselves in their culture of origin. Snakes were common in Greece, and house-snakes (*okouroi*) were kept to control vermin. The snake Erichthonius was part of the charter myth of Athens. We might then argue that the snake did not have the fearful associations found in later Christian cultures (Eve etc.). Indeed, the home of the Gorgons, the garden of the Hesperides, had a tame serpent which the nymphs fed.

Snake iconography is widespread both as enemy (Figure 1.2 shows the hero with the *Gorgoneion* shield killing a snake), and ally (the snakes on Agamemnon's shield were apotropaic). Snake-handling women

Figure 3.2. Black Figure vase from Paestum, Archaic period. Nymphs and serpent. Here, the serpent is a friend of the nymphs.

were common in Minoan culture and it has been argued that this shows a continuity between the Minoan chthonic Goddess cults and Gorgo/Medusa.

Certainly, this Kretan goddess looks remarkably like our Gorgon although she is static; her eyes are staring, possibly in a trance, and she holds the snakes up. However more than a thousand years separate these figures, and it may be stretching a point to make the connection between them. It has been argued the serpent is a symbol of Syro-Palestinian and Egyptian iconography.[5] I suggest that Gorgo/Medusa was both a magician and a priestess, a particularly Greek symbol. Rather than her magical properties, it may be that it was her sexuality which was so threatening to the new order.

One of the things instituted by Solon and later by Peisistratus were moral codes.[6] Solon opened state-controlled brothels and enacted draconian laws for safeguarding/controlling the chastity of citizen women,

Figure 3.3. Snake Goddess from the palace at Knossos, c. 1600 BCE Majolica.

including the statute that a father could sell his daughter into slavery if she lost her virginity before marriage. This enshrined in law the double standard of sexual morality. It may be that women rebelled against these laws (their voices as ever are silent) but this might explain why male domination had to be fought for again and again in the mind of the Athenian male, and the symbolism of the catastrophic defeat of rebellious women was ubiquitous.

Medusa may show the 'female violation of patriarchal order [who] has to die in order for her to be controlled'.[7] She represents the unbound woman, neither veiled nor coiffured. Gorgo/Medusa expresses the process by which women became possessions of men and lost what little agency they enjoyed. However, Homer writes of women as chattels so this cannot be laid at Solon's door. It may be that the enfranchisement of citizen males prompted the women to demand more autonomy. Certainly, the fear exemplified by the Gorgo/Medusa symbolism taught men that, if they lost control of their women, they would rise up and destroy them: a common misogynist fear that, given power, women would behave as men do. However, most mythical women who rebel do not try to rule men but instead build their own communities apart from them.[8]

After the reforms of Pisistratus, Athenian culture was ruled by men who sequestered their wives and daughters, denigrated the female role in reproduction, erected monuments to the male genitalia, had sex with the sons of their peers, and created a mythology of rape. This has been called 'the reign of the phallus'[9] and it is hard to argue with that conclusion. The story of phallic rule at the root of Western civilisation has been supressed until recently, because of the near monopoly that men have held in the field of classics, and their neglect of the rich pictorial evidence of this fact was concealed either to protect the idealised image of Athens or because of their own prudery.[10]

Certainly, the endless rapes and killing or subduing of the rebellious female in Olympian mythology illustrate the sex antagonism and gynophobia of Greek men. Women were seen as wild and untamed and represented death, chaos, and unbridled sexuality. These stood in opposition to the new values of restraint and control which can be identified as Apollonian. Indeed, it was Apollo, along with other 'heroes', who killed a serpent-like female monster or dragon at Delphi.[11] Apollo stood in direct opposition to Dionysian excess. Maenads (women who followed Dionysus) danced and celebrated the orgiastic god, hair unbound and their bodies free, reminiscent of Figure 3.1. There was a fear that the sexual licentiousness of the cult and its orgies would overwhelm family life and patriarchal order and weaken the *polis*.

Perseus did not use Medusa's head for personal power[12] but significantly he used it against followers of Dionysus. When this Eastern religion first reached Argos, the citizens rebelled against it. Perseus turned the satyrs to stone and killed the maenads with his sword. This is reminiscent of his killing of Medusa, illustrating the mix of threats these women represented: '... in the hands of Perseus the Gorgon-head was used against those of wanton intent ... [the] lewd forces of Dionysos.'[13]

Perseus' attack against the followers of Dionysus shows a 'moral development'[14] among misogynists. Olympian order and rationality destroy the 'Eastern/Barbarian' ecstatic cult and control these maddened women who are out and about and up to no good. This to me is an accurate analysis of the intention of the *polis*. The Gorgons who turn men to stone are horrifying creatures who 'unman them', or in other words, 'men who kill are heroes, women who kill are monsters'.[15] This is a revealing smorgasbord of paranoid misogyny. Perseus later killed Medusa's mother Ketos, ending her maternal line.

The depiction of women as wild and dangerous naturalises the idea that women lack control and are hypersexual.[16] The identity these images create is intended to regulate and control women and their sexuality in line with the morality laws.[17] However caution is required, as myths or representations of women's scandalous behaviour may be part of male gender performance.[18] Athenian men might not have believed what they were being told but had to act as if they did in front of other men.

Figure 3.4. Chariot plaque, bronze mid-6th C BCE. Etruscan.

At first sight, I considered this plaque to be a representation of a birthing Gorgo/Medusa who was supported by wild animals. Her face represents the transformation which occurs at birth when women contact their deepest, most animalist nature. The animals represent the struggle of birthing and the danger it brings to both mother and child. All of which would associate Gorgo/Medusa with Artemis who supported women in childbirth.

However, context is everything. This plaque was found on a war chariot, and the figure is facing outwards towards the enemy, just as the

Gorgoneion did on the warrior's shield in chapter one. It seems unlikely that a birthing woman would be placed on weaponry. The posture, the tamed wild animals and the huge snake must represent an invitation to Hades to the enemy, perhaps symbolising the beginning and the end of life, or else an insult showing the 'dangerous' female vulva. It may not be a coincidence that Neumann[19] describes Medusa as the 'Terrible Mother', the 'womb of death' which is displayed here.

The Greek word *aideomai* means to be ashamed but also to stand in awe or regard with reverence. *Aidoiod* is a term used of women deserving of respect, and *aidoion* from a similar root is used for the female genitals in the plural (*ta aidoia*). So, fear, shame, and reverence for women are all connected. By the fifth century, Medusa was the quintessential icon of *aideomai*, of fear and shame, with only a faint trace of reverence.

"The myth of Medusa is a myth of fear of women, fear of their anarchism, their self-sufficiency, their buried power."[20] Gorgo is represented as a vulva or as a face or a face in the shape of a vulva.[21] Athena's *aegis* was originally a goatskin, then later a corselet bristling with snakes which has been interpreted as the vagina dentata, implying castration.[22] The Medusa head on the *aegis* with snakes suggests pubic hair, and the aggressive associations of this image may explain why Athenian women practised partial depilation of the genital area.[23]

The connection with birth and death is epitomised in this war chariot where the Gorgon exposes her vulva as the grinning maw of death. Displaying the vulva is an apotropaic act. The *sheela na gigs* on early churches in Ireland and England are believed to repel the evil eyes (or perhaps witches, as these are Christian churches). It may be that the *Gorgoneia* on shields are protective magic to blunt or render the swords of the enemy impotent by reminding them of their mothers' genitals.[24] Or perhaps the exposure of a woman's vulva was intended to be so shocking it would disarm the soldier or it would drive away baneful influences. The cult of the phallus would make any vaginas and especially exposed vaginas threatening and terrifying, hence their use on weaponry.

Women warriors, aberrant women, foreign women, non-compliant, sexually active women, all needed to be destroyed by the Greek hero for the sake of the *polis*.[25] I believe this the cultural message of the myth. Certainly, our Gorgo/Medusas are dancing not running. They face down men and belligerently look them in the eye, or mischievously as Hesiod wrote; their hair is uncovered and sometimes flowing free, and they are noisy and wild.

46   MONSTROUS WOMEN

Figure 3.5. Gorgon dancing. Athens. Attic Black Figure Amphora c. 530 BCE.

This image is even more exuberant than Figure 3.1. This Gorgo/Medusa is forward facing and not looking in the direction of travel, suggesting she is not moving forwards but dancing. This posture, accepted by scholars, is called the *knielauf* position.[26] It was claimed she was running after Perseus, but I disagree. Her hands are forming gestures, one palm up and one facing down. This is a dance posture closely reminiscent of Indian Classical dance.

Notice the wide-legged stance, the arm and hand gestures which have sacred meaning (*Mudras*) and the tongue and staring eyes. *Bharatanatyam* dance tells mythic stories. Until the nineteenth century these dances were solely performed in temples, and were sacred dances. Then British colonialists and Christian missionaries arrived and treated these dances as part of a debased erotic culture, and its dancers prostitutes.[27] The similarity with the morality laws of Athens are evoked here: the dancing woman as sexual, debased and dangerous, who needed to be outlawed or killed.

For the Greeks dance, music, and poetry were usually experienced together as *musike*, which was believed to have a civilising and unifying effect. Music defined Greek culture, ethnicity, and gender, and was a core element of social and religious rituals, in private homes and larger urban and panhellenic festivals.[28] Greeks danced before

Figure 3.6. *Bharatanatyam* is a sacred Indian dance from Tamil Nadu believed to have originated around 500 BCE.

the hunt, at initiation ceremonies, in rituals of coming of age, in marriage celebrations, and at funerals. They danced for entertainment in symposia, competed in dance festivals, and all religious and cult activity had dance, music, and song as an integral part of their rites.[29] Dance was used to train young men for war (pyrrhic dance). It was used to educate children about social norms and morals and was viewed as essential for their physical and emotional development as well as their moral wellbeing.[30] Most importantly music provided a medium for the Greeks to communicate with the gods.[31] In some myths Athena danced in triumph when she decapitated Medusa. The dance was called the *gorgodrakontodoka* (Gorgo *drakonteios*, dragon or serpent *doka*, lying in wait for).[32]

Dance carries within it the cultural history of the group, and its myths and legends. Particular dance forms transmit teachings on ethics, gender, spiritual, and social mores which, when learned via the physical body, create deep and enduring bonds between the participants, the memory of which is deeply held in the body.³³ Anthropology may give clues to the meaning of Greek dance via cross-cultural study of dance forms. For example in the women's *Haka* of New Zealand, dancers display facial and bodily gestures which resemble those of Medusa/Gorgon (Figure 2.2). Similarly the facial and bodily movements of the Classical Indian dance *Bharatanatyam* (Figure 3.6) resemble Medusa/Gorgon.

Ecstatic dance was central to the Mystery cult of Dionysus. Dance was the fourth stage of the initiatory process, and the dance was accompanied by song, mime, and music such as the aulos and the drums, cymbals and gongs. The Maenads (*maenas* means mania) wore headdresses of vine and ivy leaves and carried a *thyrsus*, a pole entwined with ivy leaves and sometimes a snake. In Attica they were called the *Bacchae* (*bacchaevo*, meaning to revel); in Delphi, the *Thyiades* (*thyo manezo*, meaning go mad with rage); and in the Peloponnese, *Dysmaenae* (women who may go mad). The initiate became *en-theos* (overtaken by the god), which is the root of the English word enthusiasm. They also healed and prophesied. The cult was synonymous with dance. The dances were held in forests, on mountain sides, and in wild territory and were conducted at night. They were very noisy, and included crashing cymbals, drum-beating, and women screaming. Another name for Dionysus was *Bromius*, from *bremo* to "make a racket". Dancing and noise then were sacred as well as demonic.³⁴

Those who could not dance (*achoreia*) were considered brutes. If Gorgon/Medusa is shown dancing, what does that signify? Does she dance a come hither dance or a stay away dance? A 'to summon the dread goddess of death' dance or an apotropaic dance? Is she dancing the dance of life and death, birth and death, darkness and light, or just a bucolic Dionysian celebration of life and freedom? Maybe she was dancing all these dances.

Pindar wrote a Sicilian version of the myth.³⁵ He gives the home of the three Gorgon sisters in the far north.³⁶ It was a paradise, and they lived a bucolic life, without sickness and old age nor 'toil or battles', and without fear of 'strict Nemesis'. Perseus, using guile and trickery (*metis*, not heroic courage³⁷) arrived in the idyllic land of the Hyperboreans, a surprising home for these 'monstrous sisters', unlike Hades where the *Gorgoneion* lived. Pindar describes how the Hyperboreans lived:

> The Muse is always with them and is part of their customs, everywhere are maidens' dances, the song of lyres and of the

melodious flutes. They bind their hair with golden laurel-wreaths, feasting with joy. Neither disease nor wasting old age has any part in their divine home. They do not work or fight and live without the punishments of *Nemesis*.

Pythian 10:36–40

It is hard to imagine, given the communal nature of the dance, that the Gorgons were mere bystanders in these revels. They were sleeping when Perseus arrived, perhaps tired from dancing. In Figure 3.5 Gorgo/Medusa looks positively ecstatic; her face is frightening (although this might be a mask) but her stance is joyful and energetic. I believe she is not the terrifying monster that needed to be despatched by a hero, but a masked dancer. The Gorgons are dancing with the nymphs in their homeland paradise of Hyperborea.

Perseus entered this gathering,

> … he killed the Gorgon, and returned bringing stony death to the islanders, the head that radiated with hair made of serpents.

Pythian 10:46–49

This is an odd aetiological myth. How does one bring 'stony death'? Does Pindar represent here an Olympian moral/ethical objection to a sybaritic life without war and bloodshed, or perhaps a Dionysian existence? Or is Perseus a symbol of the Northern warrior tribes who invaded Greece in the twelfth century BCE,[38] and who valued nothing more than violence and power struggles, as exemplified by the Greeks in the *Iliad* destroying the palatial culture of Troy?[39] Pindar confusingly considers Medusa as beautiful and having nice cheeks as well as fierce and with horrible snaky hair.[40]

Perhaps this is the place to tell the usual story …

Perseus, showing off to King Polydektes at a banquet, boasted that he could bring him the head of Medusa. The King agreed, expecting this to be an impossible task, and that Perseus would be killed in the process. Polydektes sent him off because he wanted to marry Perseus' mother Danae who did not want to marry him. Perseus was helped by the god Hermes (possibly in the original myth).[41] Later, Pindar said it was Athena alone who helped him.[42]

Perseus went to the Gorgons' sisters the *Graeae*. They had only one eye and one tooth between them. Bullying Perseus took these and refused to give them back until they helped him. They told him where to find the nymphs. From them he received the Cap of Invisibility, a pair of winged sandals, and a wallet or *kibisis*.[43] Hermes gave him a scimitar, or curved sword. He carried a shield of bronze.

Figure 3.7. Perseus, and beheaded Medusa and Athena, Athenian red-figure hydria c. 5th BCE There is no shield here though.

This is the most famous part of the later story. Using the shield to reflect the stony gaze of Medusa (although she was sleeping ... let us not dwell on inconsistencies) he cut off her head. Mirroring her face back to her, even though she was asleep. Turning her fearsome gaze back on herself. Women and mirrors.

Mirrors in Ancient Greece were women's things; they have been found almost exclusively in women's graves. Mirrors were first encountered in excavations in Mycenaean sites dated around 1400 BCE. There is a hiatus in the archaeological record of mirrors from about 1100 until 700 BCE, when they reappear in excavations and in the visual and written records of the Archaic and Classical Greeks. Objects found at sanctuaries and in tombs suggest that during the sixth century they may have

THE DANCING GORGON   51

been made as religious offerings and possibly used by priestesses for ritual purposes.⁴⁴ Mirrors were made from an expensive metal, bronze, which was also used to make weapons and coinage. Men gave women their mirrors which were among their few permitted personal possessions. That women seem to have been exclusively responsible for the deposition of mirrors in sanctuaries and graves underscores the profound connection between mirrors and feminine agency.

Interestingly, research has found a bronze mirror showing what looks like the Kretan Labyris near Bournemouth, England in a woman's grave. She was a powerful person of the Durotriges tribe, and the grave is dated around 100 BCE. One of the grave goods was a bronze mirror. Genetic testing has found that this tribe was matrifocal, and women's graves had more grave goods than the men, who moved into the woman's tribe.⁴⁵ Bronze was a rare and expensive metal only owned by wealthy elites.⁴⁶

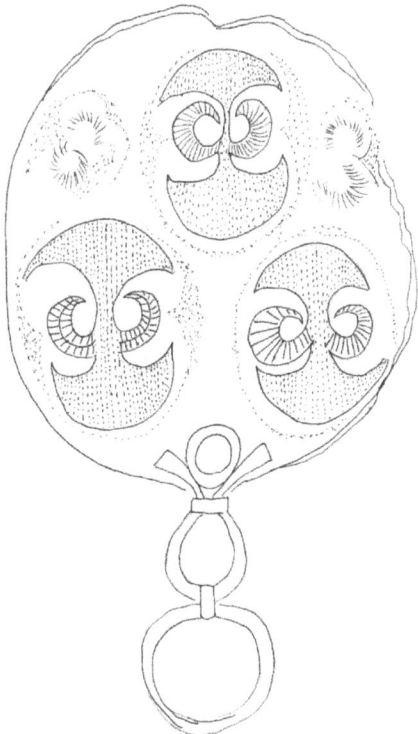

Figure 3.8. Mirror of the Durotriges Tribe c. 100 BCE Portsmouth, England.

Notice the similarity with Mycenaean jewellery.

Figure 3.9. Fresco showing Mycenean woman and her jewellery.[47]

Large caches of votive mirrors dating from the Archaic and Classical periods were discovered at the Argive Heraion (the temple of Hera) and the sanctuary of Artemis at Brauron (see Appendix 2 for a discussion of Brauron). Both goddesses were concerned with marriage, pregnancy, and childbirth among other things. In ancient Greece, mirrors were considered divine portals that connected to other realms. They were associated with foresight and knowledge, qualities that were thought to be achieved only through death; thus they had an uncanny nature. Connected to prophecy and divination, looking into a mirror could reveal the future, but also if one gazed into a mirror for too long it was believed you could lose your soul. Mirrors were seen like pools of water where souls could be trapped, a theme that is reflected in the story of Narcissus. While mirrors had their practical uses around the household, like spying on slaves and scaring away spirits, they were also feared objects. As a result, they were typically positioned with the reflective side facing toward the walls.

Catoptromancy, or divination from mirrors, comes from the Ancient Greek words, *katoptron*, mirror and *manteia*, divination. Mirrors in Greek mythology are powerful symbols. They represent truth and knowledge and are used to reflect both light and dark, as a metaphor for both deception and truth-seeking. The mirror is a medium through which the protagonist comes face to face with themselves, forcing them to reflect upon their flaws and weaknesses, which they must confront if they are to be successful in their quest.

Pausanias described the practice as follows:

> Before the Temple of Demeter at Patras, there was a fountain, separated from the temple by a wall, and there was an oracle, very truthful, not for all events, but for the sick only. The sick person let down a mirror, suspended by a thread till its base touched the surface of the water, having first prayed to the goddess and offered incense. Then looking into the mirror, he saw the presage of death or recovery, according as the face appeared fresh and healthy, or of a ghastly aspect.[48]

Using the mirror on his bronze shield, Perseus was able to reflect Medusa back on herself. He was using a masculine shield of bronze in a feminine manner, as a mirror. What can we make of that? Is the myth saying women henceforth should not look deep into their psyches, that death lived there? That too deep an inquiry would kill them, and that they should stay on the surface? In any case, it was stone to stone, ice to ice, dead eyes to dead eyes. Although she was sleeping ...

Incidentally, the sickle he used to cut off her head was made from adamant, possibly diamond or steel. A sickle made from adamant, given to him by his mother Gaia, was used by Kronos to castrate his father Uranus. Adamant then is a magical material, so what is happening here is of great significance. But what might that be? Castrating the "monster", unless her face was a mask behind which was a priestess? In a later version of the myth, Medusa is punished for having sex with Poseidon in Athena's temple, which was forbidden in sacred space. Or was coupling with the god of the sea a threat to Athena in other ways? Certainly, Poseidon and Athena were rivals for who should be the patron of Athens. Athena won. Was the sickle once again cutting short a blood line? Perhaps.

When Perseus fell upon Medusa and decapitated her, two creatures sprang forth from the wound. Pegasus, the horse with wings, and Chrysaor, the giant. Perseus fled with the head in the *kibisis*. Medusa's two sisters chased after him shrieking. The Gorgons chase after Perseus, and it is this chase that is supposedly depicted in whole body representations of the Gorgon which began to appear in the 650s BCE in both Attica and the Peloponnese (Corinth) and *Megala Hellas*.[49]

Perseus gave Medusa's head to Athena for her *aegis* in recognition for her help in his quest (or perhaps not, see above). Certainly, his actions represented violence against Medusa, who was no threat to him (she was sleeping), and instead it was a heroic quest to prove his manhood. According to legend, the head of Medusa was buried in the *agora* in Athens. Showing the Athenian domination over what exactly? Women lovers of Poseidon? Women who lived a free life with the Muses? Magical women whose souls could be trapped in a mirror? We can only speculate.

There is, however, another perspective. Scholars have argued that Gorgo/Medusa was a fertility goddess[50] and is linked with Artemis, the Great Mother, and Demeter, all ancient goddesses. The name *medousa* means queen or guardian and was a title that was also used for Athena, Artemis, and Aphrodite. Many scholars use the *Francois Krater* as further evidence of this theory.

Figure 3.10. *Potnia Theron*. The Francois Krater. Black figure Volute krater terracotta 570 BCE made in Athens, findspot Chiusi, Etruria.

The krater shows the typical winged *Potnia Theron* in profile, wearing a peplos decorated with a square pattern enriched in alternating squares with dot rosette and cross design. She is standing, grasping a spotted panther by the throat with right hand and a stag by the throat with the left. The lower border of the skirt is decorated with alternating dot rosette and cross and meander designs.

Underlying her association with the Gorgons, on the underside of the handle is a Gorgo/Medusa in motion with serpent hair, wings, staring eyes, fangs, beard, and outstretched tongue. The juxtaposition of *Potnia* and the Gorgon suggests an affinity or shared field of influence. Interestingly, Gorgo/Medusa has a masculine body (no breasts), large, muscular thighs and a bushy beard. It would be hard to identify this as a female figure unless one was familiar with the myth or the common association of *Potnia* and Gorgo/Medusa. This vase suggests the two are separate and so the identification of Gorgo/Medusa with the Great Earth Mother or Artemis is incorrect.

Figure 3.11. François Vase: Detailed drawing of the left handle, showing a Gorgon.

56 MONSTROUS WOMEN

Others believe the myth of Perseus and Medusa has nothing to do with earth goddesses; rather it represents male initiation.[51] The young *ephebe* is showing his strength and courage by killing the monster and offering the head to Athena, patron and protectress of Athens. The argument is strengthened when we examine the illustration below.

Figure 3.12. Ajax and Achilles in the Francois vase.

Here, the body of the greatest of warriors, Achilles, is carried by his brother in arms Ajax from the battlefield. This puts an entirely different light on the *Potnia* figure: she tames the wild animals, the warrior tames the enemy (or doesn't in this case) and a masculine-looking Gorgon is present, if hidden on the inside of the handle.

Three shield straps from Olympus from the early Archaic period[52] show Gorgo/Medusa along with Zeus killing Typhon, also Theseus and the Minotaur, *ephebes*[53] riding horses, lions, and other mythical beasts. It is true that the iconography of lions and horses is associated with Gorgo/Medusa. However, this does not explain why Gorgo/Medusa is female and why she needed to be killed, if she was an ally of the *ephebe*: surely, she would need to be preserved? Unless she was an enemy and not an ally. I contend that this shows Gorgo/Medusa as a warrior; not the "friend" of the warrior but instead a noble opponent.

The Perseus myth illustrates the patriarchal heroes who destroy/ neutralise/co-opt the powerful dark feminine principle, most of whom are not attacking or threatening these heroes in any way. Gorgo/ Medusa's powerful head is safe with Athena who has been stripped of her older divine traditions and supports the Olympic gods. While the "paradise" of Hyperborea with its peace and pleasure was left undefended. A cowardly warrior brought death to paradise.

The monstrous was embodied by women who epitomised the base emotions of rage and aggression,[54] but surely this is male behaviour. In Pindar it is Perseus who is base, cowardly, and aggressive, he kills a sleeping woman. If however Medusa was a threat to his way of life, then killing her by any means possible was justified. I doubt that the Athenians would have decapitated a symbol of a nature goddess. Rituals, temples, and cults to her as Artemis, Demeter, and Aphrodite continued and were supported and later financed by the state: the *Thesmophoria*, The Eleusinian Mysteries, the *Haloa* festivals to name a few. That Gorgo/Medusa represented the domination of nature and the initiation of *ephebes* is similarly unlikely, as this was Artemis' role, despite the Medusa on the temple at Corfu.[55] I argue Gorgo/Medusa was not Artemis. I believe she represented chaos, rebellion and the Barbarian Other.

To answer my original question, was the Gorgo/Medusa an example of Athenian misogyny? My answer has to be both yes and no. Yes, in the sense that giving the *Gorgoneion* a woman's body, albeit a masculine-looking one, identified woman as the problem, the monster and the Other who needed to be killed to protect the *polis*. However, by incorporating the *Gorgoneion* onto Athena's aegis, the power of Gorgo/ Medusa was acknowledged. Whether it was placed there herself or by Perseus, the potency of Gorgo/Medusa was contained and controlled by the goddess and protected the city.

Which is not to say that Athenian men did not respect the divine feminine. Festivals and cults, like *Thesmophoria* and *Haloa*, were celebrated exclusively by women and were held in the centre of the city in the political district and financed by the participants' menfolk. Athenian men understood the importance of the feminine principle to their city, even if they didn't give their women much political freedom.

Conversely my answer is no. I argue that the embodying of Gorgo/Medusa, around the time of the reforms of Solon and Peisistratus and the growing threat from Persia, was indicative of her meaning. Gorgo/Medusa represented the Other who enjoyed freedom and agency in her own right. Whether dancing with the Muses in Hyperborea or ruling countries and not marrying in Libya, her behaviour symbolised a threat to Apollonian order. The association of Gorgo/Medusa with the Amazons highlights a pervasive fear of rebellious foreign women who did not submit to the rule of men. Of course, I am not arguing for the existence or otherwise of Amazons or other female warriors. What they symbolised to the Athenians is the issue.

The fact that the symbolism of Gorgo/Medusa was widespread and developed quickly suggests that it was responding to an urgent need. Symbols in a mainly illiterate society were powerful and didactic. Myths and readings from epic poetry were performed in public as part of civic education.[56] Myths were used to promote and inculcate Athenian values, or those values that the rulers wished the populace to embrace. The monster gives society a clear visual of what is normal and what is not. Loud aristocratic women, who may have had more freedom than the lawmakers liked, who displayed their wealth and power in funerary rituals and sumptuous clothing, were constrained by Solon's reforms. It is a small step to see them as monstrous and a threat to civic order.

As discussed, this may have been performative by the men. They may have needed to appear to agree with these reforms in front of other men. Whether they believed the rhetoric is debatable. The double bias of later male writers such as Plato and Aristotle together with nineteenth century classicists, twentieth century male psychologists and anthropologists may have given Gorgo/Medusa a meaning that was never intended by Athenians.[57] The voice of Athenian women unfortunately is unrecorded.

Equally unbalanced is the wish-fulfilment of late twentieth century feminists who have 'reclaimed' Medusa while simultaneously reducing her to her genitals (something they accuse patriarchy of doing). The link with Neolithic and Minoan cultures through the Great Goddess and *Potnia Theron* is tenuous if attractive; we would love it if it were so, but to date we cannot know. However new material is always being discovered, and the history and mythology is subject to endless revision as new evidence reveals 'alternate facts'. It is important to remember that

Medusa was not attacking or threatening Perseus, and that his mission was a dare, but she was an opponent worthy of a brave warrior.

Swallowing the Demon: Meditation on the dancing Medusa

There is a saying by Native American healers: 'When did you stop dancing?' Dancing in their worldview was integral to good health and happiness. So when did you stop dancing, if you did, and why? Is there a dance you need to do? An angry dance, a healing dance, a protective dance, a loving dance? Or all of them?

Mirror magic

Look into the mirror, especially at the full moon. What do you see?

Mirrors are used in magic of all kinds, good and bad, attracting and repelling. My everyday use of mirror magic, when a creep or weirdo is staring at me, especially on the tube, is to imagine a large mirror facing them, so that I am behind the back of the mirror. They see themselves reflected and it is rare indeed that a creep or weirdo can look at this image for long. They usually turn away, get up and leave and certainly stop looking my way. This is neutral magic: you are simply returning their energy back to them.

Mirrors are used for scrying and shadow work. Temple of Chrysalis[58] describes an experiment at the University of Urbino where subjects gazed into a mirror for ten minutes. They commonly reported huge deformations of their faces (66% of respondents), fantastical and monstrous beings (48%), as well as seeing an unknown person reflected (28%), and an archetypal face, such as that of an old woman, a child, or the portrait of an ancestor (28%). Mirrors capture and reflect as well as absorb and repel, and they were believed to capture souls and trap them. Remember the Wicked Stepmother in Snow White? They have an uncanny quality.

What do you see when you look in the mirror?

Who is there?

What side of you is shown?

If you gaze at a black mirror what comes up for you?

Notes

1. Vernant 1991:136.
2. Freud 2003:84–87.
3. Bowers 1990, Alban 2023.
4. Morgan 1984:191.
5. Marinatos 2000:51–56.
6. Keuls 1993:5.
7. Khalifa-Gueta 2021:224–7.
8. Keuls 1993:34. It could be argued that it was men who feared being abandoned, consciously or unconsciously. Certainly in the 21st Century women who have freedom and their own money, the thing the patriarchy sought to deny them, have chosen in large numbers to live alone. The old trope of dying alone and miserable is busted as research has shown childless single women are the happiest people, while married men are happier than single ones and single men the most miserable of all. I am not suggesting the Greeks understood this, but perhaps they suspected women would be fine without them, as indeed Spartan women were. They were left alone a lot as their menfolk were endlessly fighting and they ran things in their absence. The same applied to women in the First and Second World Wars.
9. Keuls 1993:1.
10. Keuls 1993:1.
11. Homeric *Hymn to Pythian Apollo*, 1:254–74.
12. Howe 1954:220.
13. Howe 1954:220.
14. Howe 1954:221.
15. Keuls 1993:323.
16. Lyons 2007:36. Marinatos 2000:57.
17. Butler 1990:136.
18. Lyons 2007:40.
19. Neumann *The Great Mother* 1974:146.
20. Page du Bois, *Sowing the Body: Psychoanalysis and Ancient representations of women* (Chicago: University of Chicago Press, 1988) p.92.
21. Lubell, Winifred Milius, *The Metamorphosis of Baubo. Myths of Women's Sexual Energy.* (Nashville and London: Vanderbilt University Press, 1994) p.112.
22. Keuls, Eva, *The Reign of the Phallus. Sexual Politics in Ancient Athens* p.39.
23. Kilmer 1982.

24. Slater 1968:323.
25. Morgan 1984:186.
26. This term was invented by a word coined by German archaeologists in the 19th C. The word is borrowed from German *Knie* meaning knee, and *Lauf* meaning run.
27. Orr 2000:11–13.
28. Rocconi 2015:82.
29. Fitton 1973:254–255.
30. Lawler 1947:344–46.
31. Benešová 2012:5, Papioannou 2011:23.
32. Hardwick 1993:292.
33. Blacking 1986:10.
34. Papaioannou c. 2012:68.
35. Zolotnikova 358.
36. Pindar *Pythian Odes* 10:29–48.
37. See pg. 140 for a discussion of *metis*.
38. See Quinn 2025:93–106 for a detailed account of these Greek Dark Ages and speculation as to why the Palatial culture was literally burnt to the ground.
39. Dexter 2010:32.
40. Pindar *Pythian* 12: 6–12, 16–18.
41. Morford et al. 549.
42. Pindar, *Pythian*. 10:44–46. As the Gorgoneion ended up on the *aegis* of Athena, it is likely that the myth was changed to show Athena, patron of Athens.
43. *Kibisis* is not a Greek word; it was believed to come from Cyprus, home of Aphrodite. Morford. 561 fn.4.
44. Congdon, Lenore O. Keene. Greek Mirrors, Source: *Notes in the History of Art*, vol. 4, no. 2/3, 1985, pp. 19–25. JSTOR. http://www.jstor.org/stable/23202422. Accessed 7 Dec. 2024.
45. https://www.science.org/content/article/part-ancient-britain-was-woman-s-world-ancient-burials-reveal?fbclid=IwY2xjawH1r8hleHRuA2FlbQIxMAABHRb_I7WGLYwCqo-2PvD4Mm1dym7ye6EdItp-pommJ_IiRfYKdTeJB6BqQYw_aem_437YWZRlxzA2UZVvrRJFCA
46. There was widespread trade in the ancient world: amber from Scandinavia, lapis lazuli from Afghanistan and tin from Cornwall were found in Egypt and Krete in the Bronze Age, and Kretan goods found their way to the northern countries, see Quinn 2025:13–39.
47. Necklaces. National Archaeological Museum in Athens.

48. Pausanias *Description of Greece* 7:17–27.
49. Greater Greece, usually Italy and Sardinia where Greeks founded colonies.
50. Hagen (2007:15, 16, 23 fig. 2.7. Gimbutas 1982:152. Frothingham 1911:349.
51. Marinatos 2000:92–109.
52. Marinatos 2000:64, fig. 3.18, 104 figs. 5.11, 5.12. 103.
53. *Ephebes* are young men usually aged 18–20 who were undergoing military training.
54. Giallongo 2017:104.
55. Hagen 2007:18, fig. 2.2.
56. Giallongo 1998:66.
57. See Appendix 2 for discussion about how transmission of Greek texts distorted their meaning.
58. https://templeofchrysalis.com/mirrors-the-basics-of-mirror-magic/

CHAPTER FOUR

The Terror of Hades

The Greeks, like many people, had a complex relationship with the dead. The dead were worshipped and also feared because of how they might interfere with the living. If this sounds fantastical to a twenty-first century mind, consider in the UK and elsewhere our ceremonies around the dead. Armistice day, the eleventh hour of the eleventh day of the eleventh month, sounds pretty superstitious to me. Remembering the dead of two senseless twentieth-century wars has become fetishised. Anyone, me for example, who does not sport the red poppy around that time is likely to face pointed fingers at best and angry diatribes at worst. I have also experienced censure when I wear my white poppy of peace.[1]

Of course, ceremonies of the dead concern the living and their relationship with the dead. We, unlike the Greeks, do not believe for the most part that the dead can actually influence current events. Except they do; not perhaps by leaving Hades, but as I showed above they affect people's perceptions and behaviour. Brave is the politician or public figure who does not appear in public with their poppy in November. The dead police the living in other words. But not the actual dead; or do they? We talk about the ghosts of powerful figures. Franco, Thatcher, Marx, Stalin and other strong and divisive figures can 'haunt' present day politics. We say "he must be turning in their grave" as though they are sentient and can react to events. Our relationship with the dead is a deal closer to the superstitions of the Greeks than we care to admit.

The dead in Homer were pretty dead. They were not the ghosts they became in Classical times. The dead could be summoned, as Odysseus did in *Odyssey* book 11, by drinking the blood of a sacrificed animal (*nekuia*). Only then could they hear the living. Agamemnon and Odysseus' mother did not even recognise him until they drank the offering. Once the libation is made, the dead swarmed up from Hades like ants to spilled sugar. But the *aphradeis* (the dead) lacked mental capacity and were wisps; even after drinking blood, they had no substance. They were fated to remain in Hades and could only be summoned by sacrifice and did not and could not leave the Underworld. Odysseus travels to the ends of the world to speak to them, but the dead cannot cross the river that separates them from the living.

The restless dead, who have not crossed that river, can interact with the living, generally because they have not been accorded the correct funeral rites, e.g. Patroclus[2] and Elpenor.[3] Many cultures follow this, that correct disposal of the dead body is necessary before the dead can rest in peace. If they remain in limbo, they can harm the living. In the borderlands, Odysseus encounters the wandering lost souls of unmarried men, virgins, men killed in battle still wearing their bloody armour, and old people who have suffered ill treatment.[4] These souls frighten him, unlike the souls of the dead. He knows the restless dead could harm him.

Where the Underworld is described,[5] there are woods, groves of Persephone, tall black poplars, sterile willows and four rivers. A race of people called the Cimmerians live in eternal darkness close to the border.

The *Homeric Hymn to Demeter* shows that the boundary between the living and the dead can be crossed, at least by the goddesses Persephone and Hekate. It also introduces the idea that the dead will be punished or rewarded according to how they have behaved in life. Plato's *Myth of Er* at the end of *The Republic* goes into this in great detail.[6] The *Hymn* promises initiates of the Mysteries at Eleusis that they will have a sweet life after death, denied to the non-initiate. Sappho[7] agrees, and she says of the uninitiated,

> [dead] You will be forgotten
> And there will be no longing for you
> Because you did not share the roses of Pieria.

> Unseen in the house of Hades,
> Flown from our midst
> You will wander alone among the shadowy dead.

Pythagoras, and later Pindar and Empedocles, introduced the idea of reincarnation, that souls might be reborn in another body or the body of an animal. Plato in the *Myth of Er* gives souls some choice as to how they will reincarnate, and each soul is given a guardian spirit who accompanies them in their new life. The man who tells this story returns from the dead to tell Plato of his experiences and continues living; so he was not undead, but a messenger from the other side.[8]

Pindar[9] suggests that the oracle at Delphi approves of the dead's messages in the dreams of the living and advocates rituals the living could use to communicate with the dead. Sappho mentions Gello the soul of a dead virgin who likes children and can kill both them and pregnant women.[10]

Fifth century tragedy, which was performed at the festival of Dionysus in Athens, has a super abundance of ghostly figures. Aeschylus' *Persians* has a long monologue of the dead Persian king Darius, giving advice to his mother. Klytemnestra speaks in Euripides' *Eumendies*, and the ghost of Alcestis speaks in *Alcestis*. Another description of the Underworld is found in *Frogs*, the comedy by Aristophanes, which follows Dionysus as he goes to the Underworld.

How the dead were managed varied over time. In Classical times, apotropaic rites were intended to keep the dead happy and away from the living. Electra in *Chorephori* (the Libation Bearers)[11] takes libations to the grave of her father Agamemnon, sent by her mother Klytemnestra who is having nightmares and believes he is responsible. In Sophocles' tragedy *Electra* Chrysothemis takes offerings to be burnt on Agamemnon's grave[12] after his ghost appeared to Klytemnestra. Both rituals are similar to those performed at funerals and festivals to honour the dead.

Plutarch[13] describes how Apollo made reparations after taking over the oracle at Delphi and killing Python, to avert the anger of the *daimones*, *alastores* and *palamnaioi* (the dead who seek vengeance or supernatural agents acting on their behalf, like the *Erinyes*). Placating the angry dead was not just a personal problem; the city became involved if there were signs that the dead were angry. Punishment by the dead was contagious, and could affect the family and the community of the wrongdoer. This happened in Sparta in the mid fifth century where the angry ghost of Pausanias was believed to be causing problems.

Psychagogoi (those who lead souls away) were employed to deal with his ghost. In this case the Spartans made statues and left offerings in a deserted place to assuage the angry ghost.[14]

Two descriptions of rites performed to avoid the vengeful dead have been found from Selinus, circa 450 BCE, and Cyrene, around 330 BCE.[15] Both involve sacrificing a piglet or sheep to Zeus, purifying themselves with water and salt, perhaps also casting a circle and walking away without looking back (common in rituals involving Erinyes and Hekate). In the Selinus ritual, wine is poured through the roof of the shrine, a libation of honey and *theoxenia* is prepared, a table and couch is set up with olive branch headdresses, with more honey in cups and cakes and meat. Some or all of this is burnt.

Plato writes of men who perform rituals to cleanse the past sins of the living and the dead and to turn the angry/polluted ghost (*miaros*) into a helpful one (*katharos*).[16] The angry dead can torture the living with ancient wraths to the point of madness.[17] Indeed madness is one sure sign of an attack by the restless dead. Hekate suppers (*deipna*) were set out at the new moon as offerings to the goddess and also to address any angry dead (*hoi apotropaioi*) who might be lurking there as they wandered with Hekate, who controlled them.

The *Anthesteria*, the festival of the dead, was celebrated in Athens and Ionia.[18] Rites included opening new wine, a marriage of the queen to Dionysus, and welcoming children into rituals for the first time.

Curse tablets have been found in Sicily dating from the sixth century and in Athens from the mid fifth century, which had been left in graves, usually of those who died uninitiated or unmarried (*aoroi*), and called on these dead to carry messages to Hekate, Hermes and Persephone to command the dead to do their bidding.[19] The dead had become the means to take revenge against one's enemies. A few words were scratched on these lead tablets, and a binding song was sung (*hymnos desmios*) in this love spell:

> [May all the *atelestoi* (uninitiated) in the cemetery] ... bind her ... let her be unable to eat or drink, not be contented, not be strong, not have peace of mind, not find sleep without me ... drag her by the throat, by her hair, by her soul, to me ...[20]

So who are the unquiet dead and why do they pursue the living? There are three types that are found in many cultures: those denied proper funerary rites (*ataphoi*), the prematurely dead (*aoroi*), and those who have died violently (*biaothanatoi*). The *ataphoi* linger between the world of the living and dead, being neither one thing or another, and they can be neutralised if proper burial rites are performed, like the rites for Patroculus in the Odyssey book 19: 282–337 and for Agamemnon in Euripides' play of that name.[21]

The *biaothanatoi* are usually those who have been murdered where the culprit is yet to be punished. In Aeschylus' *Eumenides* the angry ghost of Klytemnestra, who was murdered by her son Orestes, appears demanding vengeance on her son. She charges the *Erinyes* to hunt him down and make him pay for his crime of matricide. She argues that letting him go unpunished threatens the natural order of things. Furiously she rejects the argument of the chorus (who often represent the voice of reason in tragedy) that individual claims to vengeance should be subsumed by the greater good. Her argument is that her honour after death rests on Orestes being punished, implying that the dead have their own hierarchies. As she was Queen in Argos, her loss of status is shameful to her. 'I, thanks to you, am dishonoured among the other dead.' She rages that 'not one of the divinities is wrathful on my behalf'.[22]

The *Erinyes* are her agents. She let loose these 'hounds of vengeance' in the previous play in the trilogy[23] and invokes 'Justice. Ruin and the Erinyes'. In the first play Klytemnestra identifies herself as an 'ancient bitter avenging spirit'.[24] Her ghost itself can do nothing, and she has to appeal to the *Erinyes* to take revenge. Klytemnestra links her honour with the *Erinyes*[25] and reminds them of the night-time libations she made to them.[26] She both appeals to their pity and demands that they destroy Orestes.

Klytemnestra appears in a dream to the *Erinyes*, and this is her pathway to them. Rumours and dreams are spoken of as 'women's thinking'.[27] Likewise, Agamemnon (her murdered husband) sent her a dream of a snake which terrified her.[28] Klytemnestra attacks the *Erinyes*' lack of action in their dreams, and they remain sleeping during her speech. She invokes the serpent and its terrible power: 'Powerful conspirators have drained the terrible serpent of wrath'.[29] But as a ghost or spirit (*eidolon*) she has no power. Her dream does eventually wake them, and they feel her reproach.[30]

Klytemnestra, as mother to Orestes and Iphigenia, who Agamemnon killed, calls on divine wrath for this familial crime. The ancient law demands punishment for killing blood relatives, and for that she had

68 MONSTROUS WOMEN

to kill Agamemnon. The fact that her son killed her, another crime of blood guilt, is double reason for vengeance. In the old ethics, the family (*oikos*) and blood relatives trump everything. By demanding vengeance, Klytemnestra subverts the cultural assumptions of male dominance, both sexual, political, and linguistic, and their violence.[31]

Klytemnestra is unlike Patroclus and Elpenor, the restless dead of Homer, who do not demand vengeance but a ritual burial.[32] Klytemnestra goes further and demands spilling kindred blood for the benefit of her soul that she might be restored to her previous status even though dead. This old justice is all she wishes for. The play shows her as a monstrous woman and a disruptive force in a myth of masculine divine order. She has to be crushed and defeated as indeed she is. She is given no divine support, no prophet, oracle or command from the gods as Agamemnon and Orestes have.[33] Even her champions, the *Erinyes*, who at first take her ethical claims seriously, eventually abandon her.[34] In tragedy, as well as in life, judgement was always given along gendered lines.[35] The new juries which in future will decide capital crimes will have no women on them, and their voice will be silenced.

In the Mysteries at Eleusis, the initiate was hounded in one part of the ritual by a representation of the *Erinyes*.[36] It was believed that the *Erinyes*, agents of the restless dead, could interrupt the rites and block initiation. In addition this served as a reminder of what awaited the uninitiated after death, as Sappho warns:

> In the holiest of mysteries, before the gods arrive, the emanations
> of chthonic demons manifest and visions frighten the initiates,
> distracting them from the good things the gods have to offer.[37]

The threat was severe for those with blood guilt, which is why the Lesser Mysteries were held seven months before the Mysteries, to purify initiands. The rites of the Lesser Mysteries took place after the month of *Anthesterion*,[38] the month where the dead were propitiated and placated.

Empusa, mentioned in Aristophanes' comedy *Frogs*, is an angry soul who caused problems for initiates. Of the Mystery religions. *Empousai* (f pl) are associated with Hekate who can send them out to punish people. Their names describe their behaviour. Harpies snatch their victims (*harpazein*, to snatch) while *empousai* (*empodezein*, to hinder) block their victims. Although few people would have actually been murderers, blood guilt was seen as contagious, affecting members of the family of the murderer or the tribe, and so it became a social issue.

In Homer, it is the agents of the dead, usually the *Erinyes*, who punish the living. Orestes is attacked by them after his mother's death. Both Odysseus and Achilles are threatened by the ghost of Hector that the wrath of gods will fall upon them if they do not give him a proper burial. They doubtless mean *Erinyes* who Homer calls goddesses (*theai*).[39] Homer is silent as to how the *Erinyes* punished, except to say they bring evils (*kakas*)[40] and the *Erinyes* walk through darkness (*eerophoitos*).[41]

In Classical times the dead continue to use agents which exist under a variety of names (e.g. *alastor, prostropaios, palamnaios*), but it was the *Erinyes* who were the main source of punishment. In tragedy, they drag their victims into the Underworld.[42] They become more substantial than in Homer and are described as black robed[43] children of [the] Night.[44] As mentioned above, the *Erinyes* are goddesses and not souls of the dead. However, the dead themselves become more active. A fragment of a lost tragedy describes the ghosts under Hekate's rule giving people nightmares.[45]

The Hippocratic treatise *On the Sacred Disease* traces madness, paranoia, and terror to attacks by the *biaiothanatoi* (dead through violence) as well as Hekate. Plato and Xenophon agree that the angry dead and their agents worked through mental illness.

The victim of violence "has his wrath kindled against the author of the deed ... the disembodied soul joins forces with the mind of the murderer to bring all possible disruptions on him and his labours".[46]

This may be seen as the punishment by guilt, which the murderer eventually confesses to, or goes mad, tormented by his act and his terror of being caught. Dostoyevsky's *Crime and Punishment* comes to mind; the murder was successful but the murderer cannot bear the consequences of his crime and is caught. Or those

> foully dealt with ... strike into the hearts of those who have shed their blood, and what vengeance they send to the wicked.[47]

The ghosts use the *Erinyes* to inflict madness on their victims. Why goddesses from the Underworld? It may be because of the association between madness, which lives in the dark recesses of the minds of the wicked, and the dark, tortured chambers of the Underworld. We might call this the unconscious these days.

Angry ghosts appeared in the other Mysteries. The Bacchic and Hekate's Mysteries in Aegina were renowned for their cures of madness. Later Theurgists saw the angry dead as seducing initiands away with passions of the body such as lust and gluttony rather than harming them with madness.[48]

The third type of restless dead were *aoroi*, those who had died early, before completing their earthly role and duties. They were usually the souls of women who died before having children or raising them successfully. The *aoroi* were not demons in the traditional sense of being an immortal creature, like the Harpies, but a once mortal person upon whom misfortune has fallen. These entities were called a variety of names such as Gello, Lamia, and Mormo, and were mythic creatures who described their actions through their stories. *Aoros* means untimely (*aoroi/ai* is the m/f plural) and describes the untimely death of a woman.[49] These *aorai* were responsible for women's death in childbirth, their infertility and sometimes, in the case of Gello, death before they were married. Sappho, as we saw earlier, said Gello liked children and she took them to Hades. Gello has been described as "she who strangles children and persecutes women in childbirth".[50]

Figure 4.1. Sirens or Harpies carrying dead children away detail from Lycian tomb c. 480 BCE.

Lithica (magical lore on stones) suggested that galactite be hung around the neck of a newborn to ward off Megaira (the envious woman). While aetite prevented premature delivery and miscarriages and supports a successful delivery at the right time, it also stops Gello and other *aorai* bringing terror to girls and babies. Amber protected the household from such supernatural attacks, especially on women and girls.[51] The attacker was always female and always targeted women, babies and girls.

Demeter herself recites an incantation to protect her charge. In the Greek this has a sing-song rhythm designed as a protection spell:

> I shall nurse him; nor do I expect that either an attack
> Or the Undercutter will harm him due to his nurse's negligence
> For I have a great antidote, stronger than the plant-cutter
> And I know an excellent defence against the attack that brings misfortune.[52]

In this spell, the goddess mentions *pharmakai*, herbs or poisons that might be used to attack the child.

In the aetiological myths[53] Gello died before marriage, Lamia's children died early in life, or she killed them as did Mormo. These women, embittered by their fate, were driven to make other women suffer as they had. The message was clear: failure to marry, failure to birth children and failure to raise them to adulthood was a breakdown in the primary role of a woman and an attack on the family (*oikos*) and consequently an attack on society as a whole. Their punishment was permanent exile both from the land of the living and from the dead. *Aorai* wandered and belonged nowhere. As 'failures' as women, they were denied entry into the Underworld. Because they were not fully dead, they could wander but never rest between the worlds. They could be conjured by magicians who used their powers to enact magic on earth.

Aorai were ugly, smelly and disgusting, all things mortal women were obliged not to be. Lamia was a hermaphrodite, with both male and female sexual characteristics. Mormo had a face which constantly changed, she was sometimes called *mormoluke* or 'she-wolf'. *Strix*, another *aorai*, was shown as part-woman part-owl, a bat or carrion (crow) were other manifestations. Night-hunting birds like owls, which silently fly in the night, dropping on their prey like a stone, make an easy representation of evil. Bird-like demons like the Sirens and Harpies were well-known. *Aorai* were also associated with horses and both the *Erinyes* and Medusa assumed the form of a horse to mate with Poseidon god of the untamed sea and earthquakes. Wolves were predator animals in Greece and seen as savage and dangerous, counter to the civilisation and order of the city. The *aorai* shapeshifting into animal form emphasised how far they were from the human realm, and how bestial they had become.

Lamiai were said to live in the wildernesses of Libya,[54] representing the barbarian world. Marginalised people were frightening and naturally entered the realm of the demonic in the public imagination. Fear of such a fate, for these were once mortal women, was one way that young women were kept in line within the Greek city states. Blaming a demonic entity like the *aorai* for death in childbed was also a way of shifting the blame from the women in the family using their 'evil eye' or their envy to hurt the woman and baby. Having an outsider to blame, a non-human outsider, meant the family was free of responsibility for the deaths. This meant blame was apportioned to supernatural causes and other members of the family were not accused.

The fact that the *aoria* had once been a human woman gave credence to her powers over childbearing and marriage. Because she was one of the restless dead, she was not one of the family, or tribe, but a demonic outsider who could be banished and repulsed. That she was female lent weight to her message that marriage and motherhood were the only good path for women, and misery and exile the result of failure in these roles. The *aorai* also gave a reason for unexpected infant deaths and deaths in childbirth.

As all daemons brought madness, I wonder if they were a way to explain post-partum depression and post-partum psychosis, where the new mother falls ill. Daemonic possession could be a good way of explaining these illnesses, which can seem so baffling to outsiders, as new motherhood and successful pregnancy and birth were seen as a joyful culmination of a woman's life. Of course, if the infant was deemed unfit to live, the man of the house decided this. Infanticide or the more gentle exposure happened to disabled and excess female babies. Despair and depression in the mother would be an understandable response to this cruelty and was perhaps unrecoverable from.

Swallowing the daemon: The restless dead, apathy and failure

The *aorai*, the restless dead, live in a twilight zone, neither dead nor alive. I think of all the medicated women in mental institutions, lobotomised, on tranquillisers, cowed by domestic abuse, raped and trafficked. The deadening, the numbing, the going away while still living is familiar territory for some women. We robotise our days with drudgery and so much work, we do not have the time to think or feel. Tiny moments of peace are rare as women are expected to hold up the whole sky.[55] This was the life of many of our mothers and grandmothers.

Question: where are you numb? Where are you just 'phoning it in'? Where has the fight gone out of you, so that acquiescing is easier than fighting for your rights? Where have you collapsed? Where do you feel defeated? What substances and behaviours help you to numb and carry on?

Where is your rage? Has it turned inwards into depression? The doctor Gabor Mate[56] says that seventy percent of autoimmune diseases occur in women. He believes this is because they take on all the responsibility and swallow their rage, and their body eventually consumes itself and they get sick and waste away, like the curse of the restless dead.

The daemon is collapse, the vanquisher placing yourself front and centre in your life. I use the analogy of oxygen masks in aeroplanes. They always say put your own mask on first before you tend to your children's. The same applies to life.

Notes

1. Peace poppy from the Peace Pledge Union.
2. *Iliad* 23:65–74.
3. *Odyssey* 11:71–78.
4. *Odyssey* 11:42–43.
5. *Odyssey* book 11.
6. Plato *Republic* 614b2–621d2.
7. Fragment 33, Dubnoff, Julia (trans.) *Poems of Sappho* in https://www.uh.edu/~cldue/texts/sappho.html.
8. See note 6.
9. Pindar *Pythian Odes* 4:159–64.

10. Fragment 44. Zenobius, about A.D. 130, quotes this as a proverb. The ghost of Gello was said by the Lesbians to pursue and carry off young children https://sacred-texts.com/cla/usappho/sph45.htm.
11. Aeschylus *The Libation Bearers* 523–250.
12. Sophocles *Electra* 410, 417–25, 459–60.
13. Plutarch *De Defectu Oraculorum in Moralia*. Bernardakis, N. (trans.) (1891) Teubner. Leipzig.
14. Thucydides, *The Peloponnesian War*. Book 1:134, book 4:135.
15. Johnston 1999:47–51.
16. Plato *Republic* 364b5–365a3.
17. Plato *Phaedrus* 244d5–245a1.
18. Burkert 1983:213–30.
19. Johnston 1999:72.
20. Johnston 1999:77–8.
21. The *Oresteia* was a trilogy written by Aeschylus and performed at the City *Dionysia* in Athens in 458 BCE. The first play was *Agamemnon*, the second *Chorephoroi* or the *Libation Bearers*, and the final play was *Eumenides*. It won first prize.
22. Aeschylus *Eumenides* 94–103.
23. *The Libation Bearers Choephori* 924.
24. *Agamemnon* 1433, 1501.
25. *Eumenides* 95.
26. *Eumenides* 106–9.
27. Foley 2001:207.
28. *Choephori* 523–50.
29. *Eumenides* 126–7.
30. *Eumenides* 155.
31. Foley 2001:207–34.
32. Shilo 2018:551.
33. Apollo supports them both and indeed charges Orestes with matricide. Despite his reluctance, he agrees. Athena convinces the *Erinyes* to change their behaviour and support "the rule of law" of men.
34. Shilo 2018:568.
35. Foley 2001:201–34.
36. Johnston 1999:130.
37. Proclus *Alcibiades* 340.
38. Plutarch *Demetrius* 26.1 Plutarch, *Plutarch's Lives*, with an English Translation by Bernadotte Perrin. (Cambridge, MA: Harvard University Press. London: William Heinemann Ltd. 1920). 9.

39. *Odyssey* 15:234.
40. *Odyssey* 2:130–6.
41. Johnston 1999:141 translated this as walking through air suggesting their punishments are invisible like miasmas. Liddel and Scott 1944:303 give walking through darkness which I feel better describes their behaviour. The word may be *eiaropotis:* blood drinking, Johnston op.cit. which describes their behaviour also.
42. Aeschylus *Eumenides* 245.
43. Aeschylus *Agamemnon* 462.
44. Aeschylus *Eumenides* 416:1034.
45. Johnston 1999:144.
46. Plato *Laws* 865d6–e6.
47. *Cyrus* 8.7:18–19.
48. Johnston 1999:137.
49. Johnston 1999:164.
50. *Cyranides* 2.40:35–38. Cyranides was a collection of Greek Magical texts, which was compiled in the Roman Imperial period c. 4th C CE but includes material from earlier periods.
51. Johnston 1999:167.
52. *Homeric Hymn to Demeter*.
53. Those myths which give an explanation for certain rites or beliefs or customs, from the Greek *aition* meaning cause or reason.
54. Libya is endlessly connected to barbarian and uncontrollable women. Libya of course was known as the home of the Amazons, see chapter 3.
55. There is a Chinese saying that 'Women hold up half the sky'. Modern women are often expected or forced to hold up the entire sky.
56. https://drgabormate.com/mind-body-health/ 80% of autoimmune diseases occur in women. In my opinion this is a slow wasting away like the undead or the *aorai*.

CHAPTER FIVE

The Furies

> The august Erinyes have great power among the gods
> and those below the earth,
> and it is clear how completely they achieve their will among men,
> giving songs of celebration to some,
> but to others, in turn,
> a life blinded by tears.[1]

Aeschylus' trilogy *The Oresteia* (458 BCE) is crucial in understanding the mindset of the Greeks and illustrates the social and political beliefs of the time. The myth was well known to the audience, believed to be males only. Aeschylus uses the story to show the battle, which presumably was ongoing, between chthonic and Olympian forces for the hearts and minds of the people. The struggle for domination reflected Greece's endless battles with Barbarians and the conflict between mothers' rights and the rights of women, and the fathers' rights of the patriarchy. The battle between Apollo and the *Erinyes* is played out in the final play of the trilogy, *The Eumenides*. The defeat and subordination of women is legitimised and provides the template for patriarchy going forward.

In the trilogy, we see the consequences for women if they transgress. Klytemnestra kills her husband, seizes power and takes a lover of her choosing. Her son Orestes, ordered by Olympian Apollo, kills his mother. His mother's *Erinyes* then pursue him driving him to insanity. Klytemnestra is portrayed as representative of the Archaic, vendetta-based justice, while Orestes and Apollo represent the 'civilised' future of the city state, the *polis*.

The murder of Klytemnestra unleashes the *Erinyes*, who we meet at the beginning of the play. Their appearance terrorises Orestes and he runs away. Their appearance is 'the deepest fantasies of masculine terrors'.[2] They drip and ooze from every orifice, their thoughts drop poison, and they exemplify a negative virginity and barrenness. They are female but monstrous, sterile, hideous, hunters of men. They sing a binding song to draw Orestes into Hades, to suck his blood and keep him there, insane and paralysed.

So, who were the *Erinyes*? On two linear B tablets found in Knossos, the name *Erinu*, an early form of the *Erinys*, is found alongside the early forms of the names Zeus, Athena, and Poseidon. *Erinu* then, had equal status with these other gods in Minoan times. In one tablet she is given an offering of oil as they are. Kretan *Erinu* is a *thea* (goddess) and she is described as such in Homer. The tragic playwright Aeschylus made them three in number giving them the plural *theai*.[3]

Besides the mention in the Linear B tablets, the etymology of the name is unclear. Demonic creatures usually have names which indicate their nature, for example, Mormo the fearsome one, and Empousa 'she who impedes'. The name *Erinnys*, which is the more ancient one, was perhaps derived by the Greeks from the *erinô* or *ereunaô*, meaning "I hunt" or "persecute", or from the Arcadian word *erinuô*, "I am angry". From this we can deduce that the *Erinyes* were either the angry goddesses, or the goddesses who hunt or search after the criminal, or both.[4]

In the sense of *curse* or *curses*, the word *Erinyes* is often used in the Homeric poems.[5] According to Homer the Erinyes live in Erebos (the Underworld), until they are summoned by a curse brought upon a murderer or an oath-breaker and they leave Hades to stalk their victim.[6] The crimes which they punish are disobedience towards parents, violation of the respect due to old age, perjury, murder, violation of the law of hospitality, and improper conduct towards suppliants who people are duty bound to protect.[7] The curse causes madness in the wrongdoer, destroys his family, and denies him children.[8]

The lineage of the *Erinyes* is confused. In one account she/they have a parthenogenic birth from the primeval goddess, Nyx (Night).[9] Nyx is one of the first divinities in Hesiod's *Theogony*. She is older than and stands apart from the cycle of violent patrilineal succession of the Olympians.

> O mother Night, hear me, mother who gave birth to me as a retribution for the blind and the seeing.[10]

Nyx, or Night was the primeval goddess of creation. Homer makes her an important divinity[11] who even Zeus respected and could not offend. According to Hesiod,[12] Nyx and her brother Erebus (darkness) were born from Chaos, the primaeval void. Erebus mated with Nyx, the first sexual union, to produce Aether (brightness) and Hemera (day). Nyx lived in Tartarus the deepest, darkest part of the Underworld from which she emerged every evening to bring night, as her daughter Hemera was retreating. She was the mother of dark forces such as Nemesis (retribution), Eris (strife), the Moirae (the fates), and Thanatos (death). The principle of retribution was clearly female.

Myth fragments dealing with the *Erinyes* are found among the earliest extant records of ancient Greek culture. The *Erinyes* are perpetual virgins, divine paradigms of girls who died before they could marry and bear children. 'To accompany the *Erinyes*' means to die unwed and 'wander' (*amphipoleuein*) between the worlds. That is, to become one of the restless dead or *amphipolei* who were invoked in curse tablets along with Hekate.[13] Why virgins? Because they support the mother line, mothers and unwed daughters, or maidens whose loyalty is to the mother and her family line.

Another version tells that the *Erinyes* were born when their mother Ge was being tortured by her husband and forced to swallow her babies. Ge was saved by her son, Zeus, who castrated him, and drops of the blood grew into the *Erinyes*. In this version, the *Erinyes* are born through violence, the worst violence in patriarchy, castration of the father by the son.[14]

Phallic power was at the root of the new Olympians, who raped their own mothers, daughters and sisters. Engendering children from these rapes destroys the family bond, as the child from rape is both loved and loathed by the mother and often the mother is banished from her family as though it was her fault. This is Patriarchy 101: blame the woman for men's violence and aberrant sexual appetites, humiliate her by incest-rape, and then banish her so she has no option but to stay with the rapist or kill herself from shame/loneliness/starvation.

Virgins on the other hand escape rape. They cannot be controlled in that way, and they have the freedom of non-attachment to wander between the worlds, causing trouble, attacking the patriarchal family, and denying women children. They are daughters who will not leave home to marry and have children.

Other kinds of rebellious women were *maenads* (wild, free women).[15] *Maenads* or *bacchantes* were women who worshipped Dionysus. They abandoned their families and went feral, dancing, fornicating and shrieking in the mountains. They destroy families as the *Erinyes* do by breaking the bond between mother and child. The *maenads* of Dionysus kill their children, destroying the reason women get married. They reject the patriarchal system that restricts women to brood mares. When their husbands refuse to allow them to worship Dionysus, afraid they are sexually active with other men (which of course they are) they go 'crazy wild'. Dionysus is a challenge to the status quo and to submissive women. The women become maddened or enter trance and head for the hills. They are patriarchy's worst nightmare.

Euripides'[16] Antigone calls herself a '*bacchante* of the dead' as she sings a dirge consecrated to the *Erinyes*. Similarly, when Hecuba and the other women kill Polymestor's children in revenge, they are described as '*bacchantes* from Hades'.[17] *Bacchantes* then are women who lose their minds or find their power, depending on your viewpoint. Women who contact female rage and celebrate it and act on it.

The *Erinyes* are different from the *Maenads* in that they are not wives escaping from the prison of their marriages. They seek revenge on men who abuse and murder blood kin. They do not run wild with their punishments. They are more cold-blooded and particular with their revenge which often occurs within the household. Klytemnestra called on the *Erinyes* to stand by while she murders her husband Agamemnon.[18] Murder between spouses concerns them less as these are not blood relatives. Klytemnestra kills her husband at their home in his bath, which is symbolic in itself: a man is murdered where he should feel safest.[19] She kills the man who sacrificed his daughter Iphigenia to the goddess Artemis, so that the fleet could sail to Troy. Orestes kills his mother in revenge.

The *Erinyes* pursue him for vengeance. They frighten and madden their victims despite their threat to 'suck the blood' of Orestes while he is still alive. The inflicting of madness is their favourite weapon.[20] They sing (see the Sirens for song) a binding song, and a curse spoken in rhyme has awesome power.[21] The *Erinyes* pursue matricides, as they are of the mother line. Although they are not the dead, they live with the dead in Hades or Erebus; they wear black clothes, the colour of death, and avenge the residents of Hades.

Tragedy presents the worst of human experience, and in the presentation of the *Erinyes* they appear disgusting, snaky haired, blood-lapping fiends, hideous women who take pleasure in family discord. Tragedy strongly influenced subsequent art and literature; its imagery of the *Erinyes* has persisted, although in the pot below they look more rebellious than hideous.

Figure 5.1. Pot Erinyes and Apollo, Red figure Bell Krater Paestan c. 360 BCE.

In Classical Greek tragedy, the *Erinyes* are the main avengers of the dead, probably because of their clear lineage, their connection to Homer, and their link to familial crime.[22] In Homer, they live in the Underworld, and in Tragedy they chase or drag their prey to the Underworld.[23] They are 'dwelling in its unlit gloom',[24] 'black-robed' 'children of the Night', and *'bacchantes* of Hades'.[25] Violent death calls them and 'cries forth an *Erinyes'*.[26] They are like other gods, Persephone and Hades, who are concerned with defending the rights of the dead and avenging their murder.[27] *Erinys* or the *Erinyes* punish Meleager for killing his uncle in Homer[28] which led people to suggest they were angry dead spirits.

Implacability is their traditional character. They are deaf to pleas of mercy, and they never give up; relentlessness is an essential part of their revenge.[29] For example, in his cautionary tale to Achilles, Phoenix says that the *Erinys* invoked by Meleager's mother on behalf of her slain brother has 'an implacable heart'.[30] The adjective *ameilichon* indicates that they are impervious to attempts to propitiate (*meilissein*) them. But they do not only answer for the dead; the gods, who never die, invoke them against each other.[31] They act when a crime or insult occurs within the family, by blood or marriage. They witness oaths,[32] they become guardian of young girls stolen by Harpies,[33] and they avenge an insulted beggar.[34] There is another side to the *Erinyes*, which is closer to the older, pre-tragedy version of their role.

> The *Erinyes*, that under earth take vengeance on men, whosoever hath sworn a false oath.[35]

In the Iliad, Agamemnon invokes them in the oath he swears against Priam, King of the Trojans and again when he swears an oath to Achilles, while Alcaeus calls on the *Erinyes* to punish Pittacus for breaking an oath. They become abstract symbols of justice.

The Derveni Papyrus[36] copied around 360 BCE, but dated to c. 425 BCE, was discovered partially burnt in the funeral pyre of the owner outside the Macedonian city of Lete. It contains intriguing information on the cult of the *Erinyes* and the Orphic and Bacchic Mysteries. The Bacchic Mysteries are believed to have arisen in the 6th C BCE.[37] They were concerned with the punishment after death which was meted out by the *Erinyes*. The Mysteries were secret, nocturnal, voluntary, and open to all who could pay the fee. They included a preliminary purification and a promise of a peaceful experience after death. It is believed the Mysteries were of Egyptian origin: the dismemberment of Dionysus was reminiscent of that of Osiris, the rite of Demeter resembled that of Isis, and the punishment in Hades was like those recounted in Egyptian funeral rites.

Initiands were promised escape from reincarnation, 'the cycle of grief'.[38] They dressed as nymphs, satyrs and maenads and carried daggers and snakes and danced ecstatically to the beat of drums. The initial sacrifice in these Mysteries was to the *Erinyes*, to stop them interfering with the rites. If they were not placated, they would disrupt the ceremony. The *Erinyes* also reminded initiands of the punishments that awaited those who did not sacrifice to them. The Hellenistic writer Axiochus declared that after judgement, criminals were herded by the *Erinyes* into Erebus, where they were slavered over by wild beasts and continually burned by Poinai's torches. They suffered unrelenting, eternal punishment.[39]

Wineless libations to the *Erinyes* were offered, particularly milk, water and honey. Klytemnestra reminds the *Erinyes* of the burnt sacrifices and wineless offerings she made to them at night.[40] In Athens they poured wineless libations over sacrificial honey cakes burning on the altar.[41]

Those who were hated by their parents offered these libations and swore oaths to avoid punishment. The *Erinyes* policed oath breakers, as servants or guardians of justice. Their function was to maintain cosmic justice and order, and oversee and correct those behaviours which harm the order of the cosmos.

The *Erinyes* were accustomed to being isolated from all forms of social intercourse. They are shunned by the gods, as they themselves admit in their binding song.[42] Athena does not recognize them when she first encounters them,[43] emphasizing the fact that they do not keep company with the other immortals. This exclusion is even more forcefully expressed by Apollo, who makes their isolation universal by expanding the revulsion he claims the gods feel for the *Erinyes*, to both humans and animals.[44]

> ... old women and ancient children, with whom none of the gods, nor any human nor beast, ever mingles (*meignutai*).[45]

84   MONSTROUS WOMEN

Figure 5.2. Erinyes, Krater, Magna Graeca. 4th C BCE.

In Homer there is one *Erinys*:[46]

> ... and Erinys, the mist walking,
> She of the heart without pity,
> Heard her out of the dark places [Hades].

In *Eumenides* there are three and they explain their powers:

> We are skilled in plotting, powerful in execution, and we remember evil deeds; we are revered and hard for mortals to appease, pursuing our allotted office, which is without rights, without honour,

separated from the gods in sunless light—our office that makes the path rough for seeing and dim-sighted alike.[47]

What mortal, then, does not stand in awe and dread of this, when he hears from me the law ordained by Fate, given by the gods for perfect fulfilment? My ancient privilege still remains, I do not meet with dishonour, although I have my place under the earth and in sunless darkness.[48]

Their role is protection within the home and its inhabitants:

For I have chosen the overthrow of houses, whenever violence raised in the home seizes someone near and dear.[49]

They are outcasts, women without men or children who live in the darkness and who the other gods avoid:

Zeus has considered us a blood-dripping, hateful band, unworthy of his council.[50]

And they outline their provenance:

This office was ordained for us at birth; but the immortal gods must hold back their hands from us, nor does any of them share a feast in common with us, and I have neither lot nor portion of pure white ceremonial robes.[51]

The gods will not break bread with them, nor do they expect their acolytes to wear the customary white robes for when they sacrifice to the gods. They are outcasts.

They were fated and born into the role. There are similarities in their myths between the *Erinyes* and Demeter Erinys.[52] Demeter loses her daughter to kidnapping. One aspect of the story is the strong bond between mother and daughter. For Demeter, the blood tie between her and Persephone is stronger than any marriage she might make. In patriarchy daughters leave their mothers and sometimes never see them again; certainly, they are expected to be loyal to their husband's family over their biological one. The cruelty of patriarchy tears daughters from this most powerful bond and leaves them often defenceless in the new family, where she is expected to reproduce and be a dutiful daughter. She loses support and is thrust among strangers.

Like Demeter withering the earth, the *Erinyes* threaten to poison the earth, kill the plants and make humans and animals sterile if they are not appeased.[53] Like Demeter they can also ensure there is fertility in the land and can cause barrenness. There was a plague in Sparta of infant deaths and sterility, which was reversed by offering the *Erinyes* proper cult, the lack of which was said to be the reason for the disaster.[54] Women's fertility affected the whole *polis*, and communal rituals were needed to placate the angry gods.

In the *Odyssey*, Penelope recounts the sad tale of the Pandareid sisters[55] who died before marrying and were doomed the wander for eternity with the *Erinyes*. The *Erinyes* can capture a maiden as she is leaving her biological family. Apollo insults their virginity when he claims it is involuntary (like today's single cat lady threats perhaps). In other words, they are too ugly to fuck. But perhaps they are girls who, like Artemis, choose not to marry. The Erinyes' allegiance to the mother line precludes marriage. The *Erinyes* refuse motherhood because they reject men: they do not torture women as far as we know. The fact that there were women who, exemplified by the *Erinyes*, would rather have not married and stayed with their mothers, suggests this was an issue at the time.

At the end of Aeschylus' play the *Erinyes* are persuaded to become supporters of marriage and of the primacy of the husband over the mother. Henceforth crimes of murder will be decided by an all-male jury. It could be no other way. The whole citizen male population of Athens came to these plays; they could hardly suggest otherwise. Certainly in the play women lose power as mothers; they become 'the empty vessels' in reproduction, and it is determined that killing your husband trumps matricide and filicide and all-male juries should decide these matters henceforth. The sacred mother is dead, in other words. The only way to contain rebellious, libidinous, and violent women was through patriarchal marriage which reduced her to an incubator with no personal agency. It may be no coincidence that the play begins at Delphi which is given to Apollo by Zeus after he kills the Pytho, the female dragon guarding the oracle, and claims it as his own.

The *Erinyes* were placated by offering them cult and first fruits on the birth of babies and they were told how important they were for the future of the *polis*, since children and wives are absolutely necessary for it to thrive. Blood ties and the family (*oikos*) become less important than the wellbeing of the community (*polis*). The *Thesmophoria*, a festival

THE FURIES   87

Figure 5.3. Erinye at Delphi. Red figure Bell Krater. 330 BCE Paestan.

which celebrated motherhood in Athens and was Demeter's principal cult, was funded by the husbands, and only married women could attend. It was celebrated in the centre of the city, and the lawcourts were closed during the festival. Men knew how important women's fertility was:

> If the sun exceeds its boundaries, the *Erinyes*, helpers of Justice, will seek him out.[56]

The Derveni Papyrus, alluded to earlier, sees them as 'guardians of the natural order'. Their role is to ensure that nothing is out of line with justice. The *Erinyes* as 'helpers of Justice' align with the *Erinyes*' defence of the family, where they policed infractions, and punished individuals who exceeded or broke the boundaries or limits assigned to them.[57] They prevented change from going too far (until they didn't). The *Erinyes* are defenders of traditional *nomoi* (laws/customs), revering the gods, parents and strangers, and upholding justice.[58]

In the *Odyssey*[59] when Telemachus is confronted by the suitors who wish to marry his mother Penelope, he refuses their demands even though he believes his father Odysseus is dead. He says allowing the marriage would be effectively banishing his mother from the house, and she would invoke the *Erinyes* in retaliation for his disrespect of her.

Iris warns Poseidon not to speak harshly to Zeus, because the *Erinyes* defend the rights of elders in arguments.[60] Their reach goes beyond the generations.[61] Laius' curse against his children is carried out by an *Erinys* as an instrument of Moira (fate or destiny). Hesiod[62] and Homer recognise them as the custodians of oaths. Agamemnon[63] acknowledges his imprudent decision to take Briseis, the woman originally allotted to Achilles as his war prize, for himself. He calls it an outburst of *atē* (the personification of moral blindness and error). This function of the *Erinyes* fits, as oaths are sacrosanct and are sworn in part to strengthen ties between members of the same clan or to establish a sacrosanct relationship outside one's kin.[64]

Vendetta, traditionally a male sphere, is encouraged by women lamenting loudly and at length at funerals, encouraging their menfolk on, as Electra urging her brother Orestes to kill their mother Klytemnestra. Lamentation performed by family members and professional women mourners was acted out in public settings calling for justice for the dead and reminding family members of the past, present, and future of the family. They argue that revenge protects the family line: 'the dirge is always strongest where the law of vendetta flourishes, as in Sicily'.[65] Calls for vendetta is a social throwing down the gauntlet, and funerals often give mourners the opportunity to incite rebellion against enemies or an oppressive power.

The *Semnai Theai* were a collection of Attic goddesses. They expressed the positive aspect of the *Erinyes*,[66] because all Greek gods have a positive and negative expression. For example, Hekate/Artemis protects women in childbirth but can also cause their death. In addition, like with Shakespeare's 'Scottish Play', the names of some gods, for example Persephone and the *Erinyes*, were sometimes not mentioned by name. Persephone was called *Kore* or just goddess (*thea*). Hades had a positive aspect as Pluton, the god of wealth. Aeschylus brings in the *Semnai Theai*, Euripides the Eumenides. For Aeschylus, the *Semnai Theai* would have had similar concerns as the *Erinyes*: the swearing and upholding of oaths, a concern for reproduction and a shared interest in the world of the dead, but they were neither angry nor malevolent.

Although there is little archaeological evidence for a cult of the *Erinyes*, it may be argued that they would have been worshipped under their positive attributes, *Semnai Theai* or Eumenides, in the same way Hades was worshipped as Pluton.[67] In crisis, however, the name of their dark side would be evoked to ward off disaster and to propitiate them, which is how Homer and Pausanias described their worship. Medea and Jason make offerings to them after Medea commits the crime of murdering her brother, a blood tie which is precisely their business. It can be argued, however, that the *Erinyes* were not placated as Medea's family was destroyed, in a very *Eriny*-like manner. Medea kills their sons in revenge for Jason's betrayal and then she kills his wife to be. Because she is the granddaughter of Helios, and hence partly divine, she escapes with her life and Jason is left broken and alone, a terrible punishment.

At Athens there were statues of only two Eumenides/*Erinyes*.[68] The sacrifices which were offered to them consisted of black sheep and *nephalia*, a drink of honey mixed with water.[69] White turtledoves and the narcissus were sacred to them.[70] They had a sanctuary and a grotto near the Athenian Areopagus[71] and a festival *Eumenideia* was celebrated there in their honour. Another sanctuary, with a grove which no one was allowed to enter, existed at Colonus.[72] Under the name of *Maniai* (frenzy) they were worshipped at Megalopolis.[73] They were also worshipped on the Asopus and at Ceryneia.[74]

The *Erinyes* are invoked in curse tablets or later spells of magical papyri to bring destruction on enemies and transgressors. Klytemnestra invokes them in nightly libations to stop her son avenging her husband's murder, and after her death invokes them to pursue and destroy him.[75]

The *Erinyes* had two main spheres of influence: revenge of blood kin and aiding girls' transition to motherhood. Their role in punishing the dead is linked to both of these. Murdered family members may not have anyone to avenge their deaths and maidens may be tempted or taken by ghostly maidens, *aoroi*, that died before they could marry and have children.

The goddesses were companions of Hades and Persephone in the Underworld where they oversaw the torture of criminals consigned to the Dungeons of the Damned. The *Erinyes* were similar to if not the same as the *Poinai/Poenae* (retaliations) and *Arae/Arai* (curses), both of which describe roles the *Erinyes* play.

> Retaliation, curses, extractors of justice and madness all describe their sphere and expression. They punish. Now you will hear this hymn, a spell to bind you.[76]

They dance and sing their curse. Dance, as we discovered in chapter three, is integral to Greek culture: war dances, healing dances, celebratory dances, and in this case cursing dances.

> Let us also join the dance, since we are resolved to display our hated song and to declare our allotted office, how our party directs the affairs of men … We claim to be just and upright. No wrath from us will come stealthily to the one who holds out clean hands, and he will go through life unharmed … but whoever sins, as this man has, and hides his blood-stained hands, as avengers of bloodshed we appear against him to the end, presenting ourselves as upright witnesses for the dead.[77]
>
> For this is the office that relentless Fate spun for us to hold securely. When rash murders of kin come upon mortals, we pursue them until they go under the earth; and after death, they have no great freedom.[78]

The Erinyes then represent the dark feminine, the dangerous upholder of the matriarchal line, women who do not fulfil their biological function and become mothers. The period in which the play was written was a time of endless wars, and the death of many young men. Women were left without husbands and partners, and railed against their fate and could not be silenced. Perhaps these plays were warnings to the women not to take revenge on the warmongers and to accept their fate without protest, and perhaps they did not, for if their whole lives they had been told the highest duty of an Athenian woman was to have children, and through no fault of their own they could not marry, they may have become bitter and vengeful. The *Eumenides* is saying the hatred and retribution, and non-feminine behaviour, of the *Erinyes*, can be transformed into the gentle, biddable, non-threatening *Semnai Theai* and *Eumenides*. As a later Christian source said, "It is better to marry than burn".

Meditation on the Erinyes

How does revenge sit with you? Do you hex? How do you defend yourself, your autonomy, your family? What is your dark shadow side, where does she hide? Do you lie or promise things you know you won't do? Do others do this to you? How do you respond?

"The witch who cannot hex cannot heal," writes Zsuzsanna Budapest.

In the past, witches in San Francisco hexed rapists so they might be caught and punished. Their success rate was impressive. How do you take revenge? If you don't, why not?

Where do you sweeten your rage, or do you swallow it down and lose your power?

Notes

1. Aeschylus *Eumenides* 948–55.
2. Zeitlin 1978:159.
3. Johnston 1999:250.
4. Aeschylus *Eumenides* 499. Pindar *Olympian* ii. 45, Johnston 1999:25.
5. *Iliad* ix. 454, xxi. 412, *Odyssey* xi. 280, and Aeschylus *Choephori/ The Libation Bearers* 406.
6. *Iliad* ix 571, *Odyssey* xv. 234.
7. Hom. *Il.* ix. 454, xv. 204, xix. 259, *Od.* ii. 136, xvii. 475.
8. Herod. iv. 149; Aeschyl. *Eum*. 835.
9. Aeschylus *Eumenides* 321–27.
10. Aeschylus *Eumenides* 321.
11. *Iliad* 14:256–61.
12. *Theogony* 123–5.
13. Johnston 1992:30.
14. Epimenides called them the daughters of Kronos and Euonyme, and sisters of the Moerae. Tzetz. *ad Lycophronem*. 406.
15. Euripides *Orestes* 337–8.
16. *Phaedra* 1489–1503, Johnstone 1999:254.
17. Euripides *Hecuba* 1076.
18. Aeschylus *Agamemnon* 1433.
19. This has a chilling resonance, as the majority of women who are murdered in the UK are killed at home or by a partner or ex-partner.
20. Aeschylus *Eumenides* 264–5, 307–88.
21. Johnston 1999:145.

22. Johnston 1999:143.
23. Aeschylus *Eumenides* 245, Euripides *Orestes* 255–56.
24. Aeschylus *Eumenides* 395; cf. 417.
25. Aeschylus *Th.* 699–700; cf. 977, 988 and A.462. Aeschylus *Eumenides* 416, 1034.
26. Aeschylus *Libation Bearers* 400–404.
27. Johnston 1999:144.
28. *Iliad* 9:566–72.
29. Rynearson 2013.
30. *Iliad* 9:572.
31. Johnston 1999:252.
32. *Iliad* 3:276–80.
33. *Odyssey* 20:81–82.
34. *Odyssey* 17:475.
35. *Iliad* 19:259–260, 3:278–279.
36. Janko, Richard in Most, Glenn. (ed.) *Studies on the Derveni Papyrus. Vol. 2.* (Oxford: Oxford University Press, 2022).
37. Janko 2022:157–181.
38. From the gold tablets from Thurii 5th C BCE, in Janko 2022:161.
39. Janko 2022:167.
40. Aeschylus *Eumenides* 107.
41. Janko 2022:171.
42. *Eumenides* 349–50, 360–65, 385–86.
43. *Eumenides* 406–12.
44. Rynearson 2013:68–70.
45. Sommerstein 1989:95, on *meignutai*: "holds any intercourse" whether social (cf. 55–6) or sexual. Apollo implies that the *Erinyes'* appearance and behaviour are so hideous that no male would come near them.
46. *Iliad* 9:571–2.
47. *Eumenides* 381–5.
48. *Eumenides* 389–395.
49. *Eumenides* 354.
50. *Eumenides* 364–365.
51. *Eumenides* 347–350.
52. Johnston 1999:258–265.
53. Aeschylus *Eumenides* 479, 782–78, 812–817, 829–36, 895, 903–15, 938–48, 956–60.
54. Herodotus *Histories* 4:149.2.
55. *Odyssey* 20:61–78.

56. Heraclitus, translated by Patrick, G.T.W. (1889): 91 in Heraclitus. (1989). *The Fragments of Heraclitus of Ephesus on Nature*, Patrick, G.T.W. (ed. and trans). Baltimore: N. Murray. See also: Smitherman, Valerie (2013) *Hearing the Erinyes Voices: Thoughts of the Binding Song. Eumenides 307–96.*
57. Johnston 1999:266.
58. *Eumenides* 269–72, 538–49.
59. *Odyssey* 2:130–37.
60. *Iliad* 15:200–204.
61. Pindar *Second Olympian* ll. 35–42.
62. Hesiod *Works and Days* 802–804.
63. *Iliad* 19.259–263.
64. *Xenia* is this close, bound relationship between people, for example in battle if they come across each other on opposing sides, they do not fight each other. The oath of *Xenia* is bound by the gods and breaking it is punished by them in the form of the *Erinyes*.
65. Foley 2001:34.
66. Johnston 1999:268.
67. Johnston 1999:271.
68. Schol. *ad Oed. Col.* 42.
69. Paus. ii; Aesch. *Eum.* 107.
70. Aelian, *H. A.* x. 33; Eustath. *ad Hom.* p. 87.
71. Pausanias 1. 28.
72. Sophocles *Oedepus at Colonus* 37.
73. Pausanius viii. 34.
74. Pausanius ii. 11. vii. 25. 4.
75. Aeschylus *Eumenides* 106–10.
76. Achchylus *Eumenides* 305.
77. Aeschylus *Eumenides* 310–320 see also Smitherman 2013 op. cit. for a discussion of the dancing, singing *Erinyes*.
78. Aeschylus *Eumenides* 334–336.

CHAPTER SIX

Hekate

> Hecate whom Zeus the son of Kronos honoured above all. He gave her splendid gifts, a share of the earth and the bountiful sea. She received honour also in starry heaven and is venerated exceedingly by the eternal gods.[1]

Contrary to her later appearance, early Hekate was originally seen as a great goddess with many areas of influence. The above quotation relates how Zeus honoured her with a share of the earth and the sea. In this chapter we will discover the early roots of Hekate and her dominions and see how she changed into something darker, and then lighter again.

Hekate does not appear in Homer. The first written account of the goddess is found in Hesiod's *Theogony* where she is said to be the daughter of Asteria and Perses.[2]

> Whenever a human offers rich sacrifices and prays for assistance, they supplicate Hekate. If she receives their petitions favourably, good fortune and honour comes to them.[3]

Her ability to give power, good fortune and wealth (*dunamis*) is due to her favoured status. She was a Titan, but Zeus allowed her to keep her spheres of influence despite the Titans' defeat in the war against the Olympians.[4] Hekate then is from the old order. She predates patriarchal Zeus and his gods and goddesses.

Hekate supports mortals in many ways. "August Kings in their deliberations", here she gives victory in battle to soldiers and eternal glory, she helps athletes in competitions, and supports those in the assembly who wish for honours.[5] Thus she is a benevolent goddess, should she wish to be.[6]

> If they call on Hekate, she hears them.[7]

Hekate works with other gods; for her favoured ones, she is used as an intermediary or catalyst to potentise supplications to the gods.

> Pray to Hekate and the loud crashing Earth-Shaker (Poseidon) for a good catch, though she may take it away also.[8]

The gods can be capricious, and they help and hinder depending on how they feel. The fact that Hekate is invoked with other Olympian gods does suggest that the newcomers have usurped her sphere of influence, and Zeus promotes her to placate the older goddess. Zeus courts Hekate's favour, perhaps because she did not fight for either side in the battle of the Titans[9] and was rewarded for her loyalty.[10] The only logical conclusion is that Hekate was a powerful goddess among the Titans, and Zeus wished to have her on his side. Because Hekate, like Zeus, could be negative and destructive as well as helpful. Hekate appears in the *Homeric Hymn to Demeter*:[11]

> But not one of the immortals heard her voice [Persephone's] ...
> only the tender-hearted daughter of Persaeus heard from a cave,
> Hekate with the gleaming veil.[12]

It is possible that Hekate and her cave represented the Underworld[13] whence Persephone was headed. I think of Hekate as an elder goddess, an unmarried goddess, and a non-Olympian who may have chosen to live in a cave as a solitary shamanic goddess.

Ten days[14] after Persephone's abduction, Hekate goes to Demeter and tells her what she heard, 'Hekate met with her, a torch in her hand'.[15]

The torches that Hekate is always seen with may represent the light needed to traverse the Underworld. She tells Demeter that she 'will tell quickly and honestly'[16] what she heard, which does show her as benevolent and helpful.[17]

Hekate's role as *kurotrophos* explains why in ritual a preliminary sacrifice was always made to her. Hekate was an intermediary between gods and men, both when supplicating and sacrificing to them and as a guide in times of transition.[18] For example, leading Demeter to Persephone and then embracing Persephone when she later ascends from the Underworld. Hekate is then referred to as, 'Queen Hekate *propolos* (showing the way) and *opaon* (companion) of Persephone'.[19] This suggests that the older goddess shows the younger the way, and shows her the ways of the Underworld.

Hekate is familiar with the route to the Underworld, and it is a place that as an ancient goddess she knows and understands. This contrasts with the Olympians who avoid death and the Underworld, and who cannot abide ugliness or sickness. This difference between the ancient gods and the Olympians is telling in itself. The ancient goddess understands that death and life, darkness and light, birth and death are part of the mystery of life, all are part of the whole, unlike patriarchal religion which banishes the darkness and calls it evil. We know that which is repressed persists, consciously or unconsciously. The unconscious is projected on to others, and in patriarchy, on to women, particularly aberrant women.

Retrieving and accompanying Persephone in her journey between the Underworld and the human world is something Hekate will always do. Hekate escorts her across a very important boundary, just as she was later to escort souls back and forth across that liminal space. Fear of the restless dead (see chapter Four: The Restless Dead) grew during the Classical era, perhaps as patriarchal religion became established. Goddesses who traversed these liminal spaces were especially welcomed. Olympian Hermes was a psychopomp (he could travel between the worlds) and a protector, but he never dealt with ghosts.[20]

Hekate's birthplace is thought to be in Asia Minor, probably Caria in modern day Turkey. Her temple precinct in Lagina (in Caria) was the largest of all the temples there. Friezes show Hekate may have been a Carian Cybele, goddess of the city, a mother goddess and

Figure 6.1. Hekate and Persephone. Athenian red figure Krater, 5th C BCE.

all-round benefactress. An altar dated late 6th C BCE in Miletus is inscribed to Hekate. It was found in the *prytaneum* (a public building in Greek cities) showing she was part of the official cult and not a marginal figure who associated only with ghosts.

Later, by at least the fifth century, Hekate had a temple at the city gates of Miletus, fifty miles north of Lagina (SW Turkey). At the same time in Miletus there was a guild of musicians (*molpoi*) who processed with two objects called *gulloi*. These may have been cubes of stone, or more likely woven baskets containing sacred objects (*kaneon*). One was crowned and anointed with unmixed wine and placed next to the statue of Hekate at the city gates. The first paeon sung in this ceremony was in honour of Hekate who followed the procession.[21]

There was an annual ceremony or procession of the key (*kleidos agoge*) in Hekate's name in Lagina. It is not clear what the key represents: it may be the key was to the gates of the city. In Classical Athens, High Priestesses' funerary steles (grave markers) show them holding a large key, which presumably was the key to the temple where they officiated. When new gates were built for the city of Lagina a statue of Hekate was built behind or within the city gates. By placing her statue there, the inhabitants signalled that Hekate could protect them from harm by closing and guarding the gates. A ceremony in an Archaic calendar of sacrifices mentions a rite where she was crowned.[22]

Hekate's statues were common at city gates. In Athens she had a shrine on the west road leading out of the city just outside the Sacred Gate. Hecate *Epipyrgidia* stood at the entrance of the Athenian Acropolis. This underlines her protective function for cities. Her statue is also found in front of houses of kings, which may originate from her worship in Caria, and this explains her association with Enodia, a Thessalian goddess.[23]

Guardians of thresholds, both personal and for the community, were there to ward off unhappy souls and other daemons from these liminal spaces. Hekate could also chose not to avert daemons and let them in to punish the inhabitants.[24] In the late Archaic period, the *polis* was divided into specific zones. Cemeteries were enclosed by walls and separated from living spaces; communal spaces and sanctuaries were marked by walls or boundary stones, and commercial spaces were split from non-commercial spaces. *Hekataia* were placed by doorways and entrances to cities and sanctuaries. She guarded these areas as well as defining them. A divinity at the entrance announced the special status of the space, like the sanctity of the *oikos* or the sacred space of a temple:[25]

Torch-bearing Hekate holy daughter of great-bosomed Nyx (Night).[26]

As the daughter of Nyx, Hekate's connection with the Underworld is understood. Nyx is a primordial goddess, so her daughter Hekate is one of the very first gods. Later authors Theocritus and Apollonius of Rhodes make Hekate the daughter of Zeus and Demeter. Hekate's uncertain genealogy compounds the argument that she was from an ancient lineage and making her the daughter of Zeus and Demeter was an attempt to shoehorn her into the Olympic pantheon, perhaps to give it respectability or to placate the ancient goddess.

100 MONSTROUS WOMEN

Figure 6.2. Hekate red figure vase c. 470 BCE.

The fifth century tragedian Euripides makes Enodia, who is sometimes associated with or becomes Hekate, the daughter of Demeter.[27] Enodia is an adjective used to describe Hekate as well as other goddesses such as Artemis, Selene, and Persephone (as goddess of the crossroads, liminality and journeys). Enodia was worshipped in Thessaly; little is known of their religion, but Thessaly was a known hotspot for witches, especially those who worked with medicinal herbs (*pharmaka*). Enodia is seen in references to magic, madness, the dead, and ghosts, all of which are areas of influence of Hekate and Persephone.

Enodia also means *en* (in, on, by) *odios* (the road), describes Hekate's role protecting travellers and the home, because malignant influences like ghosts and the restless dead gather both at crossroads and at the entrances to houses, buildings, and cities. Liminal spaces, inside and outside, up and down, crossroads with options as to which road to take, offer choices and the possibility of disaster. Malevolent spirits linger in these places. Liminal times, such as birth and death, are also replete with peril.

A powerful threshold for Greek women was the time between maidenhood and wifedom. One of Hekate's earliest roles was as a wedding attendant, similar to Artemis. She blessed weddings by her presence, ensuring the bride's safe transition from maiden to wife. Hekate appears on pots at marriage feasts.

> [Hekate] the golden-shining attendant of Aphrodite.[28]

Hekate also answered prayers from men who wished to marry. This supplication is from the 7th–8th C BCE:

> *Kourotrophus* [Hekate], give your ear to my prayer, and grant that this woman may reject the love-embrace of youth and dote on grey-haired old men whose powers are dulled, but whose hearts still desire.[29]

The *polis* (community) also became involved in public rituals to protect its womenfolk. Each of these rituals had a myth attached to it which explained the origin of the rites (aetiological myth). They varied from place to place but generally a maiden upsets a goddess (often Artemis) and the girl is sacrificed: Iphigenia is an example of this. She is sacrificed by her father Agamemnon and, according to one version, is snatched away at the last minute and made a priestess of the goddess Artemis in Taurus (modern Crimea).

In the second version the maiden transgresses, has sex with someone, or is raped and then she kills herself, usually by hanging. Hanging, especially from a tree, was a common form of suicide in maidens, so common that medical writers discussed it.[30] Sometimes the girl is rescued, and sometimes she becomes a statue or tree. The cult will represent this struggle and her death, and will invoke the goddess's help to protect other young women in the hazardous passage from maiden to wife/mother.

The maiden who dies is forever frozen in the neverland between the two roles, and she then becomes a problem and joins the band of the unhappy dead. In one version, Erigone, as she is hanging, curses the daughters of Athens to swing like her.[31] The girls of Athens, in a social contagion that adolescent girls are prone to, begin hanging themselves en masse. The Athenians asked the Delphic oracle for help. The Pythia instructs them to start the rite of *Aiora* (swinging), where girls swung on chairs suspended from trees to transform their frenzy. The rite was celebrated on the first and last day of the festival of *Anthesteria*.[32]

Figure 6.3. Girl on a swing. Attic red-figure hydria, c. 450 BCE.

Erigone becomes an angry ghost returning to punish the Athenians, and her curses force the maidens to hang themselves too. The *Airoa* then was concerned with the transition and sexual experience of maidens[33] and the appeasement of the angry dead. On the third day of *Anthesteria*, offerings called *eudeipnos* were made to the dead. On the previous day all the doors were painted with black pitch and buckthorn leaves were chewed to protect people and the *oikos*. There was a ceremonial cry at the end of the festival, summoning the souls to depart.[34]

A song called the *Aletis* (wanderer) was also performed by Athenian girls on the third day of the *Anthesteria* which commemorated the wanderings of Erigone. She took the name *Aletis*, as she searched and tracked Orestes, the killer of her mother Klytemnestra. Wandering is often found in these myths: Ariadne, Io and the Proetides all wander as outcasts. Wandering is associated with exile from normal life. Greek women's movements were ordinarily restricted, so a maiden wandering was both aberrant and threatening. *Aletis* was also a nickname for Medea who spent her life in exile after she murdered blood kin. Wandering ghosts roam the land because they cannot rest in the Underworld. The myth is a warning to female transgressors that they will never be at home anywhere.[35] Hekate as goddess who protects young women, and also travellers and wanderers, is thus involved in the management of angry ghosts who cannot rest in Hades but roam between the worlds menacing the living.

The dance which doubtless accompanied the song had the dual function of honouring the goddess and of putting girls of marriageable age on display, perhaps hoping they would be married before they might commit suicide. As we have seen, suicide in maidens was seen as a medical problem. Was it considered madness not to want to marry? This is reminiscent of women being sent to lunatic asylums if they 'misbehaved'. In the Hippocratic text *Concerning Unmarried Girls*, if a girl survives the terrible period of suicidal urges and returns to her senses, *manteis* (diviners) ordered the women (*gynaikes*) (probably the older women of the household) to dedicate beautiful clothes to Artemis/Hekate in thanks and in hope that the problem won't return. In this way, the angry dead can be placated by Artemis/Hekate.[36]

Hekate is

> a nurse of the young who after that day saw with their eyes, the light of all-seeing Dawn.[37]

Zeus' respect for Hekate may also be explained by the Lagina Frieze from the Hellenistic era which shows her helping him in her role of *kourotrophos* (protector of the young). She gave the stone which his father Kronos was tricked into swallowing, allowing Zeus to live and later overthrow him.[38] Hekate was there when women gave birth and she protected children after birth. Artemis-Hekate brought on labour, and she could give children to fathers who prayed to her:

> We pray that other guardians be always renewed, and that Artemis-Hekate watch over the childbirth of their women.[39]

Hekate governed the restless dead, and she could travel between worlds and protected one realm from another. The greatest liminality in human life is between the living and the dead, which is why Hekate was a goddess to help bring life into the world through her important sphere of influence of fertility. Kassandra invokes Hekate:

> Give light, O Hekate, to the marriage beds of maidens as is the custom.[40]

Writing much later, Pausanias[41] wrote that in Argos the temple of Hekate was opposite that of Eileithyia the goddess of childbirth, suggesting they had a common sphere of influence.[42]

Childbirth was a perilous time for women. Hekate, as an ancient goddess who had knowledge of the Underworld, had the power to banish vengeful spirits who could whisk away the newborn and the mother. She was invoked for their protection. *Hekataia* statues to Hekate were placed at doorways and invoking amulets were worn in the birthing chamber. Women dedicated items of clothing to Hekate/Artemis in thanks for the safe delivery of children and the hope for successful births in the future. These offerings may have also been intended to assuage the Goddess's anger and protect other women of the family or the next wife from attack if the mother died. Hekate/Artemis could both kill and cure through the agency of the *aorai* (see chapter The Terror of Hades).

During the late Archaic age when the Panhellenic pantheon was becoming fixed, divinities such as Artemis displaced local ones.

Panhellenism insisted that only a limited number of gods play a central role in myth. Because Hekate duplicated Artemis in so many ways she could not be made Artemis' mother or daughter. Hekate's varied parentage in later sources suggests that there was no strong link between Hekate and the Greek Pantheon. Destroying or co-opting mythology and religious figures is a way to impose an alien culture on the conquered. The old gods represent the old ways which the invaders wished to erase, and this is done especially through religion and myth.[43]

In another version of the myth, Artemis neither saves nor condemns Iphigenia but makes her into Hekate.[44] Although this is illogical, it shows the two have shared spheres of influence. There is a similar story with an unnamed maiden at Ephesus. It is possible that in Ephesus the original (and more ancient) goddess was Hekate and she was then replaced by Artemis. Indeed a statue of Hekate stood in the great temple of Artemis at Ephesus. Artemis was the name given by the Greeks to a local goddess in Caria, and it may be that it was to replace an older god with a new Greek god of the colonisers.

Hekate was not entirely subsumed into Artemis, but held on to her previous association with the souls of the unhappy dead, guardian entrances and liminal points as well as motherhood. She could oversee a woman's passage from girl to mother, which brought her into contact with ghosts that threatened women and babies, and she dealt with restless souls that lurk in liminal spaces. In the Greek pantheon she is the prototype for all vengeful ghosts and the goddess who controlled them. The women who by dying failed to make the transition from maiden to mother were believed to come back as vengeful ghosts to hurt and kill birthing women and babies.[45]

When Hekate entered Greece, she continued to serve as goddess of women's transitions in cult, sharing the role with Artemis. But in myth Hekate was subordinated to Artemis who took over her roles. This brought Hekate closer to witchcraft and the angry ghosts. This side of her nature moved to the forefront in myth and literature.[46]

> O Artemis, divine maiden, Diktynna, beautiful huntress. Bring your keen-nosed pack of hounds, and hunt through all the house with me, O Hekate, with flaming torches.[47]

106   MONSTROUS WOMEN

Figure 6.4. Artemis Athenian red figure Bell Krater 5th C BCE.

Hekate changed from 'goddess of the shining veil' to the 5th century BCE Hekate, who is almost entirely concerned with the Underworld and unruly ghosts:

> Do you fear that you will see a phantom in your sleep? Do you expect to be attacked by the band of chthonic Hecate?[48]

In Roman times Hekate becomes hideous and terrifying:

> Out of Erebos and Chaos the witch called Night (Nyx) and the Gods of Night invoked a prayer with long-drawn wailing shrieks to Hekate ... a groan came from the ground, the bushes paled, the grass was soaked with gouts of blood, stones bellowed and screeched, dogs began to bark, black snakes swarmed on the earth and wraithlike shapes of silent spectres drifted through the air.[49]

Hekate knew how to use magical herbs to inflict harm. Medea was her priestess. Apollonius of Rhodes, writing later (3rd C BCE) describes Medea's spell:[50]

> She drove to the Temple of Hekate in Colchis and while her twelve handmaidens readied her chariot, Medea took the magic ointment from its casket. It was named after Prometheus [who brought fire to humankind]. The body was to be anointed with it, after first making an offering to the First Maiden [*Koure mounogenes* Hekate]. This magic protected the wearer from harm by sword or fire and they would be filled with courage and strength. This came from a plant which grew from the shed blood of tortured Prometheus dropped from his flesh torn by the eagle on to the mountains of *Kaukasos* (Caucasus). This flower was like the colour of the Coricyian crocus, eighteen inches high (50cm). The root was like newly cut flesh.

Medea prepares the magical ointment:

> Dressed entirely in black, in the darkest moonless night she extracted the juice and collected it in a Caspian shell. First, she bathed in seven ever-flowing streams and called out seven times to Brimo [Hekate], nurse of the young (*kourotrophus*). Brimo, the night wanderer (*nyktipolis khthonie*), Queen of the dead (*anassa eneroi*). The dark earth shook and rumbled underneath the Titan root when it was cut[51] and the soul of Prometheus groaned in anguish.

Jason implores Medea to help him,

> I beg you, in the name of Hekate herself ... I come here as a suppliant ... bending the knee to you[52]

Medea gives Jason instructions on how to cast the spell:[53]

> At midnight bathe in a fast-flowing river, dressed entirely in black clothes. Dig a deep, round pit in the earth. Sacrifice an ewe and then on a high pyre, the fire reaching to the edge of the pit, burn it with libations of honey of the beehive and prayers to Hekate, Perses' only daughter. When it is done and you have called on the goddess, walk away from the pyre, do not look back, even if you hear footsteps or the baying of hellhounds, for you will break the magic

and you will not return alive to your companions. In the morning, melt this charm strip in water and use it like oil, rub it all over your body. Rub it also on your spear, shield and sword. This potion will protect you from the swords of others.

Jason performed the ritual once *Helice* had set:[54]

> Afterwards he withdrew and the terrible goddess (Hekate *thea deinos*), hearing his words from the abyss, came up to accept the offering. She was adorned with writhing snakes that coiled themselves round oak branches. The glitter of a thousand torches glowed in the darkness, and the hellhounds howled harshly all around her. The whole meadow trembled under her feet as she walked, and the Nymphai (Nymphs) of marsh and river who haunt the fens by the everlasting river *Phasis*[55] cried out terrified.[56]

Hekate becomes the goddess of witches, and the inventor of sorcery who was seen as wholly malevolent by the Romans. She is a favourite of necromancers, and Hekate is used to hex and torture the living. Her altars are at the crossroads, a liminal place, and her libations the blood of sacrifices. Her spirit animal was the dog, who bays at the Moon and eats flesh. Dishes of food were left for her to celebrate the New Moon (or crescent Moon as the New Moon is not visible in the sky). She appeared with packs of barking hell-hounds, snakes in her hair or on her body, dressed in black.

In *Ion* the chorus asks Hekate and her night demons to help guide the cup of Gorgon[57] poison to Ion's lips:

> Daughter of Demeter [Hekate] goddess of the crossroads, you who rule over attacks by both night and day, lead this cup full of death to whoever my queen sends it to—from the drops of the mortal Gorgon,[58] her throat cut, to the one who is grabbing at the house of Erechtheus [Athens].[59]

Hekate brought madness, like the *Erinyes*. Madness was believed to be caused by external malignant forces, like ghosts and demons. The Hippocratic *On the Sacred Disease* gave terror, fears and madness (*deimata, phoboi, paranoia*) to attacks by Hekate who sent the restless dead to torment the living. In the fifth century, the Mysteries of

Aegintea (the Greek island Egina) were famous for curing madness. They claimed to stop the dead attacking by supplicating Hekate who sent them. Dio Chrysostom writing in the first century CE said:

> Those involved with initiations and purifications (*teletai* and *katharsia*) say that by appeasing the wrath of Hekate (*hilaskomenoi*) the person recovers their senses, the angry ghosts (*phasmata*) are placated.[60]

In magical texts of late antiquity, Hekate was believed both to avert all types of ghosts (men and women) and to lead them against her victims. Hekate was assigned to this role to the exclusion of others.[61] Her association with the unquiet dead (*phantamata*), which were called *daemones* by Plutarch, had the ability to harm humans.[62]

Hekate is often depicted with a triple face or three bodies which may have represented Hekate in the Underworld, Artemis on earth and Selene in the Heavens. Hekate represented the dark terrors of the night, while Selene and Artemis were the bright light of the Full Moon.

Later Hekate became associated with the Moon. They both had a role in carrying souls or wandering *daemons* across the boundary between the earthly and celestial realms, in the same way that Hekate could open the passageway for disembodied souls to Hades.[63] Souls in limbo were under the care of Hekate, who could send them to hurt or guide humankind.

Plato[64] claimed individual souls come from the one Cosmic Soul, and that the Cosmos is a living entity with intelligence.[65] The Soul enclosing the Cosmos provides a divine and eternal source of life which contains both reason and harmony. The Cosmic Soul is a component of the human soul, along with its mortal elements.[66] The role of the Cosmic Soul was as an intermediary between the human and spiritual worlds.

Later Greek and Roman philosophers and magicians also claimed Hekate was the Cosmic Soul (*psyche*) and that she connected the divine with the human world. She was then not demonic but celestial. The Chaldean Oracles[67] are sacred texts which have only survived in fragments, but Hekate is mentioned more than any other god or goddess in them. The Chaldean Oracles were said to have been written down in the second century CE, from divine messages received from Hekate and Hermes, and they became the sacred texts of the Neoplatonists.[68]

Hekate, as we have discovered, was the goddess of liminality. She was worshipped at the crossroads, and *hekatia* were placed in the doorways of homes and at the gates of cities to protect the citizens from malefic forces. She was present at birth and marriage, liminal places for women. It was these factors which made her the ideal intermediary between humans and the divine.[69]

It was held that after death the body returned to the earth and the soul went to the Moon, where the mind separated off and went to the Sun. On reincarnation, the Sun sows new minds into the Moon and the Moon creates new souls and sows them in the earth. Mind descended to the Moon, was 'fertilised', and then descended into corporeal form on the earth.[70]

The Moon itself comes between the Sun and the Earth and was seen as an intermediary. Xenocrates argued that the Moon mediated between gods and men. Plutarch[71] agreed, and claimed the Moon marked the boundary between the Sensible and Intelligible worlds. Plutarch records that the Moon is called the lot (*kleros*) of Hekate, who is both heavenly and earthly and the Moon is her assigned place.[72]

Porphyry explains the Cosmic Hekate:

> The Moon is Hekate, and she is the symbol of the Moon's phases and of her magic, which is dependent on those phases. Therefore, Hekate's power appears in three forms, relating to the three phases of the Moon. First, there is the woman in white robes, wearing golden sandals and carrying two lit torches. She is the symbol of the new moon [the maiden]. The basket (*kanephoros*)[73] which she bears when she has mounted high is the symbol of agriculture which she makes grow due to the increasing amount of light she gives. The symbol of the Full Moon is the goddess wearing bronze sandals. Or one might judge from the olive branch she carries, that she is of a fiery nature, from the poppy that she is productive and that a multitude of souls dwell within her, just as in a city, for the poppy is the symbol of the city.[74]

Proclus wrote, "Plato gave the twelfth month to worship of chthonic deities and the Greatest goddess Hekate who closed the boundaries of things within the Cosmos, who on account of this is called the 'key-holder' (*kleidoyxos*) and is allotted the twelfth portion of the Cosmos."[75] As we have seen, the key was one of Hekate's symbols from Hellenistic times; her keys opened Hades and released the hound Cerberus. But in this instance she has the keys to the Cosmos as a celestial gatekeeper of human souls and a regulator of the Cosmos.

Hekate had three roles in the Chaldean system: firstly, as transmitter of the Ideas and thus structurer of the physical world, secondly as dividing bond between the Intelligible and Sensible worlds, and thirdly as the source of individual souls and enlivener of the physical world and humankind.

The womb of Hekate receives the Ideas from the Creative Principle (paternal mind) and these Ideas then disperse throughout the Cosmos and are manifest in the physical world. Ideas need nurturing in Hekate's womb before entering the Sensible World. In other words, her womb turns Ideas into a form, and the Demiurge can create the physical world using fire, earth, water and air. Hekate is the bond that unites and holds together the Creative Principle and the Demiurge, and her womb nurtures the Ideas and provides the structures and boundaries from which the physical world is built.[76] Hekate pours forth soul.[77] Thus Hekate connected worlds and helped to transform Spirit so it might be used by the Demiurge (creator of the material world) to make the world. As the gods were experienced as detached from the world, those that were intermediaries grew in importance, both Hekate and the Moon.

As the traditional goddess of the crossroads and liminal spaces, Hekate was the ideal goddess in the second century CE to represent the fusion of Greek religion and philosophy. From the earliest times, Hekate helped humans during periods of transition, birth to death, and she helped souls whose passage to heaven and hell she arbitrated. The Chaldean theurgist (worker in white/good magic) saw Hekate as the mediator who allowed them to contact higher spiritual powers and they also used those powers for magical operations. One fragment describes instructions by the goddess for the construction and consecration of a statue of Hekate in order to receive oracles (*tesestatic*):

> … make me a statue purified as I shall teach you
> Make the form from wild rue then add little creatures (domestic lizards) and knead a mixture of myrrh, gum and incense,
> And going outside under the crescent moon
> Finish by praying to yourself
> … make a spacious house for me with plaited laurel branches
> Then offer many prayers to my image, and in your sleep, you will see me near.[78]

Telestic (*telestika*) statues were made from plants, animals, stones, herbs, and incense.

Thus, Hekate migrated from the great Titan goddess of Hesiod to the chthonic and threatening demonic goddess of Hellenistic and Roman times, and to the celestial and beneficent goddess of the Chaldean oracles. In all cases, Hekate as mediator, as mistress of liminal spaces and boundaries who allowed spirits and the unquiet dead to cross into the land of the living and later for prayers and incantations to reach the highest levels beyond the physical world by attuning themselves to the celestial realm through symbolic preparations and incantations. Sympathetic magic works with the assumption that manipulating objects on one plane affects or reaches divine powers or Spirit.

Names by which Hekate is referred to in Hellenistic times include *megiste* (the greatest), *epiphanestate thea* (the most remarkable goddess), and *soteria* (saviour), which suggest her importance.[79] Another altar was dedicated to her in the first century under her common epithet, *phosphoros* (light bringer).

Hekate as Soul connected the microcosm and macrocosm. This relates to her earlier role as goddess of witches and mistress of *daemons*, because *daemons* were liminal creatures wandering between worlds:

> Whenever a soul is entering in partnership with a body, at birth or childbed Hekate is there; where a soul is separating from a body in burials of the dead, she is there.[80]

Hekate as goddess of birth and death naturally took control over souls who did not successfully make this transition, in or out of the body, and they were fated to wander with her. These disembodied souls or *daemons* were invoked by magicians in their rituals, but success depended on the cooperation of Hekate. Curse tablets have revealed that it was Hekate who conveyed these *daemons* to the magicians. This connection with the unquiet dead explains her identification with witchcraft and her ability to cure madness, which it was believed that *daemons* brought.

Hellenistic and Roman writers sensationalised this aspect of the goddess. Seneca[81] wrote that the baying of hounds announced her arrival from Hell.

The Sibyl wishing to enter Hades calls on and sacrifices to Hekate. The earth splits open, dogs bark, as the goddess approaches. Later the magician's art was less chthonic and more concerned with approaching the celestial realm and using the powers of light and not darkness. Hekate had come full circle.

Swallowing the daemon: Hekate the darkness and the light

Hekate collects Persephone from the Underworld. She is the light bridge between the unconscious and the conscious mind. She corrals the *daemons* who bubble up from these dark and terrifying realms and brings them into the light. The unconscious is of course unconscious, and it is hard to know what is there. It reveals itself in unconscious behaviour, patterns we find ourselves repeating, again and again, often unaware that we have been here before. You see this with relationships; we may leave one swearing never again to be with x type of person, but we find them, they find us, and we start the merry-go-round again. The tie is broken by bringing our behaviour into the light. We see things in daylight as if for the first time, and we are set free.

Consider your patterns, work, relationships, money, health and join the dots: what unconscious impulses are you acting out? Illuminating them will set you free. You may, like Persephone, have to return to the darkness, but the light will also seek you out and release you.

Notes

1. Hesiod *Theogony* 410–415.
2. *Theogony* 409–411.
3. *Theogony* 411–420.
4. *Theogony* 423–425.
5. *Theogony* 430–438.
6. West 1990:256.
7. West 283.
8. *Theogony* 440–447.
9. The Battle of the Titans (the Titonomachy) was a ten-year war (see below Fn. 3. for the number ten) between the Titans, the old gods, and the Olympians, fought out on the plains of Thessaly. The Olympians won.
10. *Theogony* 397–401.
11. The *Homeric Hymns* were a collection of thirty-three Archaic Greek hymns dated to 6th C and 7th C BCE. In antiquity they were attributed to Homer; their structure, dactylic hexameters and formulae, suggests

they were oral poems like the *Iliad* and the *Odyssey*. They influenced Apollonius of Rhodes and later Ovid. They relate the mythology of the gods and were sung accompanied by a lyre or other stringed instrument. They would have been performed to groups and were part of the educational curriculum in 5th C Athens.
12. *Homeric Hymn to Demeter* 22–26.
13. West 1990:258.
14. Ten was a mystical number for the Pythagoreans. The Tetractys was a triangle made up of four dots, three dots, two dots and one dot, adding up to ten (the Dekad) which was considered the perfect number, the number of the Creatrix. The Tetractys represented the harmony of the spheres, the principles of the natural world, the ascent to the divine and the mysteries of the divine realm. (see chapter on Sirens for the Divine realm). The four rows represented the four elements, Air, Fire, Earth and Water as well as the organisation of space, one dot zero dimensions, two dots, one dimension (a line and two points), three dots two dimensions (a three-pointed triangle) four dots three dimensions (a tetrahedron). With reference to this story, Hekate later becomes (or always was) the Cosmic womb, see below.
15. Homeric Hymn to Demeter 438.
16. HH 58.
17. West 1990:258.
18. Johnston 1999:22.
19. HH 438.
20. Johnston 1999:211.
21. Johnston 1999:206–7.
22. Johnston 1999:206.
23. Johnston 1999:207–8.
24. Johnston 1999:209.
25. Johnson 1999:210.
26. Bacchylides, Fragment 1B.
27. Euripides *Ion* 1048–1049.
28. Sappho or Alcaeus, Fragment 23 (trans. Campbell, Vol. Greek Lyric I) (Greek lyric c. 6th BCE).
29. *Homerica* 12.
30. King 1983:22.
31. Johnston 1999:221.
32. Burkert 1983:241.
33. Johnston 1999:223–4.

34. Burkert 1983:216–30, 1985:237–42.
35. Johnston 1999:221–2.
36. Johnston 1999:239.
37. Hesiod *Theogony* 450–452.
38. Johnston 1999:213.
39. Aeschylus *Suppliant Women* 674.
40. Euripides *Troades* 323–324.
41. Pausanias *Guide to Greece* 2.22.7.
42. West 1990:265.
43. Johnston 1999:245–6.
44. Johnston 1999:242.
45. Johnston 1999:247.
46. Johnston 1999:248.
47. Aristophanes, *Frogs* 1358.
48. Aeschylus, Doubtful Fragment 249 (from Plutarch, On Superstition 3. 166A) (trans. Weir Smyth) (Greek tragedy c. 5th BCE).
49. Ovid, *Metamorphoses* 10:403.
50. *Argonautica* Book 3:840–900 translation mine.
51. Was this mandrake? It has a similar mythology.
52. *Argonautica* III: 1015. Suppliants, people asking for favours and help, did so on bended knee touching the knee of the person they are asking. This follows above, where Hekate helps all invocations.
53. *Argonautica* III: 1060–1080.
54. Ursa Major, who was changed into a star by Zeus, after Hera has changed her into a bear, through jealousy (or keeping her out of harm's way).
55. Phasis was a river god of Colchis at the easternmost end of the Black Sea (modern day Georgia).
56. *Argonautica* 3:1225–1255.
57. Gorgon poison came from the spilt blood of Medusa.
58. It is said that the blood spilt when she was decapitated was powerful. It could both kill and cure.
59. Euripides *Ion* 1048–156.
60. Plutarch (*Dio* Or 4.92 2) in Johnston 1999:144–45.
61. Johnston 1999:249.
62. Euripides *Ion* 1048 The chorus asked Hekate and her spirits to bring the cup of Gorgon poison to Ion's lips. She could also send pleasing phantoms. Euripides *Helen* 569.
63. Johnson 1990:31.

64. Plato *Philebus* 30a.
65. Plato *Timaeus* 30b.
66. Johnston 1990:15.
67. Chaldea is the Ancient Greek name for Babylon. The Oracles are believed to be Hellenistic from Alexandria which was a cultural melting pot and are a mix of Persian/Babylonian, Egyptian and Semitic magical practices.
68. Johnston 1990:1–12.
69. Johnston 1990:29.
70. Plutarch *De Fac* 943.
71. Plutarch *De Is.* 368.
72. Johnston 1990:33.
73. The *kanephoros* is an office maidens held. They carried baskets on their heads in ritual processions.
74. *ap.* Eus. PE III.11, 113 c–d in Johnston 1990:130. See also *Greek Magical Papyri in Translation*. Betz, Hans. (trans.) (Chicago: University of Chicago Press, 1986). As the Crone, Hekate is the Dark Moon.
75. Proclus *Commentary on Plato's Timeus.* Book II.121:7–8 in Johnston 1990:44 and also Runia, David, Share, Michael. (2008) Cambridge University Press. Cambridge.
76. Johnston 1990:50–69.
77. Proclus Fragment 96 in Johnston 1990:63.
78. Eusebius fr 224, *PE,* V12, 200b in Johnston 1990:130.
79. Johnston 1999:205–211.
80. Rohde, Erwin, translated by Hillis, W. *Psyche: The Cult of Souls and Belief in Immortality among the Greeks.* London (1898, 1925) 297.
81. Seneca *Oedipus* 11:568.

CHAPTER SEVEN

The Sirens

> Then, you will come across the Sirens; they bewitch all men who might encounter them. Whoever unknowingly approaches them and hears the voice of the Sirens will never happily return home to his wife and small children. For the Sirens' clear, sweet song beguiles, while they sit in their verdant meadow surrounded by a great pile of rotting men, the skin around their bones dried out.
>
> Homer, *Odyssey* 12:37–46

The witch Circe (Kirke) warns Odysseus he will encounter the Sirens who will enchant him with their beautiful song, and he will die, alone and abandoned in their grassy meadow. Sirens are bird-women who have such a beautiful song no man can resist it, and only men. Their song tells of the men's great exploits and hypnotises them into abandoning their lives to sit in their luscious meadow and listen to the music until they starve to death and die where they lie. There is no violence here, but seduction.

The song of the Sirens is so sweet and compelling, men are helpless or addicted to the story they are telling. The Sirens attack warriors who cannot resist their honeyed words, they die listening to their music.

First, the Sirens control the winds, becalming any ship passing close by their island:

> Presently, the wind ceased and there was a windless calm, and a god lulled the waves to sleep.
>
> *Odyssey* 12:170

The Sirens call out to Odysseus and invite him over:

> Come here Odysseus, great glory of the Greeks! Stop your ship here and listen to the two of us! Don't let your Black ship sail past us before you have heard the honeyed voice from our lips, for if you do, it will delight you and you will leave a wiser man. For we know all about how great in wide Troy the Achaeans (Greeks) and Trojans fought because of the will of the gods. For we know all things that might happen on this all-nourishing earth.
>
> *Odyssey* 12:184–192

The Sirens are offering flattery and their version of the warrior's heroic deeds in Troy. Although arguably Odysseus' deeds were not that heroic, the Trojan Horse was his idea, which did win the war. The Greeks stormed the Trojan citadel through his trickery, not heroics. The Sirens appeal to men's vanity and sing songs of their heroism, real or imagined. Perhaps on Odysseus' ignominious journey[1] home these sweet, seductive words are balm for an uneasy conscience, as all warriors do things they would rather forget. War is bloody and rarely heroic. The Sirens seduce men with their knowledge. Such an offer would be impossible for Odysseus to resist, for he is the most inquisitive and cunning of the Greeks. He is called wily, in the Greek *metis*, a term we will meet later. This is both an insult and a compliment. Odysseus is the trickster, who gets the Greeks out of a jam, but he is not exactly valiant. Before going to fight in Troy, when Agamemnon came to find him to join his army, as Odysseus was obliged to do, he hid disguised as a woman to try to avoid fighting.

The Sirens offer stories, embroidered and with mellifluous voices, which make the man feel like a hero. They lead him to a meadow, *leimon* in the Greek, which represents a moist and grassy place. It is also a word to describe the vulva. Are the Sirens offering sex? They are bird-women so perhaps not, but there is a suggestion of a sensual component to their offering, What does the meadow represent? Safety, beauty, softness after the harsh brutality of war and the privations of sea voyages. The feminine after the hypermasculinity of combat. But men die in their meadow. They do not die violently: they starve to death and collapse in a pile of bones and dried out skin.

The imagery is reminiscent of pictures of opium addicts lying on couches and dreaming their lives away. A divine homesickness, a lassitude, where dreams and fantasies are more important than eating. These piles of bones and withered skin are from men who committed a slow somnambulant suicide while listening to transcendent, heavenly voices.

What are the stories these Sirens tell that are so fascinating and compulsive that starvation passes unnoticed? Well of course they are love-bombing, feeding the egos of passing men, recounting their 'noble deeds', seducing them with perhaps invented, but surely embellished tales of their own heroism and nobility. Who can resist such an offer? The Sirens suggest their song will record for future generations the exploits and honour of these Greek men. It gives them everlasting fame, in the Greek, *time* which is the desire of all warriors.

Indeed, the song is so sweet, so seductive, that the only way tricky Odysseus can withstand their allure, the compulsion to follow the sweetest sound, is to tie himself to the mast of his ship and have his men block their ears with beeswax.

Figure 7.1. Odysseus tied to the mast. Red Figure Stamnos c. 480–470 BCE.

Music for the Greeks can be a trivial amusement, even a distraction, but it can also be a useful tool in education and provide support for ethical development. Music was seen as a divine force manifest in nature; reason woven into chaos; beauty emerging of its own accord from the toil and turmoil of the human condition. Orpheus' fabled melodies were so potent they could charm any animal, human or god and could even bring rocks to life. Music pervaded all aspects of life from the mundane to the personal, even cosmic and supernatural.[2]

Here music is a weapon, or is it the song of women which leads men astray? Pythagoras spoke of the music of the spheres, the alignment of the cosmos through sound, mathematics and philosophy. It is believed he was following Babylonian and Egyptian magical traditions. Pythagoras famously allowed women equal status in his schools and community; the female voice to him would have been no evil force, or would it?

For the Greeks, women's voices were considered both excessive and without moderation (*sophrosune*); too loud and not silent enough. Because of their lack of moderation, they were considered *atopos* or out of place because of their excesses. The Greek general Pericles, in his funeral speech memorialising dead soldiers, reminded women:

> And if I may make mention concerning the virtue of those wives now left as widows, I will give them a brief word of advice. To be not worse than your proper nature (*phuseos*) is a great honour for you, and the greatest honour to her whose reputation among men is minimal, either for praise or blame.
>
> Thucydides, *The Peloponnesian War* 2.45

Be silent in other words, be invisible, talked about neither in praise nor blame by men. Yet in myth women's voices are everywhere and they are troublesome. Greek women's silence however was not neutral, and was equated with 'trickery and exclusion ... they are associated with a terrain of darkness that exists in opposition to the clarity ... of men'.[3] This reflects the Pythagorean table of contraries, referred to by Aristotle: bounded, light, good was male and unbounded, darkness, bad was female.[4] Although Aristotle, well-known for his misogynist viewpoint, may not be a reliable source for Pythagorean teachings. Referencing the revered Pythagoras, who left no writing, lent weight to any argument. Women were seen as 'nature' and in need of civilising by men. Although silenced, women were also liable to speak out in an exaggerated way, with no self-control (*sophrosune*), for which they were criticised. Here's the double bind. Women, due to their 'weakness' because their virtue was weaker, apparently adored their 'life of obscurity and retirement'.[5] Yet they were noisy and uninhibited.

Women in other words liked their obscurity and the chaos inherent in darkness. Yet they were not silent, and their voice was found in the very many female oracles, which were taken as truth, and in the lamentation of women, professional or not, at funerals. Pericles instituted civic funerals for the war dead, to shut the women mourners up and contain their voices as they were silenced elsewhere. And yet, the double bind: even in silence, which was associated in the Greek mind with deception, women were guilty. What were they thinking and not saying behind the backs of men, between themselves?

The voice of women[6] needed to be absorbed by the male and owned by him. Hesiod at the beginning of his *Theogony* explains how 'beautiful singing' came to him (26–28). He was a shepherd; the Muses came to him in wild nature, on Mount Helicon, and they told him:

> We know how to say many false things, and real things. And we know, whenever we want, how to utter true things.

They gave him a sceptre (or wand) from a laurel branch and they

> ... breathed into me divine voice (32)

Like the Sirens, the Muses *know*; they prophesy and endow the poet with the gift

> ... to celebrate the things that were and will be.

They *know* and can choose to speak truth or lies. To tell lies, they must know the truth. In short, they have complete knowledge. Women are teachers, prophets and voices of truth. The examples are legion: the Fates, who spin out the future; the Sirens who 'know all that comes into being';[7] the Pythia at Delphi; Cassandra the prophetess; Aspasia who teaches rhetoric to her lover, the Greek leader Pericles;[8] and Diotima who teaches Socrates about love.[9]

Women are capable of 'doublespeak'. The bees in *The Homeric Hymn to Hermes* (552–563) tell the truth if they are fed honey and lie if they are not. The Delian Maidens in *The Hymn to Apollo* can imitate voices 'of everyman who says that he himself was speaking' (157–164). Gaia in *Theogony* (463, 475, 891–3) both prophesies and devises plots (*metis* 471) and tricks (*dolos* 494). *Metis* or transformational intelligence also governs the major activity of Greek women, weaving. Spinning and weaving and 'spinning a yarn' are the same word and are connected. Silenced women weave. But also poetry or prophecy is called weaving, a metaphorical web. Words in a poem like the *Iliad* are woven together like skeins of wool on a loom. *Metis* is the ability to change shape continuously and imitate the shape of your enemy. It is the ability to intelligently devise a strategy of deception. Metis, the goddess of wisdom and her daughter Athena, the goddess of weaving, use *metis* to change Odysseus' appearance.[10] The myth of her mother, the goddess Metis, shows how *metis* was appropriated. Hesiod tells the story.[11]

Zeus was made king. He killed his father, using *metis* devised by Gaia and Rhea to keep Kronos from swallowing him as a baby.[12] Kronos could not know if the stone substituted for Zeus was his child or not; men could never know. Zeus 'married' Metis,[13] 'whose knowledge was greatest of gods and humans', but when she was about to give birth, he 'deceived her mind with a trick (*metis*) and put her in his own belly'.[14] He subsequently gave birth to Athena through his head, a ridiculous proposition. A daughter without a mother was born. By swallowing Metis, Zeus ensures only he will have her wisdom going forwards. And in myth it becomes something he always had and was his to give away. It validates Zeus' rule. In commemoration Zeus sets the stone fake baby at Delphi which henceforth becomes the oracle of his son, Apollo. Men take over prophecy, but they cannot prophesy: the seers are always women.

The Muses then are holders of truth and lies. The Muse Terpsichore is said in some sources[15] to be the mother of the Sirens. The Sirens could be deadly, dark Underworld double of the Muses, or the female rage at being silenced and having their gifts stolen and appropriated.

But are they? As female monsters the Sirens inhabit the nightmares of even the bravest warriors. There is a song, a fateful song, which will lead them astray, although Odysseus uses *metis* to avoid this fate, forewarned by another woman, the witch Kirke, who is *metis* personified.

The Homeric texts were written down sometime around the 6th C BCE (Classicists give 725 BCE as a date), but they were oral poems believed to relate to events centuries before, in the Greek Bronze Age, circa 1400 BCE, when the peaceful, goddess-loving world was overturned by invaders following the sky god from the North and East.

It has been argued that these poems are the only epic poems which have survived. Fragments of others exist. Undoubtedly there were many more: epic poetry was very popular and widespread in the Greek world. It was an oral artform, read aloud by travelling bards at festivals and banquets. Around 700 BCE they were written down and the poetry was fixed. The decision which version to save and which to discard was a political one, as it always is. One viewpoint was promoted, the warrior hero in his endless, brutal conquests, for gold, wealth, influence and power. Women were byproducts, means of exchange, booty.

But back to song. What is it that the female voice threatens, how is it so easy for the staunch warrior who has survived endless battles and reversals on his journey homewards to fall victim to the sweet sound of women's singing? And how is it that they can command the wind to stop blowing so their sound can be heard? What are these monsters?

Sirens are said to be the daughters of the River Achelous by one of the Muses: Melpomene or Terpsichore. They lived on an island Anthemoessa (flowery) located off the west coast of Italy not far from the straits where Scylla and Charybdis lived. So, they have water in their veins as well as the Muse bloodline. A mixture of sound (Air) and feeling and storytelling (Water).

Homer does not describe the Sirens, suggesting either he saw them as human, or their iconography was so well known it was unnecessary to describe them. He did, however, use *hai*, the feminine plural, when describing them, and the dual form of the verb[16] indicating there were two Sirens. By the 7th century BCE, sirens were regularly depicted in art as human-headed birds. They may have been influenced by the *ba-bird* of Egyptian religion. Greek artists partly adopted from the Orient and partly developed their own images of a series of creatures that were hybrids of human and beast, and one of these hybrids had a bird's body and a maiden's head. In early Greek art, the sirens were generally represented as large birds with women's heads, bird feathers and scaly feet.

Later they became bird-women, with the faces and voices of women and the bodies of birds, and the name Siren later came to be applied to any dangerous, alluring woman.[17] Later still, depictions shifted to show sirens with human upper bodies and bird legs, with or without wings. They were often shown playing a variety of musical instruments, especially the lyre, the kithara, and the aulos for which they would have needed human arms and not wings. Why did they become human? Perhaps, as patriarchy advanced and dug in, the need to demonise women became urgent and then embedded in the culture, so that naturally demons were female.

Figure 7.2. Sirens. Attic Oinochoe Plate c. 570 BCE.'

Figure 7.3. Siren and ritual objects. Red Figure Kylix 4th C BCE.

There is a complex reception in late Antiquity and post-Antiquity.[18] Over time, the bird body receded, and the maiden image predominated. In this vessel (Figure 7.1), Odysseus, tied to the mast, looks towards the figures as if listening to their voices and music, and this becomes standard iconography until the Middle Ages, although increasingly the number of Sirens changes from two to three.

Figure 7.4. Statue of Siren found on the site of the temple of Hera 600–550 BCE Calabria.

A later bell crater shows the Sirens holding a hand-drum (*tympanum*) and a lyre (Figure 7.2), and they have human breasts and have become less monster than beautiful woman: the Siren becomes sexualised. The seduction moves from flattery to sex, and the confrontation changes from hero to monster to man versus woman. They become a type of deviant Muse, naked and hence shameless and bestial having bird's feet. They seduce but not with knowledge. The Homeric Sirens promise to tell Odysseus everything that happens on earth, like the Muse of History, Cleo, but with sex, a taboo subject in late Antiquity. They move away from the Muse of Epic Poetry, Calliope, the aulos of Euterpe, the Muse of Dance and the lyre of Erato, the Muse of Lyric Poetry, to the farmyard, the basic instinct of sex.

In the Middle Ages the Siren changes again: she appears alone, and the bird element becomes more dominant. The Siren now embodies the corruption of the feminine, against which men of religion are warned. Maximus of Turin[19] claims the Siren song is an allegory of the dangers of the 'crags of lust' (ouch!) offered by women. Their Satanic temptation would sink the man who crosses *mare saeculum* (the worldly sea). The righteous man, naturally, is unhindered by temptations of these monstrous women.

> ... fare well in God, that on your journey across the rough sea of this world neither the treacherous arts of the beautiful Scylla deceive you nor the deadly songs of the Sirens charm you.[20]

Over time, the terrible, deadly power of the Sirens decreases, and Odysseus and his companions reverse the power dynamic, and they defeat the Sirens,[21] tossing them into the sea by their hair, drowning them or impaling them on a spear. The Sirens have become allegories of *avarita* (greed), *luxuria* (debauchery), and *vanitas* (vanity), regarded as female weaknesses. The ship of Odysseus becomes the Church sailing unharmed across the sea of the world piloted by the *miles Christi* (soldiers of Christ). The Sirens were women because

> ... nothing estranges a man's mind from God so much as the love of women[22]

The bestial aspect of the Siren was another nail in the coffin, as beasts were without souls. Sirens changed from sharers of wisdom of no specific appearance to dangerous bird-women and then tools of Satan. The adventures of Odysseus show his trials against a hostile and magical environment, which often has the upper hand, as nature will. In late Antiquity they personified war between men and women, and by the Middle Ages they had become symbols of evil to be destroyed at any cost.

But back to the Homeric Sirens. What is it about the voice or the song of the Sirens that is so beguiling? As I said before, it may be simple flattery, but I believe their song has deeper resonance. Sirens use the language of manipulation[23] using *thug-* (beguile), which is associated almost exclusively with Odysseus. The sirens beguile, Kirke beguiles,[24] *thug-* suggests the utter helplessness of the beguiled and inability to exercise rational judgement. It can make people sleep, and resistance is beyond the power of human will. They sit and listen until they die. The secret of beguiling is the content and arrangement of words, in other words their rhetorical force. The Sirens' persuasive power lies with the listener's obsession with or desire to believe what is said, be it lies, deceit or the insinuation of ideas not in the best interests of the listener. It brings with it the suggestion of seduction and flattery. The Sirens use vanity to trap their victims, and they beguile Odysseus with tales of his heroism in Troy. Flattery is a kind of aggression and those who succumb to its allure look stupid in the eyes of others:

> There is no one who does not recognise open adulation, except for the man who is entirely out of touch with reality.
>
> Cicero (*On Friendship* 99)

Plato, writing on Socrates' teachings in the 5th C BCE, argued in *The Republic* that music was a powerful force that could be used for good or evil. Pythagorean musical cosmology, which synthesised Orphic mythology and mathematics, was systematised by Philolaus (470–385 BCE) and adopted into Athenian philosophy by Socrates.[25] Pythagoras believed, according to Socrates,[26] that each Siren sang a particular musical note which linked the Sirens with the Muses[27] and to the spindle of Necessity in the afterlife.

Plato, in the myth of Er, describes the journey after death, experienced by Er, a soldier who came back to life.[28] It is a tale of reincarnation and of how souls chose their next life and how the good are rewarded and the wicked punished in the afterlife. What is interesting is how Plato describes a beam of light 'extending like a pillar, through heaven and earth, more like the rainbow … but brighter and purer'. From the 'middle of the light they saw extended from heaven the ends of chains … from these ends is hung the spindle of Necessity which spins the circles'. From these chains, circles or whorls are hung, eight whorls or circles, each one within the next. The first circle is of many colours, the seventh the brightest, the eighth reflects the seventh's colour, the second and fifth are reddish, the third whiteish, the fourth fiery red, and the sixth white. The whole spindle turns around and the circles spin in the opposite direction. They spin at different speeds, the eighth is the fastest, and the whole spindle turns on the knees of the Goddess Necessity. On the top of each circle sits a Siren who travels around with the circle, uttering one note at one pitch, and the eight together make up a single harmony.

Figure 7.5. The spheres from Plato's Myth of Er. After Chevignard, 1857.

Thus, according to Plato, the Sirens sit on these eight whorls or discs which turn at different speeds and are different colours, and on each one a Siren sings a different note. The eight notes are the eight notes in a scale. The notes of the Sirens are celestial; they connect heaven and earth.[29] Plato believed music retuned the circles of the Soul.[30] What might that mean? Music calms the savage breast, as the expression goes, and beautiful music realigns or centres the soul in its original harmony. The spinning discs regain their rhythm, the colours shine bright and the eight individual notes of the Sirens harmonise. Music, then, is the manifestation of the harmony of the universe.[31]

Plato wrote that music affects the body and mind, intellect, emotions, passions and perceptions, and more importantly, music affects the soul (*psyche*). Music can contribute to the philosophical cure of the soul and treat many psychic responses, including perception, desire, emotion and rationality. Music can resolve disorders caused to the soul while it is in the human form. Music heals the psychophysical human.

Ancient Greek music affected the soul depending on its ethical content, including the ancient use of music in religious and magical rites, for example Amphion, who moved the stones which made up the wall of Thebes (cf. the later Biblical walls of Jericho). Music was believed to form character and draw out the virtues of courage, temperance, and justice from the soul. Music was integral to the health and wellbeing of individuals and communities. Both music and dance come from a certain movement of the soul, and they transmit their nature to the soul listening to it. Music can impart qualities to the soul, and there was, according to reported Pythagorean thought, a correlation between the mathematical movements of music and the ordered movements of the soul.[32]

For this reason, according to Plato, music can be dangerous to both body and soul. Music can be a wholly sensual experience where there is no thought involved or, as Plato would have it, it can be rational and 'civilising'. Thus the type and form of music is important.[33] Music can be seen to enchant magically (*kataluein*).[34] Plato uses the example of the soothing effect of nursery rhymes on babies who do not have functioning rationality. The effect of this music on the soul is that it develops the capacity in the child to recognise love and to embrace beauty and decorum and reject ugliness.[35] This effect is obtained through habit and not reason. So, music contains an ethical potential.[36] For Plato, a rational musical education allows the person to resist the spell of fear and pleasure. Other kinds of music, for example lamentation as used by poets, encourages the worst aspect of the soul, an inability to manage one's sensual nature especially in relation to food, drink and sex.[37] It can be argued then that the music of the Sirens may have been of this kind, poetical lamentation.

Certain kinds of music were harmful, like lamenting music; and soft and convivial music which communicated drunkenness and softness, like Ionian and some Lydian musical forms, are inebriating,[38] while the Dorian and Phrygian music expressed courage and temperance.[39] Plato contends that tension and tightness in the body and in the music are vital to making good souls and good bodies.[40] So the relaxation, lethargy, and collapse of the Sirens' victims in response to slack, open, soft music makes sense. It is interesting that this type of music is impossible to resist, and it is pulling on the soul of the listener or engendering the need for repose and lethargy. To me, it sounds like a mother's soft voice, a sound you can completely relax into, held safe and passive like a baby. There is a tone mothers use to calm their children which is common to all mothers, and I have seen grown men wilt at the sound of it.

It is understandable that Plato in his ideal Republic wanted none of this softness and collapse, and perhaps mothers were anathema to him. The harm came from listening to 'sweet and mournful music' which was 'slack and lamenting' but it came especially from excessive listening.[41] Men passing by the Sirens were becalmed, because the Sirens controlled the weather. In the doldrums, sailors had no option but to 'listen excessively' and were undone.

Plato rejected the *aulos* (after Athena did) because it added nothing to wisdom (her sphere).[42] The *aulos*, used in Corybantic (frenzied) rites, such as those of Dionysus, evoked deep psychophysical effects in a way analogous to a magical formula: in other words listeners were spellbound. Helpless, they abandoned themselves to the music rather than listening to it. It is not the words or the harmony but the rhythm and the essence of this music which speaks to the soul. Bypassing reason, the irrational music of the *aulos* and Phrygian harmony is a music that cures madness with madness.[43]

Pleasure from music[44] is either hedonistic (*hedone*), from one who does not understand the mechanisms of music, or *euphrosnyne*, an emotional response from those who recognise the divine harmony in the music. Pythagoras reputedly believed music could re-order the soul with its celestial harmony.

The Sirens played instruments, which Plato also gendered. The *aulos*, inaccurately described as a double or single flute, made a sound more similar to the chanter or bagpipes.[45] It was often used in social settings and played to accompany elegiac poetry. Plato associated the *aulos* with the ecstatic cult of Dionysus. Music must cause a disturbance to overcome the disturbance of the emotions which have stormed the soul, like in Corybantic and Bacchic rites, where all reason is lost, and women become wild and hyper-sexualised.[46]

It was considered that the lyre, the *kithara*, and the *syrinx*[47] were superior instruments. There was another opposition, the lyre versus the *aulos*: freedom vs. servility and tyranny, leisured amateurs vs. professionals, moderation (*sophrosyne*) vs. excess. Music had a male or female character as well an ethical and psychological one in the notes: the Dorian male, the Phrygian female. There was also different music for men and women: for men, noble and courageous music, and for women modest and tempered music.[48] The music of the Sirens then must have been Phrygian and female. But it was impossible to resist.

Muses perform as choruses at the feasts of the gods. They have an extraordinary knowledge of past, present and future,[49] and of "all things".[50] Muses then have similarities to Sirens: both are divine beings whose prime activity is song, and they live outside settled territory and yet they know everything that happens in the world.[51] They relay this information to the bards, who sing their poetry.[52] Muses, as discussed, are 'an appropriation by the male of what he attributes to the female'.[53] In a tradition which acknowledges no female bards, the Muses are the mouthpieces of men.

Muses have a double-edged quality: they speak the truth, or lies which resemble the truth. In the *Odyssey* the Muses give both good and evil to Demodokos, blinding him and giving him the gift of song.[54] Sirens however give good news, whether truth or lies, which is fatal to the listener. They lie and claim their listeners may return home,[55] which Kirke denies. The use of the dual form may be a metaphor for their duplicity. Their deception reflects on the epic poem. Narrative can be seductive; plausible but also harmful. Narratives can be dangerous as the victims of the Sirens show. Music was also the requirement for a good death;[56] perhaps dying slowly to the sounds of the celestial spheres was deemed preferable to messy, difficult, disappointing real life.

Meditation on the Siren

What is the sound of your soul? Listen. Can you sing or hum the harmony, how are you seduced, what soothings do you use in your life, what lies do you tell yourself to feel better more at ease, more relaxed? How are you dishonest and justifying your actions?

How sweet is your voice? Does it travel, does it whisper spells and curses? Has it been silenced by 'whataboutery?'[57]

Notes

1. Odysseus has multiple trials and tribulations in the *Odyssey*; he loses all his men and is subject to several captures and threats to his life. Here, he has just escaped after being the sex-slave of Kirke for ten years.
2. Bagby, John. (2024) https://psyche.co/ideas/ancient-greek-ideas-of-attunement-can-breathe-new-life-into-music?utm_source=Psyche+Magazine&utm_campaign=0df3adc5bc-EMAIL_CAMPAIGN_2024_04_12&utm_medium=email&utm_term=0_-a9a3bdf830-%5BLIST_EMAIL_ID%5D.
3. Knowles, Adam The Gender of Silence: Irigaray on the Measureless Measure. *Journal of Speculative Philosophy*. Vol. 29. No. 3, p.303. Penn State University Press. (2015).
4. Aristotle *Metaphysics* 986a:22–27.
5. Plato *Laws* 781a–d.
6. Ann Bergren. (1983) Language and the Female in Early Greek Thought. *Arethusa*. Johns Hopkins University Press. Vol. 16. No. 1/2 pp 69–95 expands on this theme at length.
7. *Odyssey* 12:191.
8. Plato *Menexenus* 235e repeats a story Socrates told that he heard a funeral oration Aspasia composed for Pericles.
9. Plato *Symposium* 201d–212a.
10. *Odyssey* 397–403.
11. *Theogony* 886–900.
12. *Theogony* 468–478.
13. "Marriage" in this context may refer to the invading and conquering of pre-Patriarchal Goddesses. "Appropriating" or "absorbing" may be better words.
14. *Theogony* 889–890.
15. Apollonius of Rhodes 4:892–896.

16. *Odyssey* 12:47.
17. March 1998:358.
18. Moraw, Susanne, (2020) From Survival to Peril to an Ideology of Total Annihilation: Scylla and the Sirens, from Homer to Herrad of Hohenburg, in Bracker, Jacobus and Hubrich, Anne-Kathrin, *The Art of Reception.* (Newcastle-upon-Tyne: Cambridge Scholars Publishing, 2020).
19. Moraw 2020:72.
20. Moraw 2020:76 quoting Dungalus Scottus, *Letters 6.*
21. Moraw 2020:78–9.
22. Moraw 2020:82 quoting *Speculum ecclesiae* of Honorius of Atun late 12th C.
23. Ahl 1996:176–7.
24. *Odyssey* 10:212–13, 290–1, 317–18.
25. John, Bagby: https://psyche.co/ideas/ancient-greek-ideas-of-attunement-can-breathe-new-life-into-music?utm_source=Psyche+Magazine&utm_campaign=0df3adc5bc-EMAIL_CAMPAIGN_2024_04_12&utm_medium=email&utm_term=0_-a9a3bdf830-%5BLIST_EMAIL_ID%5D.
26. Plato *Republic* 617b.
27. West 1992 *Ancient Greek Music* 235, 224.
28. Plato *Republic* 616–617b.
29. Planetary association with these eight whorls, the seven visible planets, Sun, Moon, Mercury, Venus, Mars, Jupiter, and Saturn, plus one other.
30. Plato *Timmeus* 47c–e.
31. Pelosi 2010:67.
32. Pelosi 2010:29–30.
33. Pelosi 2010:6–7.
34. Plato *Laws* 790c–791b.
35. Plato *Republic* 401e1–402a4.
36. Pelosi 2010:21.
37. Pelosi 2010:24.
38. Plato *Republic* Book III 398e2, 398e10.
39. Plato *Republic* III 399a3–c6. Pelosi 2010:35.
40. Plato *Laws* 815a7–b3.
41. *Republic* 398d–e. Pelosi 2010:41.
42. Athena picked up the *aulos* and blew on it, but threw it away as it puffed up her cheeks and ruined her beauty (which seems a bit unlike cerebral Athena: perhaps she hated the sound?). The sound was supposed to be the shrieks of the Gorgons after Medusa was killed.
43. Pelosi 2010:16.

44. Pelosi 2010:66.
45. Sachs, Kurt (1940) *The History of Musical Instruments*.
46. Pelosi 2010:19.
47. Plato *Republic* 399d 7–9.
48. Plato *Laws*. 802d–e. Pelosi 2010:47.
49. Hesiod *Theogony* 38.
50. *Iliad* 2:485.
51. *Odyssey* 12:191.
52. The *Iliad* begins with an evocation of the Muse, "Sing oh Muse of the wrath of Achilles …"
53. Bergren, Ann, Language and the Female in early Greek Thought *Arethusa* 16:69–95. 1983 71.
54. *Odyssey* 8:63–64.
55. *Odyssey* 12:188.
56. Buitron-Oliver, Diana, Cohen, Beth *Between Skylla and Penelope: Female Characters of the Odyssey in Archaic and Classical Greek Art*. p. 30.
57. The silencing of women's voices telling their truth: https://whatwouldjesssay.substack.com/p/stop-asking-me-what-about-men.

CHAPTER EIGHT

Eris and the Daemons

Many of the Greek gods were *daemons* or abstract concepts. They personified emotions and states of mind. Most *daemones* were descriptive names only without any myths (see Appendix 3 for the list). A few had origin myths and or cult status, for example Eris who represented Arguments, Discord, Quarrel, Contention, Rivalry, Warmongering, and Aggression.

Eris

Eris was the personification of Conflict. She was said to be the sister of Ares, the god of War. Hesiod places her among the primordial forces as the parthenogenic daughter of *Nyx* (night):

> And Nyx (Night) bore hateful Moros (Doom) and black Ker (Violent Death) and Thanatos (Death), and she bore Hypnos (Sleep) and the tribe of Oneiroi (Dreams). And again, the goddess murky Nyx, though she lay with none, bore Momos (Blame) and painful Oizys (Misery), and the Hesperides ... Also, she bore the Moirai (Moirae, Fates) and the ruthless avenging Keres (Death-Fates) ... Nemesis (Envy) to afflict mortal men, and after her, Apate

(Deceit) and Philotes (Friendship) and hateful Geras (Old Age) and hard-hearted Eris (Strife).

Theogony 223–32

These *daemones* had no father. In a similar way, Eris gave birth to *daemones*:

But loathed Eris (Strife) bore painful Ponos (Drudgery), and Lethe (Forgetfulness), and Limos (Starvation), and the Algea (Sorrow), full of weeping, the Hysminai (Hysminae, Fighting) and the Makhai (Machae, Battles), the Phonoi (Murders) and the Androktasiai (Androctasiae, Man-slaughterers), the Neikea (Neicea, Quarrels), the Pseudo-Logoi (Lies), the Amphilogiai (Disputes), and Dysnomia (Lawlessness) and Ate (Ruin), who share one another's natures, and Horkos (Horcus, Oath) who does more damage than any other to earthly men, when anyone, of his knowledge, swears to a false oath.

Hesiod *Theogony* 226

Eris had a connection with the Erinyes:

Beware of all the fifth days [of the month]; for they are harsh and angry; it was on the fifth, they say, that the Erinyes (Furies) assisted at the birth of Horkos (Horcus, Oath), whom Eris bore, to be a plague on those who take false oath.

Hesiod, *Works and Days* 804

Discord cannot be avoided. Hesiod, ever pessimistic, said that equality and fairness have no existence beyond their name. Eris whispers into people's ears and incites family, friends, and countries to fight, and gives them the lust for victory, power, gold, and fame. For this reason, she was seen as a fearful goddess. She does not say to mortals 'look at my wicked face and quarrel', but she agitates people to compete, persuades them they are superior to others, or that their rights must dominate. For this reason, Euripides (*Phoenician Women* 799) said, 'Truly Eris is a goddess to fear'. Because all bloodshed and wars come from these quarrels. The Greek believed there were no troubles Eris could not devise.

When Justice (Dike), who nourishes harmony in human affairs, is banished she leaves Eris (Discord) in her place. And when Eris and her children have made themselves at home, Lawlessness takes over, and simple Quarrel ends in murders, and disputes feed in lies, and oath comes to trouble the forsworn, and Battles and Fighting ensues, leading the whole community to Ruin and filling it with Sorrows, Toil, and Famine. Eris escalates disputes, and whatever starts as a minor understanding can multiply and grow into violent battles. Reminiscent of those neighbours who kill each other over minor infractions, like impinging on their property or parking in their space, are all possessed by Eris. She escalates the frenzy until people lose all reason and strike out.

> Eris is the last of the gods to close an argument.
> Aeschylus *Seven Against Thebes* 1057

According to Hesiod (*Works and Days* 64) Pandora was the origin of the 'race of women'; she could 'weave a web full of artifice' and birth many, many evils as she opens the jar.[1] Like Metis (see p. 140) who ends up in Zeus' belly, Pandora opens the belly of the jar, and releases all manner of suffering, so that only hope remains. This suggests that hope, or a new beginning, arrives with the Olympians and the old order is destroyed. The feminine has been swallowed (like Zeus swallowed Metis), the 'new female' vomits up evil and a new, harsher world has been born. Hesiod harks back to a Golden Age:

> For before this [the opening of Pandora's jar] the tribes of men lived on earth remote and free from ills (*kakoi*) and hard toil (*ponoi*) and heavy sickness (*nosoi argaleai*) which bring the Keres (Death-Demons) upon men; for in misery men grow old quickly. But the woman [Pandora] took off the great lid of the jar with her hands and scattered all these [presumably the *daemon*-spawn of Eris] and her thought caused sorrow and mischief to men.
>
> Only Elpis (Hope) remained there in an unbreakable home within under the rim of the great jar, and did not fly out at the door; for the lid of the jar stopped her, by the will of Aegis-holding Zeus who gathers the clouds. But the rest, countless plagues (*muria lugra*[2]) wander amongst men; for earth is full of evils (*kakoi*) and the sea is full. Of themselves diseases (*nosoi*) come upon men continually by day and by night, bringing mischief to mortals silently.
> Hesiod, *Works and Days* 90

Woman then birthed all manner of evil. It was all her fault.

Hesiod in *Works and Days* (11–24) gives two different forms of Eris: the first is the evil daughter of *Nyx*, and the second the spirit of emulation placed in the world by Zeus to give humans a healthy sense of competition:

> There is one Eris who builds up evil war, and slaughter. She is harsh; no man loves her, but under compulsion and by will of the immortals, men promote this rough Eris (Strife). But the other one was born the elder daughter of black Nyx (Night). The son [Zeus] of Kronos (Cronus), who sits on high and dwells in the bright air set her in the roots of the earth and among men; she is far kinder. She pushes the shiftless man to work, for all his laziness. A man looks at his neighbour, who is rich: then he too wants work; for the rich man presses on with his ploughing and planting and ordering of his estate. So, the neighbour envies the neighbour who presses on toward wealth. Such Eris (Strife) is a good friend to mortals.

Eris was a woman, portrayed with wings, and had similarities with the *Erinyes*. It was Eris who threw the apple for the fairest goddess, which Paris judged, and was said to be the origin of the Trojan War.

Figure 8.1. Eris. Athenian Black Figure Kylix 6th C BCE.

The [Homeric] epic called *The Cypria*³ tells one version of the story. Zeus plans with Themis to bring about the Trojan war. Eris arrives while the gods are feasting at the marriage of Peleus and starts an argument between Hera, Athena, and Aphrodite as to which of them is the most beautiful. Zeus sends Hermes to take the three goddesses to Paris to decide. Paris chooses Aphrodite because she offers Helen in marriage to him. This leads to the strife between the goddesses and the Trojan War, as Helen is married and her husband Menelaus goes to Troy to take her back.

Lucian, in a much later version writes:⁴

> At the wedding feast of Peleus and Thetis, Eris arrived uninvited and threw an apple on the table inscribed with the words 'for the most beautiful'. Hera, Aphrodite and Athena all claimed it. Zeus decided it should be decided by Paris, who was a shepherd on Mount Ida. Paris was the son of Hecuba, Queen of Troy. Before he was born, Hecuba had a dream that the child would be the cause of the destruction of the city. So, he was exposed on Mount Ida. He was suckled by a bear and found and raised by a shepherd. Each of the three goddess offered Paris gifts to choose them. Hera promised him royal power, Athena victory in war, Aphrodite promised him Helen, the most beautiful woman in the world, as his wife. Astonished, Paris replies he has no need of Athena's gift as the land he lives on is at peace, has no desire to rule so rejects Hera's gift and accepts Aphrodite's.

This Roman version exemplifies the misogyny of the Roman author. The three goddesses are vain and care what a mortal thinks of them. This is very unlikely, they would have probably turned Paris into an insect for his insulting behaviour.

Homer has a different story,⁵ that Paris insulted Athena and Hera when they visited him but praised Aphrodite who gave him the power of being irresistible to women; hence Helen falling for him and running away from her husband and causing the Trojan War.

As discord, Eris is seen on the battlefields in the *Iliad*. Homer describes her as:

> Eris incessantly raging, sister and comrade of murderous Ares, who at first holds her head low, but thereafter strides the earth with head rearing to heaven. And now she moved through the

throng of battle, casting evil strife in their midst and ever increasing men's sorrow.[6]

With Ares she delights in the mayhem of war, increasing the lamentation of men:[7]

> She is insatiable in her desire for bloodshed, and after all the other gods have withdrawn from the battlefield, she still remains rejoicing over the havoc that she has caused.[8]

Eris is on the aegis of Athena:

> Across her [Athena's] shoulders she threw the tasselled, terrible *aigis* (aegis), all about which Phobos (Terror) hangs like a garland, and Eris (Hatred) is there, and Alke[9] (Alce, Battle Strength), and heart-freezing Ioke (Ioce, Onslaught), and the head of the grim gigantic Gorgo (Gorgon) is set upon it, a thing of fear and horror, portent of Zeus of the *aegis*.[10]

Homer describes the decoration on the shield of Achilles:

> These stood their ground and fought a battle by the banks of the river, and they were throwing bronze headed spears at each other and Eris (Hate) was there among them with Kydoimos (Cydoemus, Confusion), and Ker (Death) the destructive was holding a live man with a new wound, and another one unhurt, and dragged a dead man by the feet through the carnage.[11]

Hesiod describes the shield of Heracles:[12]

> Upon his grim brow hovered frightful Eris (Aggression) who confronts the crowds of men. She is merciless, she takes away the mind and senses of poor wretches who made war against the son of Zeus.

Aesop tells another story:

> Herakles (Heracles) was making his way through a narrow pass. He saw something that looked like an apple[13] lying on the ground and he tried to smash it with his club [violent thug that

he was]. However, the apple doubled in size when he hit it. Not having learnt his lesson, he hit it again, this time even harder and the apple grew to such a size that it blocked his path. Stunned he dropped his club and stared at it. Athena came and said, 'Herakles, don't be surprised! This object which has confused you is Aporia (Contentiousness) and Eris (Conflict). If you ignore it, it will remain small but if you try to fight it will grow to a huge size'.[14]

We have seen how Metis, Hekate and Medusa were ancient goddesses who were 'bumped aside' in the new Olympian order. Could it be that Eris, the goddess of strife, was the original warrior goddess who was co-opted and became Ares' sister and then gradually lost her dominions and faded from view?

One way to investigate this is to look at her name. Eris may relate to the Proto-Indo-European root *ere* which means both to separate and to join. Names of uncertain etymology often show a pre-Greek and then possibly Semitic or Minoan heritage. Eris derives from the noun *eris*, the stem is *erid-*, which means, strife, discord. Liddell-Scott also gives quarrel, debate, especially rivalry, contention, discord, and jealousy. In a good sense *eris agathon* connotes 'zeal for good'[15] which supports Hesiod's second expression of Eris. There are connections with the verb *orinein*, to raise, stir and excite. Several expressions use the word: for example, *erizo*, to fight, to quarrel, to rival, and to strive, and *erisma* the cause of a quarrel.

Eris then is our warrior: bad-tempered, the Black Queen, the Wicked Stepmother, Mean Girls, the Evil Twin, the Bunny Boiler. Furious, she looks for a fight, and when she finds discord she stokes it. Does she live on social media? Oh yes and trolls are a modern evocation of Eris. Where we are nasty, vicious, cruel, combative, argumentative and the goddess of everything getting totally out of proportion and then turning violent. Notice Eris remains hidden; she uses her poisonous speech secretly to enrage and engage the unwary. She loves a fight. Of course, this wholly negative view denies the power of the warrior, who fights injustice, cruelty and ignorance. War is stupid, women know this. But there are other battles to be fought; with *metis*, cunning and guile, we can defeat the enemy, using intelligence rather than the brute force of Ares (who was rather dim-witted).

I love this picture of Eris who is running or dancing (Figure 8.1). She does not look like the grim reaper of the texts, but rather jolly, or content with her winged boots and flowing locks.

Embodying Eris means looking at our dark side: the bitch, the snitch, the bully, the troll, the mean gossip. Women's words kill too.

Eris is the blowing out of all proportion event, the madness, the rage and violence of weak people. The trigger for incandescent rage and bullying. Ask yourself:

When you are triggered, do you own your part in it, or do you project it onto others?

Do you splatter your anger over people who cannot fight back, like shopworkers or children?

Anger breeds anger, are you always picking fights? Why do you feel helpless and the need to hurt others?

Being Eris is owning your anger and using it to drive your work in the world rather than attack innocent bystanders.

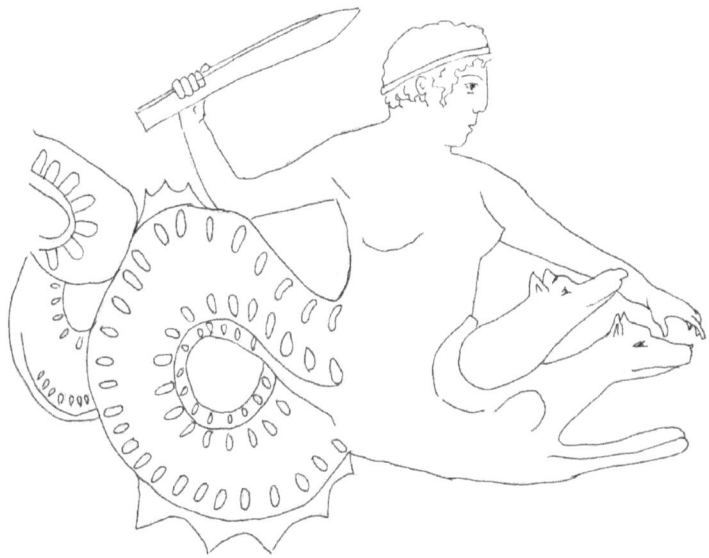

Figure 8.2. Skylla, Paestan red-figure krater c. 4th BCE.

Skylla and Charybdis

Skylla (Scylla) was a sea spirit who haunted the rocks on one side of a narrow channel of water, opposite her counterpart, the sea-swallowing monster Charybdis. The two sides of the strait are within sight of each other and so sailors attempting to avoid the whirlpools of Charybdis would pass dangerously close to Skylla and vice versa. Like other 'monsters', her origins are various. Some make her the daughter of Hekate and Phorcys.[16] The *Megalai Ehoiai* of Hesiod says her parents were Hekate and Apollo,[17] which seems rather an unlikely coupling, unless it is another "marriage" melding the Titan goddess with the Olympian god. Others make her a daughter of Typhon and Echidna.[18] Skylla may be derived from the imagery of words associated with her name, the hermit-crab (*skyllaros*—Skylla lived in a cave), and dog-shark (*skylax*), and *skyllo* meaning to rend, mangle, tear, and annoy.

Odysseus is warned by Kirke about Skylla:

> When your crew have rowed past the Seirenes (Sirens) ... Half-way up the cliff is a murky cave, facing Erebos ... inside lives Skylla (Scylla), howling horribly. Her bark is no deeper than a young puppy's, but she is a petrifying monster; no one could see her and be happy, not even a god if he went that way. She has twelve feet all dangling down, six long necks with a grisly head on each of them, and in each head a triple row of crowded and close-set teeth, filled with black death. She lurks waist-deep in the cave's recesses, then she darts out her head from that frightening hollow, and there, groping greedily round the rock, she fishes for dolphins (*delphines*) and for sharks (*kynes*) and whatever beast (*ketos*) more huge than these she can catch from the multitude that feed in loud groaning Amphitrite. No sailor ever claimed he had sailed past unharmed, whatever his vessel. For each of those heads carries one man from the dark-prowed ship. You will find the other cliff is lower, only the distance of an arrow's flight. On this there grows a great leafy fig-tree; under it, awesome Kharybdis (Charybdis) sucks the dark water down ... No, keep closer to Skylla's cliff, and row past that as quickly as may be. Far better to lose six men and keep your ship than to lose your men one and all.[19]

Odysseus askes how to escape her clutches:

> Skylla is not of mortal kind; she is an immortal monster, grim and malevolent, savage, not to be wrestled with. Against her there is no defence, and the best path is the path of flight. If you pause to arm beside that rock, I fear that she may dart out again, seize again with as many heads and snatch as many men as before.

No, row hard and invoke Krataiis (Crataeis), she is Skylla's mother; it is she who bore her to plague mankind; Krataiis will hold her from darting twice.[20]

Homer, *Odyssey* 12. 54ff

With great trepidation and we rowed on and into the strait; this side lay Skylla; that side in hideous fashion, monstrous Kharybdis (Charybdis) ... We looked at her with the fear of death upon us; and at that moment Skylla snatched up from inside my ship the six of my crew who were strongest of arm and sturdiest. When I turned back to look at the ship in search of my companions, I saw only their feet and hands as they were dragged away screaming out in anguish, calling my name, for the last time ... Skylla swayed my squirming companions up to the rocks, and there at the entrance began devouring them as they shrieked and held out their hands to me in terrible agony. Many pitiful things have met my eyes in my hardships and wandering through the sea-paths, but this was most miserable of all.[21]

According to Hyginus[22] Skylla was once a beautiful nymph desired by the sea-god Glaucus. She was not interested in him. So, he went to Kirke to ask for magical herbs (*pharmakon*) to make a love potion. Kirke wanted Glaucus for herself, but he was not to be seduced, so enraged she poured poisons into the water where Skylla usually bathed, and the nymph was turned into a monster. Another similar late tradition was that Scylla was a *Naiad*, and was adored by Poseidon, and Amphitrite, from jealousy, metamorphosed her into a monster.[23]

This makes Hekate likely to be her mother, as Skylla is another example of outraged womanhood who is punished for something she had no control over. Who after all can stop people falling in love with you? Or the revenge of jealous women? She is certainly a victim until she grows dogs from her belly or womb.

Dogs were sacred to Hekate which might explain Skylla's strange appendages. The Greeks had a curious relationship to dogs. They were both loyal companions and used as a form of abuse, especially insults directed at women. Franco[24] suggests it is because of the dog's unique status on the edge between the animal and human worlds (another liminal experience). Dogs are among the most honoured non-human species. Cats of course had a sacred status in Egypt, and house

Figure 8.3. Skylla, Paestum red-figure krater c. 450 BCE.

snakes were kept as pets, but dogs enter the domestic realm, and they eat scraps from the human's table. The human owner has to obtain the dog's co-operative loyalty, which is achieved through food and kindness. The dog becomes 'man's best friend' hopefully, and a member of the household.[25] A dog has to acquiesce to this relationship. Dogs need to be trained as hunters, companions and protectors and a deep bond often develops between dog and its owner. Dogs were named and often buried in family plots. Atalanta the famous hunter called her dog 'Avra' (meaning aura or breeze).

The dog's quasi-human position is in contrast with their natural proclivity to wolfish madness and frenzy (*lyssa*). Individual dogs may be trained (or bribed) into keeping such impulses in check, but the species as a whole remains suspect, because they can turn vicious or become a wolf in dog's clothing. There is a wariness then between human and hound, which may explain the use of 'dog' as an insult.

The Greeks' penchant to insult women in literature and comedy is well-known. *Kyon* (dog) as a slur, against a greedy, cowardly, deceitful, annoying, or crude person. In comedy, many of the sarcastic remarks aimed at impertinent women and greedy demagogues play on the figure of the dog. In Aesop's fables, the dog fares no better, being implicated in stories about unworthy behaviour, and symbolizing opportunism, greed, or cowardice.

The canine trait of attraction to carrion and corpses evoked repulsion in the Greeks. In myth, the insult is used against women who have similar canine habits: the *Erinyes*, *bacchantes*, Hecuba and Skylla. It is not the dog's noble qualities or its companionship, but its scavenger nature that relates it to female monsters and their connection to the pollution of death. These are attack dogs, dogs that hunt down offenders and terrify the living. In Skylla dog and women become one.

Wolfish

Contemplate your wolfish nature,
 How do you hunt and scavenge?
 Where do you go in for the kill?
 What do you destroy for the pleasure of doing so?
 The expression 'a dog returning to its vomit' refers to doing foolish things again and again. What are you refusing to learn?

Charybdis

Charybdis was the daughter of Poseidon and Gaia. She supported her father in his rivalry with Zeus by flooding the land with seawater. Zeus, enraged by her actions, cursed her and sent her to the bottom of the sea with a thunderbolt and plagued her with an insatiable appetite. Three times a day she swallowed and then regurgitated huge quantities of seawater which caused great whirlpools of water which pulled ships down to their doom. She sat on a rock facing Skylla, hence the expression, between Skylla and Charybdis, between a rock and a hard place.

Being Skylla and Charybdis

Being punished by the 'father' or by jealous women, obeying the rules of the patriarchy or becoming a monster, your excessive appetite as a curse. There is much to digest here. Aggrieved women eating men, or killing them, while being 'beyond the pale', monstrous and becoming one with nature, dogs and the sea.

Notes

1. Pandora did not have a box: it was always a jar.
2. The word *Lugra* (a cause of ruin and death), used above to describe the Daemons released from the jar of Pandora, is found in the works of Homer and other poets in combination with terms such as *algea, androktasie, neikos, makhai, penthos, ponoi, nosos, olethros*, and *geras*. Most of these *Lugra* are personified as children of Eris in Hesiod's Theogony. Clearly the poet imagines these as the Daemons of the jar.
3. Stasinus of Cyprus or Hegesias of Aegina, Cypria Fragment 1 (summary from Proclus, Cherstomathia 1) (trans. Evelyn-White) (Greek epic c. 7th or c. 6th BCE).
4. Lucian, *Dialogues of the Gods* 20; Loeb, vol. 3, pp. 383–409.
5. *Iliad* 24:25–30.
6. *Iliad* 4:440–5.
7. *Iliad* 4:445, 5:518, 20:48.
8. *Iliad* 5:518, 11:3, 73.
9. The *daimons* (spirits) imbued the *aigis* with its power.
10. *Iliad* 5:738.
11. *Iliad* 18:535.
12. Shield of Heracles 139ff.
13. Notice apples appear in both myths: the Judgement of Paris and this one. Apples were sacred to Hera, who pre-dated Zeus, and their unhappy 'marriage' may have reflected resistance to the usurper Olympic gods. Golden apples came from the apple tree of the Hesperides (see Chapter 3) and were guarded by a hundred headed dragon Ladon. Tiresomely, predictably Hercules stole three of these golden apples and killed the dragon. Apples also figure in the myth of Atalanta. They were sacred to the old goddesses, and Gaia in the Olympian myth gave them to Hera on her 'marriage' to Zeus. Apples then were symbols of the ancient Goddess (see *Goddess Astrology* p. 61 for more on Hera).
14. Chambry 1925/1985:129.
15. Liddell and Scott *A Lexicon*. Oxford: Clarendon Press. Oxford (1944) p. 271.
16. Apollonius of Rhodes. Book 4: 828 with the Scholiast (notes). https://books.google.co.uk/books/about/Apollonius_of_Rhodes_Argonautica_Book_IV.html?id=1M4_CgAAQBAJ&redir_esc=y.
17. Hesiod fr. 262 in *Hesiod: The Shield, Catalogue of Women, Other Fragments*, Loeb Classical Library, No. 503 (Cambridge, Massachusetts: Harvard

University Press, 2007, 2018) ISBN 978-0-674-99721-9. Online version at Harvard University Press.
18. Hyginus *Fabulae* Preface.
19. Homer *Odyssey* xii:73, 235.
20. Homer *Odyssey* 12:54ff.
21. Homer *Od.* 12:210–259.
22. *Fabulae* 199.
23. Tzetzes, John. *Ad Lycophon* 45.
24. Franco, Cristiana, Fox, Matthew (trans.) *Shameless: The Canine and the Feminine in Ancient Greece.* (Berkeley, Ca: University of California Press, 2014).
25. Franco 2013:48–49.

ENDPIECE

In our journey through the world of Greek monsters, it will have become clear that the stories and myths which have been incorporated into our social understanding have various roots and many narratives.

What has been taken as Greek myth has gone through many iterations and many pairs of eyes, all of which have looked at them through their own lenses and with their own distinct prejudices and agendas.

Myths and stories are an important part of learning cultural values, which is why it is vital to question assumptions and conventions, particularly in the case of myths around women monsters. There was and is an agenda, and history[1] and myth needs to be retold again and again to give the lie to the current interpretation which justifies misogynist assumptions and behaviours.

I remind you of the quotation of Professor Paul Cartlidge in the introduction: we make Greek myths what we wish them to be, to suit our current values. There is no neutrality in mythology. It is used didactically for good or ill, to influence our perception of ourselves as humans within our culture.

Note

1. See my *Woman Healers through History* Aeon Books (2019) for a discussion of how women's role in medicine has been hidden, denied and obfuscated.

APPENDIX ONE

Truth, Lies, and Opinions

> Consider their role in religion; for that, in my opinion, comes first. We women play the most important part, because women prophesy the will of Loxias [Apollo] in the oracles of Pheobus [also Apollo]. And at the holy site of Dodona near the Sacred Oak, women convey the will of Zeus to inquirers from Greece. As for the sacred rituals for the Fates and the Nameless goddesses: all these would not be holy if performed by men but prosper in women's hands. In this way women have a rightful share (*dike*) in the service of the gods.[1]

Until the second wave of feminism in the 1970s, the history of Ancient Greece was almost exclusively the history of elite men. Smith (2000:3) argues that 'History is constructed with gendered values' which use(d) the canon to support this (Smith:154). This historical narrative provided 'evidence' for a particular viewpoint promoted by a small group of men who produced the professional consensus ostensibly 'agreed by everyone' because they allegedly adhered to disinterested high standards to which everyone could aspire (Smith:154). A history was constructed predicated on gender, racial, and class supremacy.[2] For example, the three-volume *Social and Economic History of the Hellenistic World*, by renowned social historian Rostovtzeff (1941) carried an extensive index, with not one entry under a woman.

Women's Studies have been central in understanding the lives of women in Athens in the 4th and 5th C BCE. I begin with a brief survey of feminist analysis of history from Smith (2003). Using Lowe's (1998) analysis of scholia on the *Thesmophoria*, I argue that this women's ritual was central to the *polis* and how study of the *Arkteia* reflected the integrity of the community and the importance of women and girls. I suggest women's ritual was fundamental to Athenian identity, and interdisciplinary studies are crucial in understanding this.

Others saw women's lives filtered through masculine eyes. Wright (1923:1) considered that Athenian women lived in a type of purdah and blamed the collapse of the Greek world on this 'degradation of women'. Kitto (1951:225) disagreed, arguing that women were excluded from male spheres like politics because men were voting on things 'only men could know about'. He does concede that there was scholarly bias but only because men wrote on 'what was right and proper' (233) and illogically, the silence on women was because 'most men are interested in women, and most women are interested in themselves'. (219)

Wylie (2011:233) argues that women have only recently been 'credible knowers' because social inequality (or misogyny) affects what is regarded as knowledge and whose viewpoint is trusted. Ancient literary sources, written by elite males, and their analyses by other 'credible knowers' gave one version of the Classical World, privileging what the state/men wished to be known (propaganda).

Women were/are not respected as credible knowers, and their history, lore, and local culture was dismissed. Smith (2003:149) claims that women were seen as 'the enemy of history' because they did not embrace the universal, although arguably women as creators of life couldn't be more in touch with the universal experience of bringing life into the world.

A culture/nation state identifies and defines itself through a historical literary canon.[3] This was Homer and Archaic mythology, for both the Greeks and nineteenth and twentieth-century English and German Classicists who promoted a misogynist, racist past to justify colonialism and the suppression of women.

Traditional classicists rely on written sources, which are men writing about women. Lowe (1998:163), in his close analysis of texts, highlights the reception of these texts by 'the exegete, the philosopher, the scholiast, the Christian polemicist, the Byzantine bishop, the Cambridge ritualist, the Paris structuralist, the London seminar'. I would add 'the nineteenth-century colonialist' to this list.

Gilhuly (2009:3) considers traditional accounts of women's experience as the 'social imaginary'. The imaginary is the set of values, institutions, laws, and symbols through which people imagine their social whole. It is common to the members of a particular social group and the corresponding society. A city's self-image in the canon (literary and material) is to a large extent idealised and may be considered wish fulfilment rather than fact. Women's role in religion reveals this.

Greek religion had a social function, and the sacred infused all areas of the *polis*. Athenians would not have understood the concept of the secular. Public ritual was celebrated on the Acropolis, the religious heart of the city. Life was arranged around the religious calendar, based on the phases of the moon, and the most sacred day was the beginning of a lunar cycle.

There were approximately 170 festival days in Athens.[4] Citizen women were involved in many of these rituals, so for at least half of the year priestesses, celebrants, ritual workers, and temple helpers and keepers of its sacred objects would be abroad in the city, going to and from temples, contradicting the commonplace of the perpetual seclusion of Athenian women.

The *Thesmophoria* was the most widespread and conspicuous of women's festivals, celebrated in late summer throughout the Greek world.[5] These rites were ancient, chthonic and only initiates, citizen women, could attend. A ritual space was created in the heart of the male city (Lowe 1998:149) in the *Thesmorphorion* sanctuary of Demeter, close to the *pynx*, the men's assembly.[6]

Anthropologist James Frazer (*The Golden Bough* 1922:616) argued that the *Thesmophoria* was a fertility festival. Goff (2004:126–7) considered it a fertility festival for the 'the correct management of desire' because women fasted and remained celibate throughout. Burkert (1985:242) agreed that it honoured Demeter, and women celebrated by imitating the ancient way of life before the discovery of civilisation (243). The concept of 'fertility magic' became the dominant interpretation of the *Thesmophoria*[7] long after the fertility paradigm was discounted by anthropologists such as Leach (1978).[8] Classicists nevertheless still subscribe to this theory.[9]

Lowe (1998:149–170) explores the *Thesmophoria* and its role in the *polis* using scholia on *Dialogues of Hetaerae* (Documents A and C) a thirteenth-century manuscript of Lucian (Rhode 1870), Clement of Alexandria's attack on Greek mystery cults in chapter two of *Protrepticus* dated around 190 CE (Document B), and a scholium on Lucian's *Council of the Gods*, six manuscripts dated between early tenth and fifteenth centuries (Document D).

These documents provide two versions of a pair of texts, where A and C give an account of the *Thesmophoria*. Lowe contends that these four texts are traceable to a single ancient source, a fact unnoticed by other scholars (1998:150), and that they represent our only account of the mysteries and explain what the *Thesmophoria* meant to the writer (151).

Source A was the first and only detailed evidence for fertility magic, which Frazer then extrapolated into a general meaning of Greek ritual. Close reading of the text is more nuanced: the scholium gives two explanations (*logoi*) for the ritual. The first was mythical (*muthodesteros*) or aetiological.[10] The *Thesmophoria* re-enacted an episode from the Eleusinian myth: the swineherd Eubouleus witnessing Kore's kidnap. Celebrants threw piglets into a pit beforehand; later their rotted remains were collected by women called diggers. These remains were placed on the altar.

The second *logos* is physical (*phusikos*) concerning fertility which attracted the attention of Frazer who assumed the decaying remains were scattered on the fields to increase the fertility of crops (and by sympathetic magic, the women participants), but this is not what the text says.

The reason for scattering the offerings is not an act of sympathetic magic (rotting remains = fertiliser) but an offering of thanks (*charisterion*) to Demeter. *Charisterion*, translated as 'placatory offerings, and a token of gratitude'[11] are offerings to a god for a particular purpose. Pigs and pine leaves were chosen not to transfer this effect to something else (agriculture and womenkind) because they are symbols of generation (*sunthemata tes geneseos*), but as a thanksgiving offering to Demeter for civil society (*hemeros*). The purpose of the mystery is thanksgiving and commemoration for the gift of civilisation.

Growing crops, sowing, reaping, harvesting, and preparing grain requires a settled population which in turn becomes interdependent; and rules, customs and civil society then develop. This *logos* reflects the most ancient and pervasive Greek/Eleusinian belief that agriculture is the key to civilisation.[12] Demeter is a Panhellenic culture goddess, responsible for the gift of corn, but more importantly for the consequent rise of civilisation.[13]

The ritual objects, symbols of human reproduction, are not manipulated to promote fertility but are potent representations of the gift of grain and its effect on human behaviour.[14] The sexual abstinence of the participants was not ritual management of desire as Goff (128) argues or a concentration of energies needed for reproduction,[15] but likely a gathering of power before the great work. The text provides both aetiology and allegory to explain the ritual. The *Thesmophoria* is the female invocation and celebration of civilisation.

Scholia D describes a similar aetiological myth of Dionysus' revenge on farmers (with penis cakes) again not to promote male fertility but to give thanks for and commemorate the gift of wine and its profound effect on human behaviour and society.[16]

This explains the site of the *Thesmophoria*, on the *pynx*. If it were purely an agricultural festival, as Goff suggests (128), there would be no reason to celebrate it in the centre of Athenian political life, and a rural setting would be more appropriate. The lawcourts and the assembly were closed for the three-day duration of the festival. Male citizens paid their wives' expenses for the *Thesmophoria* just as they funded other religious rites. Imagine a group of women holding a three-day festival in Parliament Square, from which men were excluded, while all the business of the government and the lawcourts stopped. Seen in this way, the *Thesmophoria* can be considered as crucial a ritual at the heart of the *polis* as the city *Dionysia* where the successes of the Athenian state were celebrated. Burkert (246) hints at this: 'the Greeks interpreted Demeter as the bringer of order, the order of marriage, civilisation and of life itself', but his argument is not developed. He accepted its agrarian aspect but suggested this did not explain 'all its peculiarities' (245).

In tracking the transmission and reception of the text, Lowe illustrates how the erroneous explanation of the rites became the orthodoxy. The two long texts A and C went through 'a drastic process of repeated abridgement, precis, rewording, reshaping, and reordering in the course of transmission, resulting in several different kinds of obscurity and *non sequitur* all too characteristic of scholiastic literature in general'.[17]

Furthermore, D 'shows signs of interference by a Christian editor with a distinctive line in baroque Greek and a tendency to strange prudish circumlocutions and indignation at the excesses of paganism'.[18]

For example, C.18 τα αισχιστα (*aischista*) is translated as 'the most disgusting things' while Diggle (2021) gives 'ugliness, insult, or abuse'. Goff (129) relates this to Iambe telling risqué jokes to Demeter to cheer her up.[19] Goff suggests women's ribaldry without respect for rank evokes a sense of community among the participants who reject the *sophrosune* (decorum) which men expected of women and which women only practise for masculine ears. Alone, women speak the unspeakable.[20]

What is 'unspeakable' is female sexuality or desire, particularly among celibate priests who were the main transmitters of Greek culture. The derogatory translation of women's ὑβριστικῶς κινηθῆναι (hubristikos-outrageous, kinethenai-movement) is revealed by Diggle who offers 'outrageous ideas, insulting deportment and insurrection' (2021). Surely not what Christians would have wanted to promote? Burkert (1979:242) wrote 'the absence of men gives a secret and uncanny quality to the festival of women' and continues (243) 'women enter contact with the subterranean, with death and decay, *phalloi*, snakes, fir cones, sexuality and fertility are present', with 'obscenity and blood worship of the pudenda'. He cites the *Thesmophoria* in Cyrene where *sphaktriai*, their faces smeared with blood, swords in hand, castrated a man who spied on them. Burkert associated Demeter with a rage that demanded sacrifice (244). Goff (35) suggests women's rituals around birth and death, seen as 'polluting', references their affinity with 'darkness' before birth and after death, and 'was mobilised by patriarchal ideology to disqualify women from fuller participation in public discourses other than ritual'.

Lowe (1998:163) claims these texts are crucial to understanding the process by which a later male writer looked for meaning in an exclusively female experience. Lowe reasons (161) that it is unlikely this information came from a woman breaking a sacred oath, given the strict penalties for doing so (usually execution). The interpretations were probably constructed by outsiders, reporting the rumoured or imagined (through male eyes). Lowe (163) questions the agenda of the scholia. Women priestesses held equal rank in Greek religion; Christianity broke that tradition. These interpretations, and the history of the transmission, reception, and interpretation, were misogynistic propaganda against pagan religions. It is unlikely, at least in Christendom, that other interpretations were allowed or preserved.

When reading men writing about women, scholars need to examine the context critically before 'facts' are taken as read. Whose voice do we hear? Lowe counsels against favouring our own culturally biased, ideologically gendered, interpretations over the sources, when discussing what women's religion meant to Athenians. This misinterpreted text was used as the standard for all later scholarship. The document 'was not an inert or innocent source but created by complex layers of textual and intellectual history'. He disputes that Greek religion was "as dogma free, as empty of indigenous 'meaning' as scholars have claimed, who inserted their own meaning" (163).

APPENDIX ONE   157

Perhaps women were not as silent as we have been led to believe. Modern research has found fragments of women's voices. Anticipater of Thessalonika (c. 10 BCE–c. 38 CE) wrote a catalogue of famous women poets:

> These women Mt. Helicon and Macedonian Rock of Pieria
> raised—with godlike tongues for songs:
> Praxilla, Moero, the voice of Anyte,
> Sappho, the ornament of the fair-tressed Lesbians,
> Erinna, Telesilla of wide fame, and you, Korinna,
> singing of the impetuous shield of Athena,
> Nossis of womanly tongue, and sweet-sounding Myrtis—
> all of them composers of pages that will last for all time.
> Great Heaven created nine Muses, but Earth
> bore these nine, as everlasting delight for mortals.[21]

Praxilla (fl. 451 BCE) was a lyric poet from Sicyon in the Gulf of Corinth. Only fragments of her work survive: some versions of myths, some drinking songs, and religious choral lyric poetry. A fragment of her hymn to Adonis is quoted by Zenobius (117–138 CE):

> The most beautiful thing I leave behind is the sun's light;
> second, the shining stars and the moon's face;
> also ripe cucumbers and apples and pears.[22]

She was well-known in antiquity; a bronze sculpture of her was made by Lysippus, and Aristophanes parodied her in his plays *The Wasps* and *Thesmophoriasusae*. She was still well-known in the twelfth century, when Eusatathias of Thessalonika (1110–1198 CE) listed her as one of five female poets.[23] But later her work was lost or destroyed, presumably by misogynist male scholars.

Lowe's micro-examination of a text concerning women is contrasted with the macro-examination of the girl's festival of *Arkteia*. We move from the centre of the *polis* to its outermost edge:

> I had my saffron robe (*krokotos*) and was a bear at the *Brauronia*.
>   Aristophanes, *Lysistrata* 638–47

The *Arkteia* or 'playing the bear'[24] was a rite for girls held in Brauron, 37 kilometres from Athens. Artemis was often worshipped at the physical margins of a community in liminal sacred space:[25] this reflected the marginality of the celebrants, in this case girls.[26] Wilderness is the nature of Artemis, and Burkert (1985:149) describes her as mistress of the animals, (*potnia theron*), wild and uncanny. Sourvinou-Inwood (1988:24) examined pottery fragments of black and red figure *krateriskoi*, found at Brauron (1988: figs1–7) and reports that the *arktoi* were aged between five and ten. The number and status of the girls attending the quadrennial *Arkteia* is unclear and likewise whether there was a greater and lesser *Arkteia*. The *krateriskoi* depict naked girls running, hair streaming behind them, as well as young women dancing clothed and unclothed, processing to an altar, and holding torches and wreaths.[27] Sourvinou-Inwood (31) reminds us that interpreting the meaning of images is never objective and analysis is subject to the same biases as written texts. Often what is expected is what is seen.

Cole (1984:242) argues girls were 'purged of their wildness' in *Arkteia* in preparation for their marriage. Goff (109) contends that the girls' nudity as they ran addressed their developing sexuality; however, as girls as young as five performed these rituals, this interpretation seems unlikely. The *Arkteia* was completed by age ten. Sourvinou-Inwood (24) claims that Artemis presided over menarche to 'bring female transitions under male control', to regulate this period of biological change which culminated in menarche at age fourteen. She argues men needed control of the female body.[28] This seems far-fetched and similar to the 'fertility' trope of the *Thesmophoria*. Is their biology the only thing girls can celebrate? Here, Women's Studies are still limited by the western worldview of women and girls.

In the liminal spaces these girls entered they took on animals' forms. 'Playing the bear' relates to a myth of Artemis but may be symbolic. Possibly as 'Mistress of the Wild Things', Artemis encouraged girls to inhabit, exercise, and enjoy their natural bodies, in a way they could not within the confines of the *oikos* as girls and as wives. Cole (242) agrees but argues the purpose of the rites is to exorcise this wildness in preparation for the straitjacket of marriage. Dowden (2011:488–9) suggests that the *Arktaeia* was an initiation rite for girls, as initiation often happens in liminal spaces, while Blundell (29) considers the ritual was more concerned with communal benefit than personal initiation.

Hughes (1990:193) sees Artemis as the virgin goddess of untamed nature. Civil and religious law forbade hunting in these large sanctuaries, creating extensive nature reserves. Hughes (196) claims the worship of Artemis protected these Greek wildernesses for centuries. Artemis' relationship to hunters referenced her ancient roots to an era of pre-agriculture. She protected both wild and untamed women and wild animals, such as the bear. By the fifth century bears were rare in Attica and girls wore saffron robes (*krokoton*) instead (195). Artemis demanded both reverence for life and its conservation as a sacred obligation (194). She protected young children (*paidotrophos*) and in the rites of *Arkteia*, goddess, girl, and bear became one, honouring all life as sacred. Artemis, the goddess of conservation, taught girls to protect nature, so they would later teach their children. Male hunters sacrificed to Artemis before the hunt, and they learned at their mothers' knee her punishment for profane killing.

Figure 1. Artemis. Athenian Red Figure Lekythos. 5th C BCE.

Childbirth, when a woman comes closest to her animal nature, is a journey close to death, bringing life, for which women need extraordinary stamina, the strength of a bear, to survive. I suggest the *Arkteia* connected girls to this animal nature in a positive, life-affirming way, to use later during labour. A 6th C BCE bronze relief from Perugia depicts a Gorgon, perhaps (or perhaps not) another aspect of Artemis, showing childbirth, labouring braced by wild animals, which may support my argument[29] (illustration mine from Neumann:80).

A man whose wife miscarried when he was out hunting examined his behaviour for insults against Artemis,[30] giving men a sacred, protective role in childbirth. Hughes' analysis offers a more holistic sense of the lives of men and women, and their relationship with the numinous power of nature. This was antipathetical to later Christian teaching that animals had no souls.

When rituals excluded males, females had only divine protection. If girls could worship safely in Brauron, it meant the *polis* was secure and at peace. Conversely, violation of these rites demonstrated threat from neighbours.[31] Breaking Artemis' taboos was punished by famine, plagues, and infertility of the women of the *polis*.[32] Epigraphical evidence of offerings to Artemis at Brauron (Lefkowitz and Fant 1992:284) demonstrates the importance of this cult. Guettel (41) argues engraving these sacred inventories on public documents reveals the crucial part these rites played in the wellbeing and survival of the *polis*.

They reminded the community both of individual thanks for safe delivery in childbirth and the importance of the performance of public ritual by girls, the most vulnerable members of their community.

Lefkowitz (1986.2007:x) argues that the Greeks neither hated nor disliked women's sexuality, nor excluded them from culture (xiii). Men saw women as essential to the functioning of the *polis*, for their service to the gods as well as the *oikos*. Feminist scholars have examined the canon to challenge to the orthodoxy of the Classics, once the bedrock of elite, white, male privilege. To that extent Women's Studies have had a profound effect on understanding the Classical World. Their analyses may be applied to written sources and material culture. There is no objective eye; scholarship arrives through the lens of the gender, culture, religion, and motives of the interpreter. However, bias runs in both directions. Hughes' analysis via Conservation Studies provides a refreshing perspective free from patriarchal prejudice, which feminist scholars can lack. Both have revealed a previously misinterpreted area of the Classical World greatly enriching our understanding.

Notes

1. Euripides, *Melanippe* (Fr.494.9–22 TGrF=WLGR 34) in Lefkowitz 2007:95.
2. Smith:156.
3. Smith 2003:148.
4. Morford 2015:157–8.
5. Goff 2004:125.
6. Burkert 1985:242.
7. Versnel 1994:236. Simon 1983:21. Burket 1985 [1977]:244.
8. For contemporary social anthropologists, the category fertility god is as meaningless as totemism.
9. Burkert:242, Goff:126, Pomeroy 1994:77.
10. Lowe:154.
11. Diggle, 2021:1495.
12. Lowe:155.
13. Graf 1974:158–81.
14. Lowe:155.
15. Goff:127.
16. Lowe:156.
17. Lowe:152.

18. Lowe fn. 16 p.172.
19. *Homeric Hymn to Demeter* 200–4.
20. Goff:130.
21. Synder, Jane, *The Woman and the Lyre: Women Writers in Classical Greece and Rome*. (Carbondale: Southern Illinois University Press, 1989) p.9.
22. Praxilla 747 in Campbell.
23. Campbell, D.A. 1992:371 *Greek Lyric IV: Bacchylides, Corinna, and Others*, Harvard University Press.
24. Goff:105.
25. Cole 1998:27.
26. Dowden 2011:489.
27. Sourvinou-Inwood:24, Goff:107.
28. Sourvinou-Inwood:30.
29. I make a counter argument in page 67.
30. Hughes:193.
31. Blundell:28.
32. Blundell:30.

APPENDIX TWO

The political situation in Athens in the 5th century and its effect on the *aegis*

Homer does not mention Perseus in connection with the *aegis*. Marx (1993:227–268) argues that sources reporting that Perseus gave Athena the *aegis* occurred late, in around 540 BCE. Hartswick (1993:274) suggests that the first mention of Athena receiving the *Gorgoneion* from Perseus and placing it on her *aegis* is in the first half of the fifth century by Pherekydes. Although it appeared on red-figure vases c. 540–520 BCE,[1] Hartswick (1993:278 fn. 36) suggests that Peisistratus added the *aegis* into his version of the *Iliad* (5, 741–743) which had previously been an oral poem and was written down around that time. By so doing he gave this new form an ancient pedigree. Hartswick (1993:283) argues the *aegis* was a symbol deliberately promoted by the tyrant to bring Perseus into the text. The *aegis* increased the power of the goddess and cemented her relationship with Perseus (who did the decapitation) and represented the alliance between Athens and Argos.[2]

However, Marx (1993:266) through painstaking analysis of extant material culture demonstrates that the placing of the *Gorgoneion* on Athena's shield and *aegis* did not occur during the reign of Peisistratus (546–510 BCE) as a propaganda tool. Instead, the connection between the *Gorgoneion*, Athena and Perseus fell out of use at that time. Either because the myth was considered old-fashioned in the new *polis*, or to disassociate Athens from Argos, which had once been their ally but betrayed them.[3]

The latter seems a more likely explanation: Perseus/Argos the friend and then the enemy and then the friend again. Another explanation is the conflation of Perseus and the Persians who were enemies of Athens. Whatever the truth of the matter, these theories underline the importance given to the symbolism of the *aegis* and Gorgo/Medusa's head. Care is needed to ascribe meaning to supressed or promoted iconographic features as the majority of decorated vases were destined for export, so local political issues may have been irrelevant.[4] Nevertheless, the *Gorgoneion* was added and then removed and then reinstated on Athena's *aegis* for some social or political reason.

With regard to the embodiment of the *Gorgoneion*, Feldman (1965:488) argues unconvincingly that the body was attached later to give it mobility and action but does not explain why this was necessary as the *Gorgoneion* was mobile. Howe (1954:215–6) claims that the body was restored as an afterthought, as the head must have had a body. Again, this explains nothing as the *Gorgoneion* was a magical being, and it could be anything including a disembodied head. Howe continues that a 'slayer' was needed to decapitate her and therefore Perseus was an afterthought. I believe the symbolism of Perseus the hero and Gorgo/Medusa the monster was not accidental but carried the 'script' that Athens and others wished to create.

Marx (1993:266) considers the myth less an attack on women than a response to domestic unrest in Athens in the time of Peisistratus as his reforms were strongly resisted, and Morgan (1964:187) and Kirk (1970:194) agree. Marx (1993:266) proposes that the Perseus tale relies heavily on magic and that Athenians in the sixth and seventh century, when aristocrats held absolute power, looked to others to provide solutions to their political, social, and economic problems, and were consequently attracted to stories of divine intervention.

Peisistratus' era was characterised by pragmatism and a 'can do' attitude and a hero rather than divine intervention was needed to deal with any threats.[5] This argument has some validity because illustrations of the Perseus/Medusa myth returned after Peisistratus, perhaps because when the Persians advanced on the city, the Athenians again looked for miracles to solve their problems.[6] I like this explanation, which matches the pragmatism of Athens and reflects events on the ground.

Morgan (1984:187, fn.15 p.234) suggests that in the move from *oikos* to *polis* with its strain on family bonds, the increased individualism pitted family against clan loyalty. Also, political and economic insecurity were factors in the development of the embodied Gorgon, and a public enemy was needed, a scapegoat to blame. Kirk (1970:194) disagrees, claiming ongoing family tensions rather than social conditions are the reason for the development of Gorgo/Medusa, but this does not explain why at this particular time family tensions should necessitate a female demon.

Vase painting, a reflection of social mores, changed during the fifth century. Women were increasingly depicted doing domestic chores such as childrearing, wool working, water gathering etc. to reinforce women's roles and status during a time of warfare. Interestingly, these images were often contrasted with mythical figures like the Amazons, showing how 'good women' behaved. The images reinforced the value women had in their domestic and childbearing roles.[7] It suggests that, in a time of war, when so many women were left widowed, they may have rebelled against domesticity or mourned the lack of opportunity to marry and have children. They may have made new demands on the *polis* because of their now single and independent status.

Evidence does not support this, you say. I would point you to Appendix 1 which outlines the evolution of the transmission of a text through many hands, with many prejudices, to arrive at what we consider evidence and common practice today. We cannot be sure; we can only make our own judgement. My contention does fit in with Thucydides' speech in which he encouraged women to be invisible and silent, presumably because they were being noisy and visible. It can be argued then that the *Gorgoneion* became a political symbol for Athens' growing power and independence and that literary sources, the updated *Iliad*, and visual images were used to convey political and civic propaganda in a time of unrest and change.

Notes

1. Hartswick 1993:275–6.
2. Hartswick 1993:283.
3. Marx 1993:266.
4. Hartswick 1993:285 fn. 62.
5. Marx 1993:264.
6. Marx 1993:265.
7. Smotherman 2023.

APPENDIX THREE

Daemons

Many of the Greek gods were *daemons* or capitalised nouns. They personified emotions and states of mind, such as Joy and Grief, Laughter, Hope and Fear, Sexual Desire, Love and Hate etc. They described the mortal experiences such as Pleasure and Pain, Youth and Old Age, Wealth and Poverty, Hunger and Disease, Birth and Death, Ease and Toil, and Fate and Opportunity. They symbolised characteristics such as Stupidity, Wisdom, Strength, Beauty, and Grace. They represented moral virtues and vices such as Moderation, Arrogance, Modesty, Moderation, Courage, Mercy, Insolence, Lies, Truth, Impiety, Justice, Fame, Oath-taking, Curses, Laments, Gossip, Respect and Disrespect. They characterised utterances such as Lies, Quarrels, Eloquence, Prayer, Criticism, Persuasion, Counsel, Messages, and Call to Arms. *Daemons* epitomised actions such as Murder, Fighting, Victory, Competition, Force, Rivalry and Work as well as general conditions such as Peace and War, Law and Lawlessness, Good Governance, Justice and Injustice.

Most *daemons* were descriptive names only without any myths. A few had origin myths and or cult status: for example, Eris (Strife) and Hypnos (Sleep), Eros (Love), Nike (Victory) and Nemesis (Annihilation).

I have added the list here as they may be used in ritual or spells for specific purposes:

Achos (Akhos): Pain of Body, Pain of Mind, Grief, Distress (Latin *Dolor*)

Adephagia: Gluttony

Adicia (Adikia): Injustice, Wrongdoing

Aedos (Aidos): Reverence, Respect, Shame, Self-Respect, Modesty (Latin *Pudicitia*)

Aergia: Idleness, Laziness, Do Nothing, Sloth (Latin *Socordia*, *Ignavia*)

Aeschyne (Aiskhyne): Shame, Sense of Shame, Modesty, Honour (Latin *Pudicitia*)

Aglaea (Aglaia): Beauty, Splendour, Glory, Magnificence, Adornment

Agon: Contest, Struggle

Alala: War-Cry, Battle-Cry

Alastor: Blood Feud, Vengeance

Alce (Alke): Battle-Strength, Prowess, Courage

Aletheia: Truth, Truthfulness, Sincerity (Latin *Veritas*)

Algea (plural): Pain of Body, Pain of Mind, Grief, Distress, Suffering (Latin *Dolor*)

Amechania (Amekhania): Helplessness, Want of Means

Amphilogiae (Amphilogiai, plural): Disputes, Debate, Contention (Latin *Altercatio*)

Anaideia: Ruthlessness, Shamelessness, Unforgivingness

Anance (Ananke): Necessity, Compulsion (Latin *Necessitas*)

Androctasiae (Androktasiai, plural): Slaughter of Men in Battle

Angelia: Message, Tidings, Proclamation

Ania: Grief, Sorrow, Distress, Trouble (Latin *Dolor*)

Anteros: Reciprocated Love

Apate: Trick, Fraud, Deceit, Guile, Treachery (Latin *Dolus*, *Fraus*)

Aporia: Difficulty, Perplexity, Want of Means (Latin *Egestas*)

Arae (Arai, plural): Curses, Imprecations

Arete: Virtue, Excellence, Goodness, Manliness, Valour (Latin *Virtus*)

Ate: Delusion, Infatuation, Folly, Reckless Impulse, Rash Action (Latin *Nefas*, *Error*)

Bia: Force, Power, Might, Bodily Strength, Compulsion (Latin *Vis*)

Cacia (Kakia): Vice, Moral Badness

Caerus (Kairos): Opportunity, Critical Time, Advantage, Profit (Latin *Occasio*, *Tempus*)

Calleis (Kalleis): Beauty

Calocagathia (Kalokagathia): Nobility, Nobleness, Goodness

Charis (Kharis): Beauty, Grace, Favour—the Graces

Charites (Kharites, plural): Grace, Favour, Beauty (Latin *Gratiae*)

Coalemus (Koalemos): Stupidity, Foolishness

Corus (Koros): Satiety, Surfeit, Insolence, Disdain

Cratus (Kratos): Strength, Might, Power, Bodily Strength, Rule (Latin *Potestas*)

Ctesius (Ktesios): Home, House, Domestic Property

Cydoimus (Kydoimos): Din of Battle, Confusion, Uproar, Hubbub

Deimus (Deimos): Terror-Fear, Dread (Latin *Pavor*, *Formido*)

Democracia (Demokrakia): Democracy

Dicaiosyne (Dikaiosyne): Justice, Righteousness

Dike: Justice, Rights by Custom and Law, Righteous Judgment (Latin *Justitia*)

Dolus (Dolos): Trickery, Cunning Deception, Craftiness, Guile, Treachery (Latin *Dolus*)

Dysnomia: Lawlessness, Bad Civil Constitution

Dyssebia: Impiety, Ungodliness (Latin *Impietas*)

Eirene: Peace (Latin *Pax*)

Ececheria (Ekekheiria): Truce, Armistice, Cessation of Hostilities

Eleus (Eleos): Pity, Mercy, Compassion (Latin *Misericordia*, *Clemencia*)

Elpis: Hope, Expectation (Latin *Spes*)

Epiales: Nightmare

Epidotes: Ritual Purification

Epiphron: Prudence, Shrewdness, Carefulness, Thoughtfulness, Sagacity

Eris: Strife

Eros: Love, Sexual Passion (Latin *Amor*, *Cupidos*)

Eucleia (Eukleia): Good Repute, Glory

Eudaemonia (Eudaimonia): Happiness

Eunomia: Good Order, Civil Order, Good Laws, Lawful Behaviour

Eupheme: Good Words, Praise, Acclamation, Applause

Euphrosyne: Good Cheer, Cheerfulness, Merriment, Joy, Mirth

Eupraxia: Good Conduct

Eusebia: Piety, Filial Respect, Loyalty (Latin *Pietas*)

Euthenia: Prosperity, Abundance, Plenty

Euthymia: Good Cheer, Joy, Contentment

Eutychia (Eutykhia): Good Fortune, Luck, Prosperity, Success (Latin *Fortuna*)

Gelus (Gelos): Laughter (Latin *Risus*)

Geras: Old Age (Latin *Senectus*)

Harmonia: Harmony, Marital Harmony, Concord, Union, Joining (Latin *Concordia*)

Hebe: Youth, Youthful Prime (Latin *Juventas*)

Hedone: Pleasure, Enjoyment, Delight, Sensual Pleasures (Latin *Voluptas*)

Hedylogus (Hedylogos): Sweet Talk, Flatter

Hesychia (Hesykhia): Quiet, Rest, Silence, Stillness (Latin *Quies, Silentia*)

Himerus (Himeros): Sexual Desire, Longing, Yearning

Homadus (Homados): Din of Battle, Battle-Noise, Tumult

Homonoea (Homonoia): Concord, Unanimity, Oneness of Mind (Latin *Concordia*)

Horcus (Horkos): Oath, Punishment of Perjury (Latin *Jusjurandum*)

Hormes: Effort, Impulse to Do, Setting Oneself in Motion, Eagerness, Starting Action

Hubris (Hybris): Insolence, Violence, Excessive Pride, Wantonness, Outrageous Behaviour (Latin *Petulantia, Superbia*)

Hygeia: Good Health (Latin *Salus*)

Hypnos (Hypnos): Sleep, Sleepiness (Latin *Somnus*)

Hysminae (Hysminai, plural): Fighting, Fights, Fist Fights, Combat (Latin *Pugna*)

Ioke: Onslaught, Battle-Tumult, Pursuit, Rout

Keres (plural): Death, Doom of Death, Plague (Latin *Letum, Tenebrae*)

Lethe: Forgetfulness, Oblivion (Latin *Oblivio, Letum*)

Limus (Limos): Hunger, Famine, Starvation (Latin *Fames*)

Litae (Litai, plural): Prayer, Entreaty

Lupe: Pain of Body, Pain of Mind, Grief (Latin *Dolor*)

Lyssa: Rage, Martial Rage, Fury, Raging Madness, Frenzy, Rabies (Latin *Ira, Furor, Rabies*)

Machae (Makhai, plural): Battle, Combat

Maniae (Maniai, plural): Madness, Crazed Frenzy, Insanity (Latin *Insania*)

Methe: Drunkenness, Inebriety

Mnemosyne: Memory (Latin *Moneta*)

Moirae (Moirai, plural): Fate, Destiny, Portion (Latin *Parca, Parcae*)

Momus (Momos): Mockery, Ridicule, Blame, Reproach, Stinging Criticism (Latin *Querella*)

Morus (Moros): Fate, Destiny, Doom, Death (Latin *Fatum*)

Music (Mousika): Music

Neicea (Neikea, plural): Quarrel, Feud, Grievance (Latin *Altercatio*)

Nemesis: Righteous Indignation, Karma, Jealousy, Wrath (Latin *Invidia*)

Nike: Victory (Latin *Victoria*)

Nomus (Nomos): Law, Laws, Ordinances, Statutes

Nosi (Nosoi, plural): Sickness, Disease, Plague (Latin *Morbus*)

Oizys: Woe, Misery (Latin *Miseria, Tristitia*)

Olethrus (Olethros): Day of Doom, Destruction, Death

Oneiri (Oneiroi, plural) Dream, Dreams (Latin *Somnium, Somnia*)

Ossa: Rumour (Latin *Fama*)

Palioxis: Backrush, Flight, Retreat in Battle

Paregoros: Comfort, Consolation, Soothing Words (Latin *Consolatio*)

Peitharchia (Peitharkhia): Obedience to Command

Peitho: Persuasion, Suasion, Seduction (Latin *Suadela*)

Penia: Poverty, Need, Penury

Penthus (Penthos): Grief, Sorrow, Mourning, Misery (Latin *Luctus*)

Pheme: Rumour, Report, Common Talk, Gossip, Fame, Reputation (Latin *Fama*)

Philia: Affectionate Regard, Friendship (Latin *Amicitia, Gratia*)

Philophrosyne: Friendliness, Kindliness, Welcome

Philotes: Friendship, Love, Affection, Sex (Latin *Amicitia, Gratia*)

Phobus (Phobos): Panic-Fear, Flight, Rout (Latin *Metus, Terror, Fuga*)

Phoni (Phonoi, plural): Murder, Killing, Slaughter

Phrice (Phrike): Horror (Latin *Horror*)

Phthisis: Wasting Away, Perishing, Decay (Latin *Tabes*)

Phthonus (Phthonos): Envy, Jealousy, Ill-Will, Malice (Latin *Invidia*)

Phyge: Flight, Escape, Flight from Battle, Exile, Banishment (Latin *Fuga*)

Pistis: Trust, Honesty, Faith, Trustworthiness (Latin *Fides*)

Plutus (Ploutos): Wealth

Poinae (Poinai, plural): Retribution, Vengeance, Recompense, Punishment, Penalty, Blood Money (for murder and manslaughter) (Latin *Ultio*)

Polemus (Polemos): War, Battle

Pompe: Religious Procession

Ponus (Ponos): Hard Work, Toil, Labour (Latin *Labor*)

Porus (Poros): Expediency, Means of Accomplishing or Providing, Contrivance, Device

Pothus (Pothos): Sexual Longing, Yearning

Praxidicae (Praxidikai): Exacting Justice, Exacting Penalties

Proioxis: Onrush, Pursuit in Battle

Prophasis: Excuse, Plea

Pseudologi (Pseudologoi, plural): Lies, Lying Words, Falsehood (Latin *Mendacium*)

Ptocheia (Ptokheia): Beggary

Sophia: Wisdom

Sophrosyne: Moderation, Temperence, Self-Control, Prudence, Discretion (Latin *Continentia, Sobrietas*)

Soter: Safety, Deliverance and Preservation from Harm

Soteria: Safety, Deliverance and Preservation from Harm

Techne (Tekhne): Art, Craft, Technical Skill

Telete: Consecration, Initiation

Thalia: Festivity, Banquet

Thanatus (Thanatos): Death (Latin *Mors*, *Letus*)

Thrasus (Thrasos): Overboldness, Rashness, Insolence

Tyche (Tykhe): Fortune, Chance, Providence, Fate (Latin *Fortuna*)

Zelus (Zelos): Rivalry, Zeal, Emulation, Ambition, Envy

BIBLIOGRAPHY

Primary Sources

Aeschylus, *The Eumenides*, translated by A. Sommerstein. (Cambridge: Cambridge University Press, 1989)

Apollodorus, *Biblioteca, Book 2*, translated by James Frazer. (Cambridge, Mass: Loeb Classical Library, Harvard University Press, 1990)

Apollonius of Rhodes, *Argonautica*, translated by R.C. Seaton. (Cambridge, Mass: Loeb Classical Library, Harvard University Press, 1912)

Aristophanes, *Lysistrata and Other Plays*, translated by A. Sommerstein. (London. Penguin, 1973)

Diodorus Siculus, *The Library of History*, translated by C. Oldfather. (Cambridge, Mass: Loeb Classical Library, Harvard University Press, 1933)

Dio Chrysostom *Collected Works*, translated by H.L. Crosby. (Cambridge, Mass: Loeb Classical Library, Harvard University Press, 1989)

Euripides, *Ion*, translated by W. Di Piero. (Oxford: Oxford University Press, 1996)

Euripides, *Medea*, translated by P. Vellacott. (Harmondsworth: Penguin, 2004)

Euripides, *Bacchae*, translated by J. Davie and R. Rutherford. (Harmondsworth: Penguin, 2006)

Hesiod, *Theogony, Works and Days*, edited by G. Most. (Cambridge, Mass: Loeb Classical Library, Harvard University Press, 2006)
Hesiod, *The Shield, Catalogue of Women and other fragments*, translated and edited by G. Most. (Cambridge, Mass: Loeb Classical Library, Harvard University Press, 2018)
Homer, *Iliad*, translated by Richmond Lattimore. (Chicago: University of Chicago Press, 1962)
Homer, *Odyssey*, translated by Richmond Lattimore. (New York: Harper Perennial, 1967)
The Homeric Hymn to Demeter: Translation, Commentary, and Interpretive Essays, translated and edited by Helene Foley. (Princeton, NJ: Princeton University Press, 1993)
Ad Lycopon (Tzetes, John (trans.) Scholia to Lycophron's Alexandra, marginal notes by Isaak and Ioannis Tzetzes and others, from the Greek edition of Eduard Scheer (Weidmann 1881)
Ovid, *Metamorphoses*, translated by David Raeburn. (London: Penguin, 2004)
Palaephatus, *Unbelievable Tales*, translated by Jacob Stern. (Wauconda, Illinois: Bolchazy-Carducci Publishers, 1996)
Pausanias, *Descriptions of Greece*, translated by James Frazer. (New York: Biblo and Tannen, 1965)
Pindar, *Olympian Odes, Pythian Odes*, translated by William Race. (London: Loeb, 1997)
Pindar, *Odes*, translated by Diane Arnson Svarlien. (1990). https://www.perseus.tufts.edu/hopper/text?doc=Perseus%3Atext%3A1999.01.0162%3Abook%3DP.%3Apoem%3D10. Accessed 10.7.2023.
Plato, *Timmeus* and *Critias*, translated by T. Kjeller and D.J. Lee. (London: Penguin, 2008)
Plato, *Republic*, translated by H.D.P. Lee and D. Lee. (Penguin. London, 2007)
Plato, *Philebus*, translated by J. Wood. (London: Broadview Press, 2019)
Plato, *Symposium*, translated by C. Gill. (London: Penguin, 2003)
Plutarch, Aeschylus, *Doubtful Fragment 249* (from Plutarch, On Superstition 3. 166A), translated by Weir Smyth. (London: Reprint Books)
Plutarch, *De Facie Quae in Orbe Lunae Apparet*, translated by W. Goodwin. (Boston: Little, Brown, and Company, 1874)
Plutarch, *De Defectu Oraculorum in Moralia*, translated by N. Bernardakis. (Leipzig: Teubner, 1891)
Plutarch, *Plutarch's Lives*, translated by Bernadotte Perrin. (Cambridge, MA: Harvard University Press, 1920)
Pseudo-Apollodorus, *Apollodorus, The Library 1*, translated by James Frazer. (Cambridge, Mass: Loeb Classical Library, Harvard University Press, 1921)

Pseudo-Hesiod, *Shield of Heracles*, translated by Hugh Evelyn-White. (London: Loeb Classical Library, 1995)
Sappho, *Poems of Sappho*, translated by Julia Dubnoff. (University of Houston, Texas). https://www.uh.edu/~cldue/texts/sappho.html.
Seneca, *Phaedra and Other Plays*, translated by R. Scott Smith, R. (London: Penguin, 2011)
Thucydides, *The Peloponnesian War*, translated by R. Warner. (Harmondsworth: Penguin, 1954)
Virgil, *The Aeneid*, translated by D. West. (London: Penguin, 2003)

Secondary Sources

Alban, Gillian. M. E. *The Ferocious Medusa: The Petrifying, Apotropaic Gaze and Matrixial Vulva of Medusa, alongside Genital Display Figures.* Journal of Feminist Studies in Religion, 39(1) (2023). https://link-gale-com.libezproxy.open.ac.uk/apps/doc/A749906513/AONE?u=tou&sid=bookmark-AONE&xid=b79cd236. Accessed 2.3.2023.
Alexandridou, Alexandra, *The Early Black-Figured Pottery of Attica in Context c. 630–570 BCE.* (Leiden, Boston: Brill. Leiden, Boston, 2011)
Altman, Meryl, "παρθενοι to Watch Out For? Looking at Female Couples in Vase-Painting and Lyric." (CAMWS, 2009, Print)
Baglione, Maria and Gilotta, Fernando. Galeotti, Lorenzo, *Corpus speculorum etruscorum. Italia 6: Roma Museo nazionale etrusco di Villa Giulia.* Review by: Pol Defosse (2011) Source: Latomus, T. 70, Fasc. 2 (Juin), pp. 580–582. Société d'Études Latines de Bruxelles Stable. https://www.jstor.org/stable/41548197. Accessed 10.7.2023.
Barnes, Hazel, *The Meddling Gods* (Lincoln: University of Nebraska Press. 1974)
Baumbach, Sibylle, *Medusa's Gaze and the Aesthetics of Fascination. Anglia: Journal of English Philology.* 128, no. 2. (2010).
Belson, Janer, *The Gorgoneion in Greek Architecture.* Ph.D. diss., Bryn Mawr College. (1981).
Benesova, Eva, *Dance in Ancient Greece including Arkteia.* PhD thesis. University of Masarykova. (2012). https://www.academia.edu/36534599/Dance_in_ancient_Greece_text?email_work_card=view-paper. Accessed 12.3.2023.
Berger, John, *Ways of Seeing.* (Harmondsworth: Penguin Books, 1982)
Berggreen, Brit and Marinatios, Nanno, *Greece and Gender.* (Bergen: The Norwegian Institute at Athens, 1995)
Betegh, Gabor, *The Derveni Papyrus, Cosmology, Theology and Interpretation.* Vol. 1. CUP. (2004).
Betegh, Gabor, *Studies on the Derveni Papyrus.* Vol. 2. (Cambridge: Cambridge University Press. Cambridge, 2004)

Blundell, S. Williamson, M. (eds.), *The Sacred and the Feminine in Ancient Greece*. (London and New York: Routledge, 1998)

Boardman, John, *Early Greek Vase Painting. 11th-6th centuries BC*. (London: Thames and Hudson, 1998)

Boutsikas, Efrosyni, The Role of Darkness in Ancient Greek Religion and Religious Practice. *The Oxford Handbook of Light in Archaeology* (2017): 43–63. (Oxford: Oxford University Press, 2017)

Bowers, Susan, Medusa and the Female Gaze. *NWSA Journal* 2, no. 2. (1990). http://www.jstor.org/stable/4316018. Accessed 12.2.2023.

Bremmer, Jan. (ed.) *Interpretations of Greek Mythology*. (London: Croom Helm, 1987)

Bron, Christiane, The Sword Dance for Artemis. *The J. Paul Getty Museum Journal* 24 (1996). http://www.jstor.org/stable/4166661. Accessed 6.7.2023.

Brooke, Elisabeth, *Goddess Astrology*. (London: Aeon Books, 2022)

Burkert, Walter, *Structure and History in Greek Mythology and Ritual*. (Berkeley, CA: University of California Press, 1979)

Burkert, Walter and Raffan, John, (trans.) *Greek Religion: Archaic and Classical*. (Oxford: Blackwell, 1985)

Burkert, Walter, *Oriental and Greek Mythology: The Meeting of Parallels* (Routledge London. 2014)

Burkert, Walter, *The Orientalizing Revolution*. (Cambridge, MA: Harvard University Press, 1992)

Campbell, Joseph, *Occidental Mythology*. (New York: Viking Press, 1964)

Carter, Jane Burr, "The Masks of Ortheia." *American Journal of Archaeology*, vol. 91, no. 3, 1987. JSTOR. https://doi.org/10.2307/505359. Accessed 11 July 2023.

Cartledge, Paul, *The Greeks. A Portrait of Self and Other*. (Oxford: Oxford University Press, 2002)

Chambry, Emile, *Aesop's Fables*. (Paris: Belles Lettres. Paris, 1925/1985)

Cohen, Beth, *The Distaff Side. Representing the Female in Homer's Odyssey*. (Oxford: Oxford University Press, 1995)

Cole, Susan, Domesticating Artemis. In Blundell, Sue and Williamson, Margaret, *The Sacred and the Feminine in Ancient Greece*. (London, Routledge, 2005)

Connelly, Joan, Ritual Movement through Greek Sacred Space: Towards an Archaeology of Performance. In Chaniotis, A. (ed.), *Ritual Dynamics in the Ancient Mediterranean: Agency, Emotion, Gender, Reception*. (Stuttgart, 2011). https://www.academia.edu/21951394/RITUAL_MOVEMENT_THROUGH_GREEK_SACRED_SPACE_Towards_an_Archaeology_of_Performance. Accessed 2.6.2023.

Dawkins, Richard. et al. Laconia: I. Excavations at Sparta. *The Annual of the British School at Athens*, vol. 13. (1907). http://www.jstor.org/stable/30096368. Accessed 31 July 2023.

Dawkins, Richard. et al. The Sanctuary of Artemis Orthia at Sparta. *Journal of Hellenic Studies*. vol. 50, no. 1, 1930. (1929). https://doi.org/10.2307/626172. Accessed 23.7.2023.

De-Gaia, Susan, The Gorgon. In *Encyclopaedia of Women in World Religions: Faith and Culture across History: African Religions to Hinduism*. (London: Bloomsbury Books, 2019)

Destrée, Pierre and Murray, Penelope, *A Companion to Ancient Aesthetics*, (London: John Wiley & Sons. Blackwell, 2015)

Dexter, Miriam. The Ferocious and the Erotic: "Beautiful" Medusa and the Neolithic Bird and Snake, *Journal of Feminist studies in religion*, 26(1). (2010). https://doi.org/10.2979/FSR.2010.26.1.25. Accessed 14.4.2023.

Dietrich, Moira, *Death, Fate, and the Gods*. (London: Athlone Press, 1965)

Diggle, B.L. Fraser, P. James, O.B. Simkin, A.A. Thompson, S.J. (eds.), *The Cambridge Greek Lexicon*. (Cambridge: Cambridge University Press, 2021)

Dillon, Matthew, *Girls and Women in Classical Greek religion*. (London: Routledge, 2002)

Dodds, Eric, *The Greeks and the Irrational*. (Berkeley, CA. University of California Press, 1964)

Doherty, Lilian Eileen, *Siren Songs. Gender, Audiences and Narrators in the Odyssey*. (Ann Arbor: University of Michigan Press, 1995)

Doherty, Lilian Eileen, *Gender and the Interpretation of Classical Myth*. (London; Duckworth, 2001)

Dowden, Ken, *Death and The Maiden: Girls' Initiation Rites in Greek Mythology*. (London: Routledge, 1989)

Eliade, Mircea, translated by Trask, Willard, *The Sacred and the Profane: The Nature of Religion*. (New York: Harcourt. New York, 1956)

Eliade, Mircea, translated by Trask, Willard, *Rites and Symbols of Initiation: The Mysteries of Birth and Rebirth*. (Woodstock, Conn. Spring Publication, 1995)

Farnell, Lewis, *Cults of the Greek States*. Cambridge: Cambridge University Press, 1909/2011)

Feldman, Thalia, Gorgo and the Origins of Fear. *Arion: A Journal of Humanities and the Classics*. Autumn. Vol. 4. No. 3. Boston University. (1965). https://www.jstor.org/stable/20162978. Accessed 2.5.2023.

Fitton, J.W. Greek Dance in *The Classical Quarterly*. Vol. 23 no. 2 November. (1973). https://philpapers.org/rec/FITGD-3. Accessed 1.4.2023.

Foley, Helene (trans.), *The Homeric Hymn to Demeter: Translation, Commentary, and Interpretive Essays*. (Princeton NJ: Princeton University Press, 1993)

Foley, Helen, *Female Acts in Greek Tragedy*. (Princeton NJ: Princeton University Press, 2001)

Frazer, James, *The Golden Bough*. (New York: Macmillan, 1922)

Freud, Sigmund, The Medusa Head (1922). In Garber, Marjorie and Vickers, Nancy, *The Medusa Reader*. (London: Routledge, 2003)
Fontisi-Ducroux, Francoise, The Invention of the Erinyes. In Kraus, Chris, Goldhill, Simon, Foley, Helen, P. Elsner, Jas. (eds.), *Visualizing the Tragic. Drama, Myth, and Ritual in Greek Art and Literature*. (Oxford: Oxford University Press, 2007)
Frothingham, Arthur, Medusa, Apollo, and the Great Mother. *American Journal of Archaeology* 15, no. 3. (1911). https://doi.org/10.2307/497414. Accessed 4.7.2023.
Gamkrelidze, Thomas and Ivanov, Vjaceslav translated by Nichols, Johana, *Indo-European and the Indo-Europeans. A Reconstruction and Historical Analysis of a Proto-Indo-European language and a Proto-Indo-European Culture*. (Berlin and New York: Mouton de Gruyter, 1995)
Gantz, Timothy, *Early Greek Myth: A Guide to Literary and Artistic Sources*. 2 vols. (Baltimore and London: Johns Hopkins University Press, 1993)
Garber, Marjorie, *Vested Interests: Cross dressing and cultural anxiety*. (New York: Routledge, 1992)
Garber, Marjorie and Vickers, Nancy, *The Medusa Reader*. (London: Routledge, 2003)
Gershonson, Daniel, The Beautiful Gorgon and Indo-European Parallels. *Mankind Quarterly* 29, no 4. (1989).
Giallongo, Angela and Forster, Anna. *The historical enigma of the snake woman from antiquity to the 21st century*. Cambridge Scholars Publishing. Newcastle upon Tyne. *ProQuest Ebook Central* (2017). http://ebookcentral.proquest.com/lib/open/detail.action?docID=5487779. Accessed 12.6.2023.
Gianvittorio-Ungar, Laura, Narratives in Motion: The Art of Dancing Stories in Antiquity and Beyond, *Greek and Roman Musical Studies*, 8(1) (2020). https://doi.org/10.1163/22129758-12341367. Accessed 12.4.2023.
Gilhuly, K. *The Feminine Matrix of Sex and Gender in Classical Times*. (Cambridge: Cambridge University Press, 2009)
Gilmore, David, *Monsters, Evil Beings, Mythical Beasts and All Manner of Imaginary Terrors*. (Philadelphia: University of Philadelphia Press, 2002)
Gimbutas, Marija, *The Goddesses and Gods of Old Europe*. (Berkeley: University of California Press, 1982)
Glennon, Madeleine, Medusa in Ancient Greek Art. In *Heilbrunn Timeline of Art History*. New York: The Metropolitan Museum of Art. (2000). http://www.metmuseum.org/toah/hd/medu/hd_medu.htm.
Goff, B. *Citizen Bacchae: Women's Ritual Practice in Ancient Greece*. (Berkeley: University of California Press, 2004)
Goldberg, Marilyn. Archaic Greek Akroteria. *American Journal of Archaeology*, vol. 86, no. 2, 1982. JSTOR. https://doi.org/10.2307/504832. Accessed 11 July 2023.

Gombrich, Ernst, *Meditations on a Hobby Horse and Other Essays on the Theory of Art*. (London: Phaidon Press, 1963)
Gomme, A.W. *Essays in History and Literature*. (Oxford: Blackwell, 1937)
Gómez, Espelosin, Iberia in the Greek Geographical Imagination. In Dietler, M. and López-Ruiz, C. (eds) *Colonial Encounters in Ancient Iberia: Phoenician, Greek, and Indigenous Relations*. (Chicago: Chicago University Press, 2009)
Goulimaris, Dimitrios, et al. Dancing mania as healing proceedings in the context of religious worship in ancient and contemporary Greece. *Aethlon: The Journal of Sport Literature*, vol. 22, no. 2, Spring. Gale Academic OneFile. (2005). link.gale.com/apps/doc/A157655514/AONE?u=tou&sid=bookmark-AONE&xid=fbc8037b. Accessed 21 June 2023.
Graves Robert, *The Greek Myths*. Vols. 1 & 2. (Harmondsworth: Penguin Books, 1960)
Griffin, Miranda, Sex and the Serpent. In *Transforming Tales: Rewriting Metamorphosis in Medieval French Literature*. (Oxford: Oxford University Press, 2015)
Grimal, Pierre, translated by Maxwell-Hyslop, *The Dictionary of Classical Mythology*. (Oxford: Blackwell, 1951/1986)
Hall, Edith, *Inventing the Barbarian. Greek Self-Definition through Tragedy*. (Oxford: Clarendon Press, 1989)
Hall, Edith, *The Ancient Greeks. Ten Ways they Shaped the Modern World*. (London: Vintage, 2015)
Hall, Nor, *The Moon and the Virgin*. (London: Harper and Row, 1980)
Halperin, David, Winkler, John, Zeitlin, Froma. (eds.) *Before Sexuality. The construction of Erotic Experience in the Ancient Greek World*. (Princeton, NJ: Princeton University Press, 1990)
Hardwick, L. *Reception Studies, Greece & Rome*, New Surveys in the Classics no. 33, Oxford: Oxford University Press, pp. 1–11. (2003).
Harrison, Jane, *Prolegomena to the Study of Greek Religion*. (New York: Meridian Books, 1903/1955)
Hartswick, Kim. The Gorgoneion on Aigis of Athena. Genesis, Suppression and Survival. *Revue Archeologique*. (Paris: Presses Universitaires. Paris, 1993). http://www.jstor.org/stable/41738384. Accessed 12 Aug. 2023.
Henle, Jane, *Greek Myths: A Vase Painter's Notebook*. (Bloomington and London: University of Indiana Press, 1973)
Hirvonen, Kaarle, *Matriarchal Survivals and Certain Trends in Homer's Female Characters*. (Helsinki: Suomalainen, 1968)
Hopkins, Clark. Assyrian Elements in the Perseus Gorgon Story. *American Journal of Anthropology*. Vol. 38, 3, July-September. (1934). https://doi.org/10.2307/498901. Accessed 30.7.2023.
Hornblower, Stephen and Spawforth, Anthony, *The Oxford Companion to Classical Civilisation*. (Oxford: Oxford University Press, 1998)

Howe, Thalia, P. The Origin and Function of the Gorgon-Head. *American Journal of Archaeology*. Vol. 58. No. 3. *STOR* (1954). https://doi.org/10.2307/500901. Accessed 13.5.2023.

Hughes, D.J. *Artemis Goddess of Conservation*. Forest & Conservation History Vol. 34, No. 4 (Oct., 1990), pp. 191–197 (7 pages) Oxford University Press. https://www-journals-uchicago-edu.libezproxy.open.ac.uk/doi/pdfplus/10.2307%2F3983705. Accessed 14.5.2022.

Inge, Simon, *The Natural History of the Eye*. (London: Bloomsbury, 2007)

Janko, Richard. The Cult of the Erinyes, the Villa of the Mysteries, and the Unity of the Derveni Papyrus in Most, Glenn. (ed.) *Studies on the Derveni Papyrus. Vol. 2*. (Oxford: Oxford University Press, 2022)

Johnston, Sarah Iles, *Hekate Soteira. A study of Hekate's Roles in the Chaldean Oracles and Related Literature*. (Atlanta: Scholars Press, 1990)

Johnston, Sarah Iles, Defining the Dreadful: Remarks on the Greek child-killing Demon. In Meyer, M. and Mirecki, P. (eds.) *Ancient Magic and Ritual Power*. (Leiden: Brill, 1995)

Johnston, Sarah Iles, *Restless Dead. Encounters between the Living and the Dead in Ancient Greece*. (Berkeley, CA: University of California Press, 1999)

Johnston, Sarah Iles and Struck, Peter, T. (eds.), *Mantike. Studies in Ancient Divination*. (Leiden: Brill, 2005)

Joplin, Patricia, Rape and Silence in the Medusa Story, in Garber, Marjorie and Vickers, Nancy, *The Medusa Reader*. (London: Routledge, 2003)

Jung, Carl, *The Archetypes and the Collective Unconscious* in The Collected Works of C.G. Jung. Vol. 9 (part 1) (Princeton NJ: Princeton University Press, 1948)

Karoglou, Kiki, *Dangerous Beauty: Medusa in Classical Art*. Exhibition catalogue. Metropolitan Museum of Art. New York (2018)

Kerenyi, Karl. *The Gods of the Greeks*. (London: Thames and Hudson, 1951)

Keuls, Eva. *The reign of the phallus: Sexual politics in Ancient Athens*. (Berkeley, Ca. University of California Los Angeles, 1993)

Khalifa-Gueta, Sharon, Medusa Must Die! The Virgin and the Defile in Graeco-Roman Medusa and Andromeda Myths. *Athens Journal of Mediterranean Studies*. 7, no. 3. (2021). https://www.researchgate.net/publication/351722441_Medusa_Must_Die_The_Virgin_and_the_Defiled_in_Greco-Roman_Medusa_and_Andromeda_Myths/citation/download. Accessed 2.6.2023.

King. H, Bound to Bleed: Artemis and Greek Women, in Cameron, A. and Kuhrt, A. (eds.) *Images of Women in Antiquity*. (London: Croom Helm, 1983)

Kirk, Geoffrey, *Myth; its Meaning and Function in Ancient and Other Cultures*. (Cambridge: Cambridge University Press, 1970)

Kitto, H.D.F. *The Greeks*. (Harmondsworth: Pelican, 1951)

Kopanias, Konstantinos, Some Ivories from the Geometric Stratum at the Sanctuary of Artemis Orthia, Sparta: Interconnections between Sparta, Crete and the Orient during the Late Eighth Century BC. *British School at Athens Studies*, vol. 16. *JSTOR* (2009). http://www.jstor.org/stable/40960628. Accessed 23 July 2023.

Kraus, Chris, Goldhill, Simon, Foley, Helen P. Elsner, Jas, (eds.) *Visualizing the Tragic. Dram, Myth, and ritual in Greek Art and Literature*. (Oxford: Oxford University Press, 2007)

Kristeva. Julia, translated by Gladding, Jody, *The Severed Head. Capital Visions*. (Columbia OH: Columbia University Press, 2012)

Lacey, W.K. *The Family in Classical Greece*. (Ithaca, New York: Cornell University Press, 1968)

Larrington, Carolyne, *The Feminist Companion to Mythology*. (London: Pandora, 1992)

Larson, Jennifer, Artemis and the Nymphs: Handmaidens of Artemis. *The Classical Association Journal*. Vol. 92. No. 3. (Feb-March) (1997). https://www.academia.edu/27564557/Handmaidens_of_Artemis_Classical_Journal_92_3_249_57_1997_?email_work_card=view-paper. Accessed 12.7.2023.

Lawler, Lillian, The Dance of the Holy Birds. *The Classical Journal*, vol. 37, no. 6. *JSTOR* (1942). http://www.jstor.org/stable/3292318. Accessed 7.7.2023.

Lawler, Lillian, A Lion among Ladies (Theocritus II, 66–68). *Transactions and Proceedings of the American Philological Association* 78. (1947a). http://writings.raftis.org/wp-content/uploads/2020/08/Lawler-A-Lion-among-Ladies-1947.pdf. Accessed 11.7.2023.

Lawler, Lillian B. Snake Dances. *Archaeology* 1, no. 2. (1948). http://www.jstor.org/stable/41662498. Accessed 6.7.2023. Accessed 11.7.2023.

Lawler, Lillian B. The Dance in Metaphor. *The Classical Journal* 46, no. 8. (1951). http://www.jstor.org/stable/3292556. Accessed 6.7.2023.

Lawler, Lilian B. *The dance in ancient Greece*. (London: A. & C. Black Ltd. 1964)

Lawler, Lillian B. Are They Dancing? *The Classical Journal* 60, no. 6. (1964). http://www.jstor.org/stable/3294283. Accessed 6.7.2023.

Lazarou, Anna, Prehistoric Gorgoneia: A Critical Reassessment. *Studia Antiqua et Archaeologica*. 25 (2) (2019). https://www.academia.edu/42320486/Prehistoric_Gorgoneia_a_Critical_Reassessment. Accessed 23.9.2023.

Lazarou, Anna, Liritzis, Ioannis. Gorgoneion and Gorgon-Medusa: A Critical Research Review. *Journal of Ancient History and Archaeology*. Vol. 9, Issue 1. (2022). https://www.academia.edu/78588819/Gorgoneion_and_Gorgon_Medusa_JAHA. Accessed 3.6.2023.

Lazarou, Anna, Liritzis, Ionannis. Gorgoneion and Gorgon Medusa: A critical research review. *Journal of Ancient History and Archaeology*. 9.1. (2022).

https://www.academia.edu/78588819/Gorgoneion_and_Gorgon_Medusa_JAHA?email_work_card=view-paper. Accessed 19.9.2023.

Leeming, David, *Medusa: In the Mirror of Time*. (London: Reaction Books, 2013)

Lefkowitz, Mary, *Women in Greek Myth*. (Baltimore: Johns Hopkins Press, 2007)

Lefkowitz, M.R. Fant, M. B. *Women's Life in Greece & Rome: A source book in translation*. (Baltimore: Johns Hopkins University Press, 1982, 1992)

Lefkowitz, M.R. *Women in Greek Myth*. (Baltimore: Johns Hopkins University Press, 1986, 2007)

Lewis, D.M. *Notes on Attic Inscriptions* (II) Annual of the British School at Athens. (1955).

Liddell, Henry, Scott, Robert, *A Lexicon. Abridged from Liddell and Scott's Greek-English Lexicon*. (Oxford: Clarendon Press, 1944)

Lloyd-Jones, Hugh, Artemis and Iphigenia. *Journal of Hellenic Studies*. 103, 87–102. JSTOR. (1983). https://doi.org/10.2307/630530. Accessed 5.5.2023.

Lonsdale, S.H. *Dance and Ritual Play in Greek Religion*. (Baltimore: Johns Hopkins University Press, 1993)

Lowe, N.J. Thesmophoria and Haloa: myth, physics and mysteries in Blundell, S. Williamson, M. (eds.) *The Sacred and the Feminine in Ancient Greece*. (London & New York: Routledge, 1998)

Lubell, Winnifred, *The Metamorphosis of Baubo: Myths of women's sexual energy*. (Nashville and London: Vanderbilt University, 1994)

Lykesas Georgios, Papaioannou, Christina, Dania, Aspasia, Koutsouba, Maria, Nikolaki, Evgenia, The Presence of Dance in Female Deities of the Greek Antiquity. *Mediterranean Journal of Social Sciences*. Vol. 8, no. 2, MSCR Publishing. Rome (March 2017). https://www.academia.edu/93691623/%CE%A4he_Presence_of_Dance_in_Female_Deities_of_the_Greek_Antiquity. Accessed 14.7.2023.

Lykesas, Georgios, Papaioannou, Christina, Aspasia, Dania, Koutsouba, Maria, Nikolaki, Evgenia, The Presence of Dance in Female Deities of the Greek Antiquity. *Mediterranean Journal of Social Sciences*. Vol. 8, No. 2, March. (Rome, Italy: MCSER Publishing, 2017). https://www.academia.edu/93691623/%CE%A4he_Presence_of_Dance_in_Female_Deities_of_the_Greek_Antiquity?email_work_card=view-paper. Accessed 12.8.2023.

Lyons, Deborah, The Scandal of Women's Ritual, in Tzanetou, Angeliki, Parca, Maryline, *Women's Rituals in the Ancient Mediterranean*. (Bloomington: University of Illinois Press, 2007)

Macintosh, Fiona, (ed.) *The Ancient Dancer in the Modern World: Responses to Greek and Roman Dance*. (Oxford: Oxford University Press, 2010). https://ebookcentral.proquest.com/lib/open/detail.action?docID=3054510. Accessed 14.7.2023.

McPhee, Ian, *Myth, Drama and Style in South Italian Vase-Painting*. (Uppsala: Astroms Forlag, 2016)

March, Jenny, *Dictionary of Classical Mythology*. (London: Cassell, 1998, 2002)

Marinatos, Nanno, *The Goddess and the Warrior. The Naked Goddess and Mistress of Animals in Early Greek Religion*. (London: Routledge, 2000)

Marler, Joan, An archaeomythological investigation of the Gorgon. *ReVision*, vol. 25, no. 1, summer. (2002) *Gale Academic OneFile*. link.gale.com/apps/doc/A91397851/AONE?u=tou&sid=bookmark-AONE&xid=82feb765. Accessed 27 July 2023.

Marx, Patricia, Introduction of the Gorgoneion to the Shield/Aegis of Athena. *Revue Archeologique* no. 2. Paris: Presses Universitaires. *JSTOR* (1993). http://www.jstor.org/stable/41738383. Accessed 12 Aug. 2023.

Morford, Mark, Lenardon, Robert *Classical Mythology*. (Oxford: Oxford University Press, 2015)

Morgan, Wendy, *Constructing the Monster: Notions of the Monstrous in Classical Antiquity*. Unpublished PhD dissertation, Deakin University, Australia (1984).

Morris, Ian, *Burial and Ancient Society: The Rise of the Greek City State*. (Cambridge: Cambridge University Press, 1989)

Most, Glenn (ed.) *Studies on the Derveni Papyrus. Vol. 2.* (Oxford: Oxford University Press, 2022)

Napier, David, *Foreign Bodies: Performance, Art, and Symbolic Anthropology*. (Berkeley, CA: University of California Press, 1992)

Neumann, Erich, translated by Manheim, Ralph, *The Great Mother. An Analysis of the Archetype*. (Princeton NJ: Princeton University Press, 1974)

Nicholson, Adam, *The Mighty Dead. Why Homer Matters*. (London: William Collins, 2014)

Nilsson, Martin, *The Mycenaean Origin of Greek Mythology*. (Cambridge: Cambridge University Press, 1932)

Oesterley, William, *The Sacred Dance. A Study in Comparative Folklore*. (Cambridge: Cambridge University Press, 1923)

Ogden, Daniel, *Perseus*. (London and New York: Routledge, 2008)

Orr, Leslie, *Donors, Devotees, and Daughters of God: Temple Women in Medieval Tamilnadu*. (Oxford: Oxford University Press, 2000)

Osborne, Robin, *Archaic and Classical Greek Art*. (Oxford: Oxford University Press, 1998).

Osmun, George, Palaephatus. Pragmatic Mythographer. *The Classical Journal*, vol. 52, no. 3, p. 131–37. *JSTOR*. (1956). http://www.jstor.org/stable/3294901. Accessed 24 Aug. 2023.

Padgett, Michael, *The Berlin Painter and His World. Athenian vase painting in the early fifth century B.C.* (New Haven: Yale University Press, 2017)

Padgett, Michael, *The Centaur's Smile: The Human Animal in Early Greek Art*. (New Haven and London: Princeton University Art Museum, 2003)

Palmer, Jennifer. *The Seated Goddess and Animal: A Case Study in Iconographic Transfer and Transformation* Rosetta 12.5: 58–65. (2013). http://www.rosetta.bham.ac.uk/Colloquium2012/palmer_goddess.pdf. Accessed 2.2.2023.

Papaioannou, Christina, Lykesas, Georgios, The role and significance of dance in the Dionysian Mysteries. *Studies in Physical Culture and Tourism*. 19. 68–72. (2012).

Pelosi, Francesco, *Plato on Music, Soul and Body*. (Cambridge: Cambridge University Press, 2010)

Pollard, John, *Seers Shrines and Sirens. The Greek Religious Revolution in the sixth century B.C.* (London: George Allen and Unwin, 1965)

Pomeroy, S.B. *Goddesses, Whores, Wives and Slaves: Women in Classical Antiquity*. (London: Pimlico, 1975)

Pomeroy, Sarah, Burstein, Stanley, *A Brief History of Ancient Greece. Politics, Society and Culture*. (Oxford: Oxford University Press, 2009)

Pratt, Annis, Aunt Jennifer's Tigers: Notes towards a Preliterary History of Women's Archetypes. *Feminist Studies* 4: February. JSTOR. (1978). https://doi.org/10.2307/3177634. Accessed 30 July 2023.

Pucci, Pietro, The Song of the Sirens in Schein, Seth, *Reading the Odyssey, Selected Interpreted Essays*. (Princeton NJ: Princeton University Press, 1996)

Pucci, Pietro, *The Song of the Sirens. Essays on Homer*. (New York and Oxford: Rowman and Littlefield, 1998)

Rabinowitz, Jacob, *The Rotting Goddess*. (New York: Autonomedia, 1998)

Rabinowitz, Nancy, Women as Subject and Object of the Gaze in Tragedy. *Helios*. Vol. 40, Nos. 1–2. Texas Tech University Press. (2013). https://www.researchgate.net/publication/265952447_Women_as_Subject_and_Object_of_the_Gaze_in_Tragedy. Accessed 2.4.2023.

Reid, Heather, Tanasi, David. (eds.) *Philosopher Kings and Tragic Heroes. Essays on Image and Ideas from Western Greece*. (Sioux City, Iw: Parnassos Press, 2016)

Revermann, Martin, Wilson, Peter. (eds.) *Performance, Iconography, Reception: Studies in Honour of Oliver Taplin*. (Oxford: Oxford University Press, 2008)

Robb, John, Harris, Oliver, *The Body in History: Europe from the Palaeolithic to the Future*. (Cambridge: Cambridge University Press, 2013)

Robinson, David, An Illustration of Hesiod on a Black-Figured Plate by the Strife Painter. *American Journal of Archaeology*, vol. 34, no. 3. JSTOR (1930). https://doi.org/10.2307/497989. Accessed 11 July 2023.

Rocconi, Eleanora, The Culture of Musike in Archaic and Classical Greece. In Destrée, P. et al. *A Companion to Ancient Aesthetics*, John Wiley & Sons. (2015). *ProQuest Ebook Central*. https://ebookcentral.proquest.com/lib/open/detail.action?docID=2044683. Accessed 3.3.2023.

Roccos, I. J. Perseus. *Lexicon Iconographicum Mythologiae Classicae VII, I* Zurich. (1984). https://archive.org/stream/limc_20210516/Lexicon%20Iconographicum%20Mythologiae%20Classicae/LIMC%20V-1%20Herakles-Kenchrias_djvu.txt. Accessed 12.9.2023.

Rose, Herbert, *Handbook of Greek Mythology*. (London: Methuen, 1928)

Rostovtzeff, M.I. *The Social and Economic History of the Hellenistic World*. 3 vols. (Oxford: Clarendon Press, 1941)

Rynearson, Nicholas, Courting the Erinyes: Persuasion, Sacrifice and Seduction in Aeschylus's Eumenides in *Transactions of the American Philological Association 143*. 1–22. (2013). https://www.academia.edu/12728652/Courting_the_Erinyes_Persuasion_Sacrifice_and_Seduction_in_Aeschyluss_Eumenides?email_work_card=view-paper.

Schaps, D.M. *Economic Rights of Women in Ancient Greece.* (Edinburgh: Edinburgh University Press, 1979)

Segal, Charles, Afterword: Jean Paul Vernant and the Study of Ancient Greece. *Arethusa 15*: 221–34. JSTOR. (1982). https://www.jstor.org/stable/26308111. Accessed 4.5.2023.

Shearer, Anne, *Athena: Image and Energy.* (London: Viking, 1996)

Shay, Jonathan *Odysseus in America.* (New York: Scribner, 2002)

Shilo, Amit, The Ghost of Clytemnestra in the Eumenides: Ethical Claims beyond Human Limits, in *American Journal of Philology*. Vol. 139, Number 4 (Whole Number 556), Winter 2018, pp. 533–576. Johns Hopkins University Press.

Siebers, Tobin, *The Mirror of Medusa*. (Berkeley CA: University of California Press, 1983)

Six, Jan, Some Archaic Gorgons in the British Museum. *The Journal of Hellenic Studies*. Vol. 6. (1885) The Society for the Promotion of Hellenic Studies. https://www.jstor.org/stable/623402. Accessed 2.4.2023.

Slater Phillip, *The Glory of Hera: Greek Mythology and the Greek Family*. (Princeton NJ: Princeton University Press, 1968)

Smith, Bonnie G. *The Gender of History: Men, Women, and Historical Practice*. (Cambridge, Mass: Harvard University Press, 2000). https://hdl-handle-net.libezproxy.open.ac.uk/2027/heb.04359. EPUB. Accessed 1.1.2022.

Smith, Tyler Jo, Reception or deception? Approaching Greek dance through vase-painting. In Macintosh, Fiona. (ed.) *The Ancient Dancer in the Modern World. Responses to Greek and Roman dance*. (Oxford: Oxford University Press, 2010)

Smith, Tyler Jo, *Komast Dancers in Archaic Greek Art*. (Oxford: Oxford University Press, 2010)

Smotherman Bennett, Danielle, My Fair Lady: Exploring Social Change through Athenian Vase-Painting in the Fifth Century BCE.

In *The Athenian Empire Anew: Acting Hegemonically, Reacting Locally in the Athenian Arkhē*, edited by Aaron Hershkowitz and Michael McGlin. Special issue, Classics@ 23 (2023).

Soar, Kathryn, Aamodt, Christina, *Archaeological Approaches to Dance Performance*. BAR International Series 2622. (Oxford: Archaeopress, 2014)

Sourvinou-Inwood, C. *Studies in Girls' Traditions. Aspects of the Arkteia and Age Representation in Attic Iconography*. (Athens: Kardamitsa, 1988)

Toler, Vasil S. *Odyssey and Sirens: A Temptation towards the Mystery of the Iso-polyphonic Regions of Epirus A Homeric theme with variations*. https://www.academia.edu/50062598/Vasil_S_Tole_Odyseus_and_Sirenes_converted?email_work_card=view-paper. Accessed 18.7.2024.

Tsiafakis, Despoina, ΠΕΛΩΡΑ: Fabulous Creatures and/or Demons of Death? In Padgett, J.M. *The Centaur's Smile: The Human Animal in Early Greek Art*. (New Haven and London: Princeton University Art Museum, 2004)

Tsakiropoulou-Summers, Tatiana, Kitsi-Mitakou, Katerina (eds.) *Women and the Ideology of Political Exclusion*. (London: Routledge, 2018)

Tsakiropoulou-Summers, Tatiana, Solon's Legislation and women's incompatibility with state ideology. In *Women and the Ideology of Political Exclusion*. (London: Routledge, 2018)

Turner, Frank, *The Greek Heritage in Victorian Britain*. (New Haven: Yale University Press, 1981)

Vernant, Jean-Pierre, *Mortals and Immortals. Collected Essays*. Zeitlin, Froma (ed & trans) (Oxford: Princeton University Press, 1991)

Weinberg, Saul, Corinthian Relief Ware: Pre-Hellenistic Period. *Hesperia: The Journal of the American School of Classical Studies at Athens*, vol. 23, no. 2. (1954). https://doi.org/10.2307/146692. Accessed 11.7.2023.

Warner, Marina, *From Beast to the Blonde: Fairy Tales and their Tellers*. (New York: Farrar, Straus & Giroux, 1995)

West, David Reid, *Some Cults of Greek Goddesses and Female Daemons of Oriental Origin*. Thesis unpublished University of Glasgow. (1990).

Wilk, Stephen, *Medusa: Solving the Mystery of the Gorgon*. (Oxford: Oxford University Press, 2000)

Wright, F.A. *Feminism in Greek Literature from Homer to Aristotle*. (London: Routledge, 1923)

Wright, F.A. *Greek Social Life*. (London & Toronto: J.M. Dent & Sons Ltd. 1925)

Wylie, A. Epistemic Justice, Ignorance, and Procedural Objectivity: Editor's Introduction, *Hypatia*, vol. 26, no. 2, pp. 233–5. (2011).

Zarifi, Yana, Chorus and Dance in the Ancient World. In Marianne McDonald. Walton Michael. (Eds.) *The Cambridge Companion to Greek and Roman Theatre.* (Cambridge: Cambridge University Press, 2007). doi:10.1017/CCOL9780521834568.013. Accessed 1.7.2023.

Zeitlin, Froma, The Motif of the Corrupted Sacrifice in Aeschylus' Oresteia. (1965) *TAPA* 96: 463–508.

Zeitlin, Froma, The Dynamics of Misogyny: Myth and Mythmaking in the Oresteia. *Arethusa*. Spring and Fall. Vol. 11. No. ½, Women in the Ancient World (Spring and Fall 1978). pp. 149–184.

Zeitlin, Froma, *Playing the Other: Gender and Society in Classical Greek Literature.* (Chicago: University of Chicago Press, 1996)

Zolotnikova, Olga, A Hideous Monster or a Beautiful Maiden? Did the Western Greeks Alter the Concept of Gorgon? In Reid, Heather, Tanasi, David (eds.) *Philosopher Kings and Tragic Heroes: Essays on Images and Ideas from Western Greece.* (Fonte Aretusa: Parnassos Press, 2016). https://doi.org/10.2307/j.ctvbj7gjn.23. Accessed 3.7.2023.

INDEX

Achilles, xxiii, 8
    and Ajax, 4
    in *Francois Krater*, 56
    shield, 12, 140
achoreia, 48
adamant, 53
aegis, 13, 14, 29, 30, 61, 163–165
Aeneid (Virgil), xxii
Aeschylus, xx, 74, 77, 88–89, 137
Aesop, xx, 140, 146
aetiological myths, 71, 75, 101
Agamemnon, x, xxiii, 4, 67–68, 82, 88, 118
Agamemnon (Aeschylus), xx, 74
aideomai, 45
aidoiod, 45
Aiora, rite of, 102
aischista, 155
aition, 75
Ajax, 17
    and Achilles, 4
    in *Francois Krater*, 56
Ajax (Sophocles), xxi, 17

Alcestis (Euripides), xxi
Aletis (wanderer), 103
Altman, M., 36
Amazons, x, 11, 25–26, 58
Anthesteria, 66
Anticipater of Thessalonika, 157
Antigone (Sophocles), xxi
aoroi, 67
aoros, 70
aphradeis, 64. See also death
Aphrodite, xxiii, 139
Apollonian, 43
Apollonius of Rhodes, xxii, 107, 114
Apollo, x, xxiii, 12, 14, 43, 65, 74, 81, 86
Apology (Plato), xxii
apotropaic symbol, 1, 7
apples, 138–141, 147
Archaic Period, xxx
Archanians (Aristophanes), xxi
Ares, 135, 140
Argonautica (Apollonius of Rhodes), xxii
Aristophanes, xxi, 65, 68, 157

Aristotle, xvi, xxii, 58, 120
Arkteia, 157–160
Artemis, xxiii–xxiv, 31, 34–35, 157–159
    Artemis-Hekate, 103–105
    Athenian red figure Bell Krater, 106
    Potnia Theron and, 37
Aspasia, 121
ataphoi, 67
Atê, 17
Athena, xxiv
    aegis, 13, 14, 30, 61
    aulos, 133
    Birth of Athena, 14
    gorgodrakontodoka, 47
    Gorgoneion on aegis, 163–165
    Medusa and, 29
    Perseus, and beheaded Medusa and, 50
Athenian
    black figure Amphora, 4
    black figure Kylix, 138
    men, xi, 23, 42, 44
    misogyny, 57–58
    politics and aegis, 163–165
    red figure Bell Krater, 106
    red-figure hydria, 50
    red figure Krater, 98
    red figure Lekythos, 159
    ritual, 153
aulos, 130, 131, 133

The Bacchae (Euripides), xxi
bacchantes, 80
Bacchic Mysteries, 82–83
Bacchylides, xx
Battle of the Titans (Titonomachy), 96, 113
Bharatanatyam, 46, 47
biaothanatoi, 67
Bird Goddess, 34
The Birds (Aristophanes), xxi
bird-woman motif, 33–34. *See* Sirens
Birth of Athena (Stesichoros), 14
Blau, R. De P., 18
Blundell, S., 158
Bricolage, ix

Bromius. See Dionysus
Budapest, Z., 91
Burkert, W., xi, 153, 155, 156, 158

Callimachus, xxii
Cartlidge, P., 149
carved chalcedony gemstone, 40
catoptromancy, 52–53
ceremonies of dead, 63
Chaldea, 116
    Chaldean Oracles, 109
    Chaldean theurgist, 111
Charisterion, 154
Charybdis, xxvii, 123, 142–146. See also daemons
Chrysaor, 53
Cicero, 127
Cimmerians, 64
Classical period, xxx–xxxi
Clouds (Aristophanes), xxi
Cole, S., 158, 160
Concerning Unmarried Girls (Hippocrates), 103
Cosmic Soul, 109
Council of the Gods (Lucian), 154
Crime and Punishment (Dostoyevsky), 69
The Cypria (Homer), 139
Cyranides, 75

daemones, xv. *See* unquiet dead
daemons, 112, 135, 168–174
    Charybdis, 142–146
    epitomised actions, 167
    Eris, 135–142
    Lugra, 147
    Skylla (Scylla), 142–146
    wolfish, 146
Danaids, x
dance, 46, 90, 103, 129
    Bharatanatyam, 46, 47
    ecstatic, 48
    gorgodrakontodoka, 47
    Gorgon dancing, 46
    Haka or war dance, 26
    healing power of, 59

INDEX 193

death, 8
   agents of, 69
   Anthesteria, 66
   aoroi, 67, 70–72, 73
   aoros, 70
   ataphoi, 67
   biaothanatoi, 67, 69
   ceremonies of, 63
   curse tablets, 66
   Eumenides, 67–68
   ghosts and afterlife, 65
   madness and vengeful, 69
   mythic female spirits, 70–72
   placating angry dead, 65–66, 103
   protection spell, 71
   reincarnation, 65
   restless, 63–65, 66, 73, 104
   Sirens, 70, 72
   supernatural policing of women's roles, 71–72
   unquiet dead, 66–67
   untimely deaths of women, 70
De Generatione (Aristotle), xvi
Demeter, 154
   Erinys, 85–86
Derveni Papyrus, 82, 87
Descent to the Goddess (Perera), 18
Dexter, M., 15
Dialogues of Hetaerae (Lucian), 153
Diggle, B. L., 155, 156
Dio Chrysostom, xxii, 109
Diodoros, 25
Dionysus, xxiv
   aetiological myth of, 155
   maenads of, 43, 80
   Mystery cult of, 48, 131
Diotima, xxi, 121
Discord. *See* Eris
Dostoyevsky, F., 69
Dowden, K., 158

Early Dark Age, xxx
ecstatic and idyllic gorgons, 48–50
eerophoitos. *See eiaropotis*
eiaropotis, 69, 75
Electra, xxiv

Electra (Euripides), xxi
Electra (Sophocles), xxi, 65
embodied gorgon, 20
Empedocles, 65
Empousa, 78
Enodia, 100
en-theos, 48
ephebes, 56, 57, 62
Erinyes, xv, 77–90
   and afterlife punishment, 83
   as agents of vengeance and madness, 80–81
   appearance, 78
   characteristics and role, 82
   in cult and tragedy, 89
   as dark feminine, 90
   and Demeter Erinys, 85–86
   Erinye at Delphi, 87
   etymology, 78
   in *Eumenides*, 84
   as guardians of natural order, 87–88
   Homer, 78, 84
   invocations, 89
   in Krater, 84
   lineage of, 78–79
   and *Maenads*, 80
   as outcasts, 84–85
   patriarchy and suppression of female, 86
   Pot Erinyes and Apollo, 81
   and restless dead, 79
   rituals and, 83
   Semnai Theai, 88–89
   transformation into Eumenides, 90
Eris, xv, 135. See also *daemons*
   and aporia, 140–141
   Athenian Black Figure Kylix, 138
   on battlefield, 139–140
   embodying, 142
   etymology, 141
   forms of, 138
   and judgment of Paris, 139
   in modern age, 141
   nature, 136–137
   Pandora, 137

194   INDEX

The Eumenides (Aeschylus), xv, 74, 77
    biaothanatoi, 67–68
    Erinys, 84–85, 89, 90
Euripides, xxi, 80
    Enodia, 100
    Eris, 136
    Ion, 29, 115
Eusatathias of Thessalonika, 157

Feldman, T., 164
Franco, C., 144
Francois Krater, 54
    Ajax and Achilles in, 56
    Medusa in, 55
    Potnia Theron in, 54–55
Frazer, J., 153, 154
Frieze, L., 104
Frogs (Aristophanes), xxi, 65, 68

Gaia, xxiv
Gello, 65, 70, 71, 74
Giallongo, A., 15
Gilhuly, K., 153
goddess-mother, 12–13
Goff, B., 153, 155, 156, 158
Gorgo/Medusa, xiv, xv, 54, 164
    on archaic shield straps, 56–57
    Athena and, 29
    Chariot plaque, 44
    dance of, 46–50
    as demonized feminine, 20
    in *Francois Krater*, 55
    gorgodrakontodoka, 47
    Hesiod's, 21–22
    iconography and power, 39–40
    myth, 24–26, 45, 53, 56
    and patriarchal fear, 42–43
    Perseus, and beheaded Medusa
        and Athena, 50
    Pindar's Hyperborean myth,
        48–50
    politics of Otherness, 23–24
    Shield of Heracles, 22
    symbolism, 57–59
    on temple of Artemis, 30–31
    as warrior queen and fertility
        goddess, 29–30
    'womb of death', 44–45
gorgon(s), xiv, 1
    Baubo figure, 3
    black figure pot, 23
    cultural significance, 46–48
    ecstatic and idyllic, 48–50
    etymology, 5, 15
    Gorgo/Medusa, 1, 14
    Gorgon dancing, 46–48
    Gorgoneion, 1, 2
    Korkyra Gorgon, 31
    origins, 1, 15
    Palaephatus and Gorgon myth
        interpretation, 24–25
    Potnia and, 33–34
    Shield of Heracles, 22
    Tlaltecuhtli, 27–29
Gorgoneion, xiv–xv, 1, 2, 7
    as apotropaic symbol, 7, 8
    on Athena's aegis, 163–165
    bulging eyes of, 9
    Chigi vase, 6
    diving into the abyss, 14
    gaze of, 9–10, 11
    Gorgoneion anti-fix roof tile, 6
    Homer and, 3, 5, 9
    iconography, 4
    khthonia, 8
    Kylix Black-Figure pot, 12
    Odyssey, 7–8
    origin, 15
    political transformation of, 19
    pre-*Gorgoneion*, 1, 2
    representation of ignominious
        death, 8
    shaggy faced Gorgoneion, 5
    snakes, 12–13
    symbolism, 4, 12–13
    on warrior shields, 4
Greece, ancient
    dogs, 144–146
    ethical gendering of instruments, 131
    ghosts and afterlife, 65

"Greek woman", xi
music, 129–130
re-evaluation of women's
    importance, 151–161
Thesmophoria, 153, 154, 155
women and control, x, 63–73
women's voices, 120–121, 123,
    127
Greek mythology, ix, 149
blindness and divine
    retribution, 11, 17
fear of female agency, 45
goddess-mother in, 12–13
Otherness, xii
women and control, x

Hades, 48, 82, 88. *See also* death
'bacchantes from Hades', 80
companions of, 89
eidolon, 8
Hagen, 37
Haka, 26–27, 48
Harpies. *See* Sirens
Hartswick, K., 163
Hekate, xv, 95
Anthesteria, 102, 103
Artemis-Hekate, 103–105
in Caria, 97–99
Cosmic, 110
Cosmic Soul, 109
early origins, 95
Enodia, 100
epithets of, 112
as goddess of witches,
    108–109
as guardian of childbirth, 104
as guide of unconscious, 113
Homeric Hymn to Demeter, 96
liminal spaces, 99, 101, 110, 112
Medea, 107–108
and Persephone, 96–97, 98, 113
red figure vase, 100
rite of *Aiora*, 102
roles, 96, 101–103, 111
in Roman times, 106

thresholds, 99
and Underworld, 96–97, 99
Hellenistic Period, xxxi
Herodotus, xiii, xx, 13, 20, 25
Hesiod, xiii, xix, 1, 20, 88, 121, 143
Athena, 14
Eris, 135–136, 138, 141
Gorgons, 21
Hekate, 95
Medusa, 21–22
Nyx, 79
Pandora, 137
Perseus, 22
shield of Heracles, 140
hexing, 91
Hippolytus (Euripides), xxi
Histories (Herodotus), xx
The History of the Peloponnesian War
    (Thucydides), xxi
Homer, xiii, xv, xix, 20, 42, 95, 113–114,
    117, 163
aegis, 5
and Archaic mythology, 152
dead, 64, 68, 82
decoration on shield of Achilles,
    140
epics, 3
Erinyes, 69, 78, 84
Eris, 139–140
Gorgo/Medusa, 1
and *Gorgoneion*, 3, 5, 9, 23
Homeric Texts, xxxi, 122
male gaze, 10
modern scholarship of, xxxi
Nyx, 79
Sirens, 123, 126, 127
Homeric Hymns (Homer), 64, 96,
    113–114, 121–122
Howe, T., P., 164
How the World Made the West (Quinn),
    xvii, xxxi
Hughes, D. J., 158–159, 160, 161
Humbaba, 15
Hyginus, 144
Hyperboreans, 48–50

196   INDEX

Iliad (Homer), xix, 82, 134, 139
Inanna: Queen of Heaven and Earth
    (Wolkstein), 18
Innana, myth of, 18
Ion (Euripides), 29, 115

Jason, xxiv, 89, 107–108

Kalypso (Calypso), xxiv–xxv
kanephoros, 116
Kassandra (Cassandra), xxv
Keres, 8, 16
Keuls, 60
kibisis, 50, 53, 61
kinethenai-movement, 156
King Oedipus (Sophocles), xxi
Kirke (Circe), xxv
Kirk, G., 164, 165
Kitto, H. D. F., 152
Klytemnestra (Clytemnestra), x, xxv
knielauf position, 46, 61
Korkyra Gorgon, 31
kourotrophos, 104
krateriskoi, 158
Kretan goddess, 41
Kronos (Cronos), xxv

lamentation, 88
Lamia (Neath), 24, 71, 72
Lazarou, A., xiv
Leach, E. R., 153
Lefkowitz, M. R., 161
Levi-Strauss, C., ix
Libya, 13, 24, 25–26, 75
Lithica, 71
Lowe, N. J., 152, 153, 155, 156, 157
Lucian of Samosata, 139, 153, 154
Lugra, 147
Lysistrata (Aristophanes), xxi

maenads, 43, 80, 48
male gaze, 10
Marinatos, N., 37
marriage, 122, 132
Marx, P., 163, 164
Mate, G., 73
matriarchy, myth of, x

Maximus of Turin, 126
Medea, xxv, 89, 107–108
Medea (Euripides), xxi
Medusa. *See* Gorgo/Medusa
Medusa in Wells (Blau), 18
Megaira, 71
menstruation, stigmatization of, 36
Metamorphoses (Ovid), xvi, xxii
Metis, x, xxv, 14, 122, 137
metis, 118, 122
miasma, 16
Middle Bronze Age, xxix–xxx
mirror(s), 50, 59
    of Durotriges tribe, 51
    Perseus and mirror shield, 53
    prophecy and divination, 52–53
misogyny, xiii, 139, 152
    Gorgo/Medusa, 57
    of Greek, ix
    Hesiod, 14
    paranoid, 43–44
Mistress of the Wild Things. *See potnia*
    theron
monsters, xiii
Moralia (Plutarch), xxii
Morgan, W., 40, 164
Mormo, 71, 78
Muses, xxvi, 122, 131
music, 46, 129–130
    ethical gendering of instruments,
    131
    harmful, 130
    molpoi, 98
    Plato, 127, 129
    Pythagoras, 120, 127
musike, 46
Mycenean woman and jewellery, 52
Mystery cult of Dionysus, 48
myth(s), 149. *See also* Greek mythology
    aetiological myths, 71, 75, 101
    Innana, 18
    of matriarchy, x
    mythic female spirits, 70–72
    Pindar's Hyperborean myth, 48–50
    of rape, 43
    violence in, 79
Myth of Er (Plato), 64, 65, 127, 128

INDEX   197

Neumann, E., 45
nymphs and serpent, 41
Nyx (Night), xxvi, 78–79, 99, 135

Odes (Pindar), xx
Odyssey (Homer), xix, 64, 86, 88, 132
    Gorgoneion, 7–8
    Odysseus, xxvi, 118–119
    Sirens, 117
    Skylla and Charybdis, 143–144
Oedipus at Colonis (Sophocles), xxi
Olympian gods, xiii, xxvi, 20
On Friendship (Cicero), 127
On the Sacred Disease, 69
The Oresteia (Aeschylus), xx, 74, 77–78
Orestes, xxvi
Otherness, xii
Ovid, xvi, xxii, 114

Palaephatus, 24, 25
Pandareid sisters, 86
Pandora, 137, 147
Panhellenism, 104–105
Parallel Lives (Plutarch), xxii
patriarchy, 85
    blaming women for male
        transgression, 79
    fear of female autonomy, 42–43
    marriage, x
    Perseus myth, 57
    and stigmatization of menstruation,
        36
    and violence in myth, 79
Pausanias, 53, 65, 89, 104
Pegasus, 53
Peisistratus' era, 164
The Peloponnesian War (Thucydides), 120
Perera, S. B., 18
Pericles, xx, 120, 121
Persephone, 82, 88, 96, 100
    companions of, 89
    Hekate and, 96–97, 98, 113
    Underworld, 7, 64
Perseus, xxvi, 20–21, 22, 24–25, 163
    adamant sickle, 53
    and beheaded Medusa and
        Athena, 50

    against Dionysus followers, 43
    and mirror shield, 53
    myth, 48–50, 56
    politics of heroism and domination,
        54
    symbolism, 164
Persians (Aeschylus), xx
Phaedra (Euripides), xxi
phallus
    phallic charms, 11
    'reign of phallus', 43
Phasis, 115
Pherekydes, 163
Philoctetes (Sophocles), xxi
Philolaus, 127
Pindar, xx, 25, 48, 49, 57, 65
Plato, xx, xxi, 58, 64, 69, 109, 127, 128
    aulos, 130, 131
    music, 129–130
    Platonic Love, xxi
    Sirens, 127–129
    spheres from Plato's Myth of Er,
        128
Plutarch, xxii, 65, 109, 110
polis, 99
Porphyry, xxii, 110
Poseidon, xxvi, 11, 53, 72
potnia theron, 31–34, 37, 158
    Artemis Orthea sanctuary, 32
    in *Francois Krater*, 54–55
Praxilla, 157
Proclus, 110
Prometheus Bound (Aeschylus), xx
protection spell, 71
protective spirits, 35
Pythagoras, xx, 65, 120, 127, 130
The Pythia, xix
The Python (Pytho), xxvi

Quinn, J., xvii, xxxi

rape, mythology of, 43
'reign of phallus', 43
reincarnation, 65, 83, 110, 127
The Republic (Plato), xxii, 64, 127
restless dead, 63–65, 73, 79, 104. *See also*
    death

restless female spirits, 63–73. *See also* death
Rhea, xxvi–xxvii
Rostovtzeff, M. I., 152

Sappho, xix–xx, 64, 70
Scylla. *See* Skylla (Scylla)
Semnai Theai, 88–89
Seneca, xxii, 112
Seven Against Thebes (Aeschylus), xx, 137
Shakespeare, W., 88
Shield of Heracles, 22
Sirens, xv, 70, 117
    allegorical meaning, 126
    allure of, 117–118
    Attic Oinochoe Plate, 124
    Homeric, 127
    instruments, 131
    interior, 132
    meadow (*leimon*), 118–119
    in Middle Ages, 125, 126
    Muses, 122, 131
    Odysseus, 118–119
    origins and early description, 123–125
    Plato, 127–129
    and ritual objects, 124
    song, 119–120, 127
    spheres from Plato's Myth of Er, 128
    statue on temple of Hera, 125
    women's voices, 120–122, 123
Skylla (Scylla), xv, xxvii, 142. *See also daemons*
    origins, 143–144
    Paestan red-figure krater, 142, 145
    transformation, 144–146
Smith, B. G., 151, 152
snake-cults, ancient, 13
Snake Goddess, 12, 24, 42
snake iconography, 40
    Black Figure vase from Paestum, 41
    Kretan goddess, 41
    nymphs and serpent, 41
    Snake Goddess, 12, 24, 42
    snake symbolism, 12–13

Social and Economic History of the Hellenistic World (Rostovtzeff), 151–152
'social imaginary', 153
Socrates, xxi, 127
Solon, 22–23, 58
    laws, 19–20
    sexual morality and women control, 41–42
Sophocles, xxi, 65
Sourvinou-Inwood, C., 158
Stesichoros, 14, 25
Suppliants (Aeschylus), xx
symbols, xii, xiv, 12–13

The Tetractys, 114
Thanatos, 8
Thebes (Aeschylus), xx
Theocritus, xxii, 99
Theogony (Hesiod), xix, 79, 95, 121, 135
Thesmophoria, 153, 154, 155
Thesmophoriasusae (Aristophanes), 157
Thevet, A., 36
Thucydides, xxi, 120, 165
Titanomachy, 11
Titans, xxvii
Titonomachy. *See* Battle of the Titans
Tlaltecuhtli, 27–29
The Trojan Women (Euripides), xxi

unconscious, 69, 97, 113
unquiet dead (*phantamata*), 66, 109, 112
Ursa Major, 115

vase painting, 165
Virgil, xxii

The Wasps (Aristophanes), xxi, 157
Wilk, S., 15
wolfish, 146. *See also daemons*
Wolkstein, D., 18
women
    Arkteia, 157–160
    childbirth, 159–161
    deconstructing female ritual, 156
    'doublespeak', 121–122

gaze, 9, 11
insults, 145–146
kinethenai-movement, 156
lamentation and call for vendetta, 88
metis, 122
monsters, xii, xiv
  rebellious, 80
  re-evaluation of importance, 151–161
  revenge and hexing, 91
  rituals, 153–161
  sexuality regulation, 44
  suicide in maidens, 101–103
Thesmophoria, 153, 154, 155

'unspeakable', 156
voices, 120–121, 123, 127
Women of Trachis (Sophocles), xxi
Works and Days (Hesiod), xix, 136, 137, 138
Wright, F. A., 152
Wylie, A., 152

Xenia, 93
Xenocrates of Chalcedon, xxii, 110
Xenophanes, 25
Xenophon, 69

Zenobius, 74, 157
Zeus, xxvii, 11, 14, 95, 96, 122, 139

www.ingramcontent.com/pod-product-compliance
Ingram Content Group UK Ltd.
Pitfield, Milton Keynes, MK11 3LW, UK
UKHW021925181125
465179UK00001B/3